MACHINE DRAWING

DR. O.P. JAKHAR
Associate Professor
Department of Mechanical Engineering
Government Engineering college, Bikaner

AMIT MATHUR
Assistant Professor & Head
Department of Mechanical Engineering
Government College of Engineering & Technology, Bikaner

KHANNA BOOK PUBLISHING CO. (P) LTD.
Publisher of Engineering and Computer Books
4C/4344, Ansari Road, Darya Ganj, New Delhi-110002
Phone : 011-23244447-48 **Mobile:** +91-9910909320
E-mail : contact@khannabooks.com
Website : www.khannabooks.com

Dear Readers,

To prevent the piracy, this book is secured with HIGH SECURITY HOLOGRAM on the front title cover. In case you don't find the hologram on the front cover title, please write us to at contact@khannabooks.com or whatsapp us at +91-99109 09320 and avail special gift voucher for yourself.

Specimen of Hologram on front Cover title:

Moreover, there is a SPECIAL DISCOUNT COUPON for you with EVERY HOLOGRAM.

How to avail this SPECIAL DISCOUNT:

Step 1: Scratch the hologram
Step 2: Under the scratch area, your "coupon code" is available
Step 3: Logon to www.khannabooks.com
Step 4: Use your "coupon code" in the shopping cart and get your copy at a special discount
Step 5: Enjoy your reading!

Price: ₹ 525.00

ISBN: 978-93-86173-28-7

Machine Drawing
by O.P. Jakhar, Amit Mathur

First Edition: 2018
Reprint: 2025

To view complete list of books, Please scan the QR Code:

KPH

Published by:
Khanna Book Publishing Co. (P) Ltd.
CIN: U22110DL1998PTC095547

Visit us at: **www.khannabooks.com**
Write us at: **contact@khannabooks.com**

Printed in India.

PREFACE

This book is designed for the student of Engineering and Technology as well as specially for Mechanical Engineering Degree and Diploma students. The teaching of this course faces difficulty in explaining the various concept of machine drawing viz., orthographical projection, sectioning, complicated mechanical assembly drawing etc. Sometimes explanation requires some three dimensional and complicated drawings to be drawn on the black board which is quite impossible due to the time constraint of class.

This book is an outcome of the strong need felt by students persuing the course and the teaching faculty members. The teacher can explain the related concepts, drawing methods and uses of various parts being drawn etc. in each practical class without wasting time on the black board.

We tried to compress the subject matter from the view point of Mechanical Engineering students. We have taken assistance in preparing this book from large number of text books.

We have also added Basic Drawing Softwares in this book which describes about the basics of Auto-CAD, CATIA, PROE, ANSYS etc. which is useful for today's need of Engineering & Technology. Readers are requested to communicate the comments, suggestions to improve the book.

Dr. O.P. Jakhar
Amit Mathur

ABOUT THE AUTHORS

Dr. O.P. Jakhar started his teaching carrier in 2000 as lecturer in Mechanical Engineering Department at Shri Balaji College of Engineering and Technology (SBCET), Jaipur. Further he served Stani Memorial College of Engineering and Technology, Phagi, Jaipur and Ajmer Institute of Technology, Ajmer as Senior Lecturer. Dr. Jakhar joined Maharana Pratap University of Agriculture and Technology, Udaipur as Assistant Professor in 2005. At presently he is serving at Govt. Engineering College, Bikaner as Associate Professor in Mechanical Engineering department since 2008. His areas of interest are Heat Transfer, Fluid Mechanics and Machines, Steam Power and Thermal Engineering.

Dr. Jakhar is life member of ISTE and Indian Geological Congress (IGC) He has guided 10 M.Tech. dissertations and published more than 40 research papers.

Dr. O.P. Jakhar got commissioned as Lieutenant in NCC in 2005 and presently he is serving as Captain at 7 Raj. BN. NCC, Bikaner.

Amit Mathur is presently Assistant Professor & Head in the Department of Mechanical Engineering at Govt. College of Engineering & Technology, Bikaner. He has done B.E. (Mechanical Engineering) from Govt. Engineering College, Ajmer and M.E. (Manufacturing Technology) from NITTTR, Chandigarh. He has an experience of more than 10 years in the field of Teaching & Research. He has published more than 06 papers in National Conference Proceedings & Journals. He is also an Associate Member of Institution of Engineers, India.

CONTENTS

1

BASICS OF MACHINE DRAWING

1.1 INTRODUCTION

Machine Drawing is the systematic representation of a machine or machine components by different lines on the sheet or paper. It is the communicating medium used in industry to furnish all the information required for manufacturing and assembly of different parts of a machine. It is essential in Machine Design.

Machine drawing comprises of its own rules for projections, its idioms in conventional practices and its observations in symbols. It is the shortest way to communicate the basic idea of any machine component or its assembly. Even a small error committed by an engineer in the drawing may misguide or confuse the worker or operator and ultimately spoil the product.

1.2 TYPES OF MACHINE DRAWING

From engineering point of view, the subject of machine drawing can be divided into the following categories:

1. **Production Drawing:** Production drawing shows complete information for the production or manufacturing of a machine or structure.

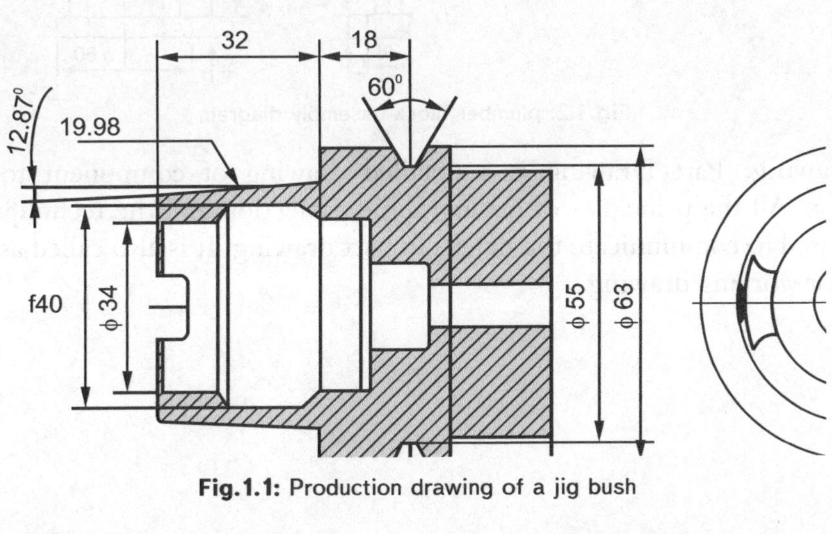

Fig.1.1: Production drawing of a jig bush

2. **Assembly Drawing:** Assembly drawing consists of a drawing of a complete machine or structure in which all the parts are arranged or assembled in accordance with their functional positions.

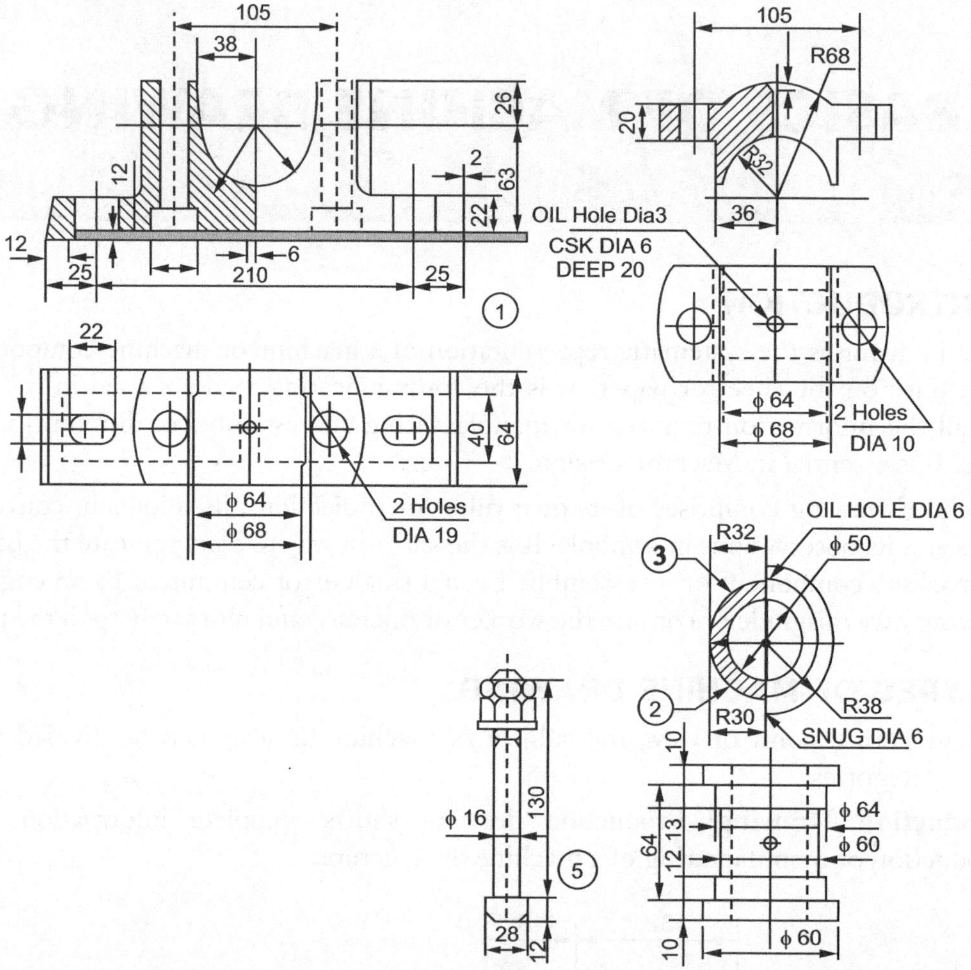

Fig.1.2: plumber block assembly diagram

3. **Part Drawing:** Part Drawing is a detailed drawing of component to facilitate its production. All the principles of orthographic projection and the techniques of graphic must be used to communicate the details in part drawing. It is also called as a production drawing or working drawing.

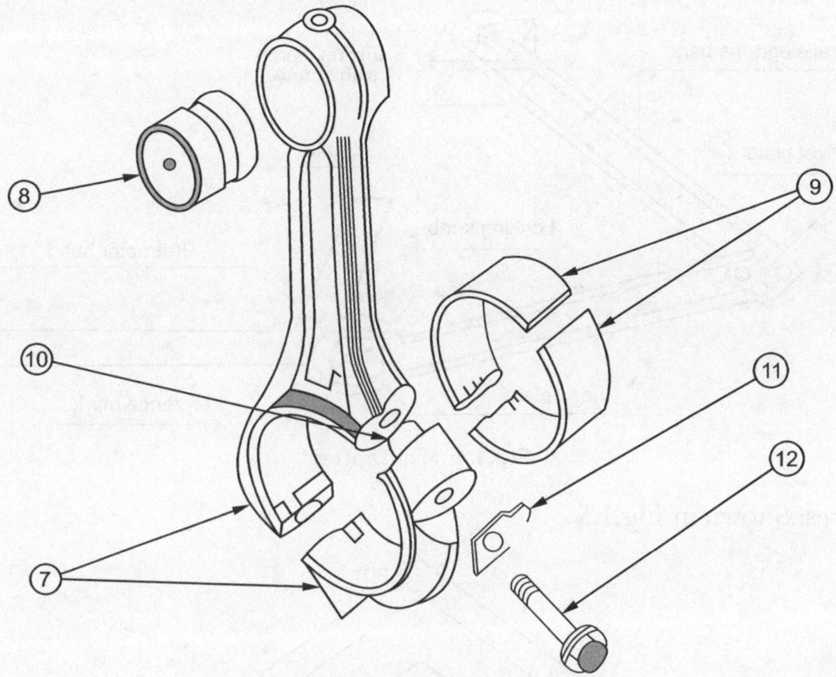

Fig.1.3: Connecting rod parts drawing

1.3 DRAWING INSTRUMENTS

A brief list of drawing instruments is shown below:

1. Mini Drafter: Shown in Fig.1.4. Where & how used?

A smaller than usual drafter is a significant gadget utilized for planning drawing rapidly and precisely. The calling of common and mechanical architect depends on smaller than normal drafter. The mini drafter is an adaptable device and can be utilized for nearly everything and can be utilized to draw parallel lines, perpendiculars, slanted lines of any degree with unmatched speed, it comprises of one long scale and one little scale and the scales are formed in L shaped and by a smaller than normal drafter we can complete 3 sorts of works i.e. drawing of lines, drawing perpendiculars for the lines and can utilize as a protractor all the while.

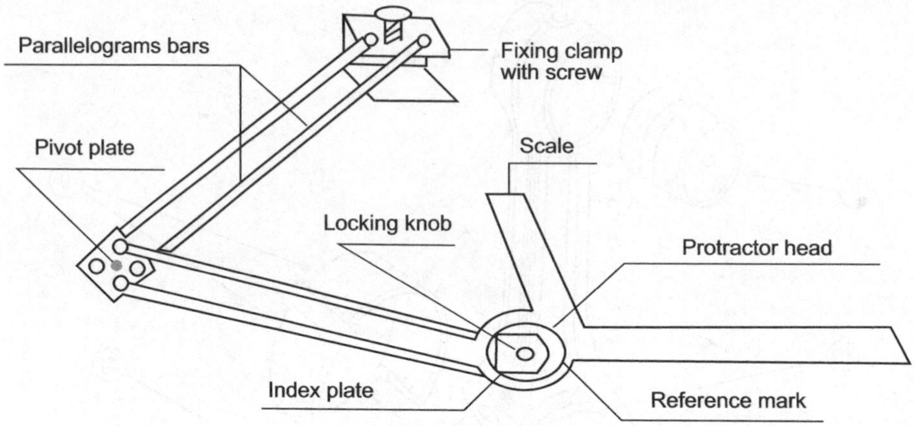

Fig.1.4: Mini Drafter

2. Set Squares: Shown in Fig.1.5

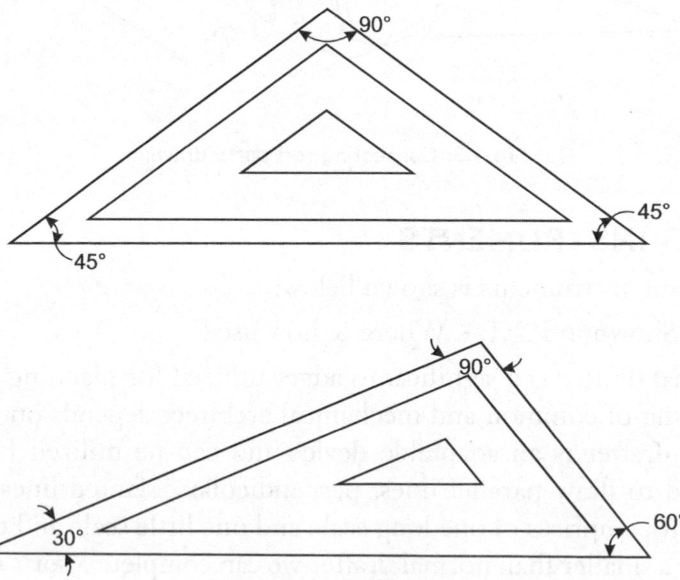

Fig.1.5: Set Squares

3. Instrument Box: Shown in Fig.1.6

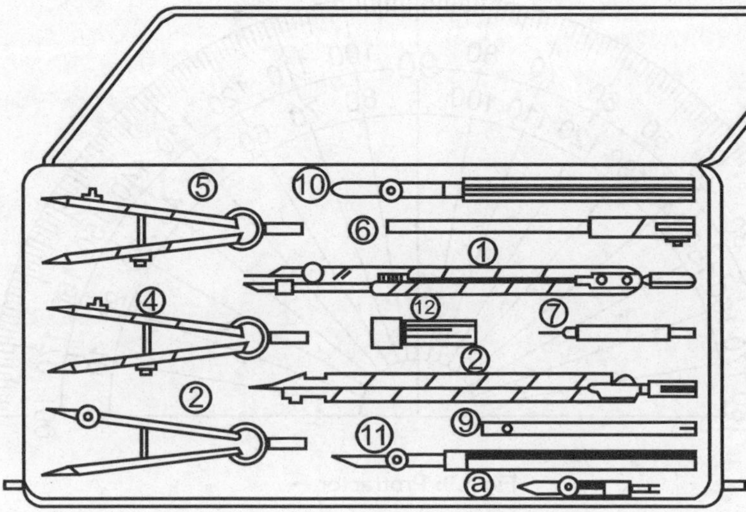

Fig.1.6: Instrument Box

4. Scales: Shown in Fig.1.7

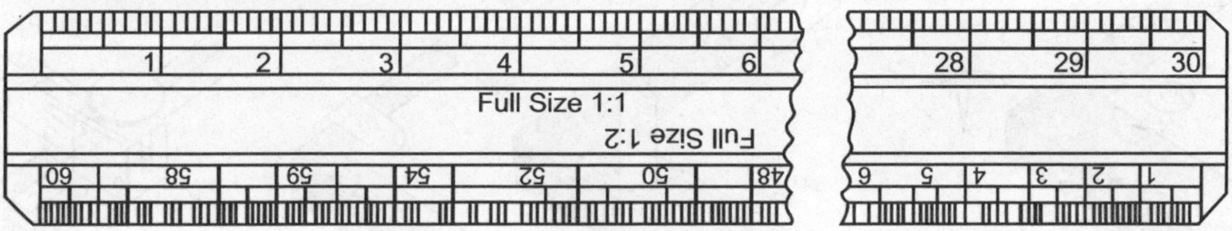

Fig.1.7: Scale

5. Set of Pencils: Shown in Fig.1.8

The "HB" grade pencil is medium soft and dark in black colour, whereas 1H, 2H, grade pencils hard and light in black colour.

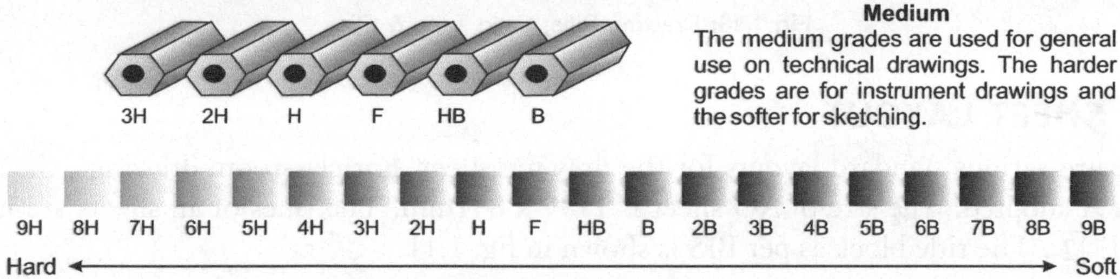

Fig.1.8: Set of Pencils

6. Protractor: Shown in Fig.1.9

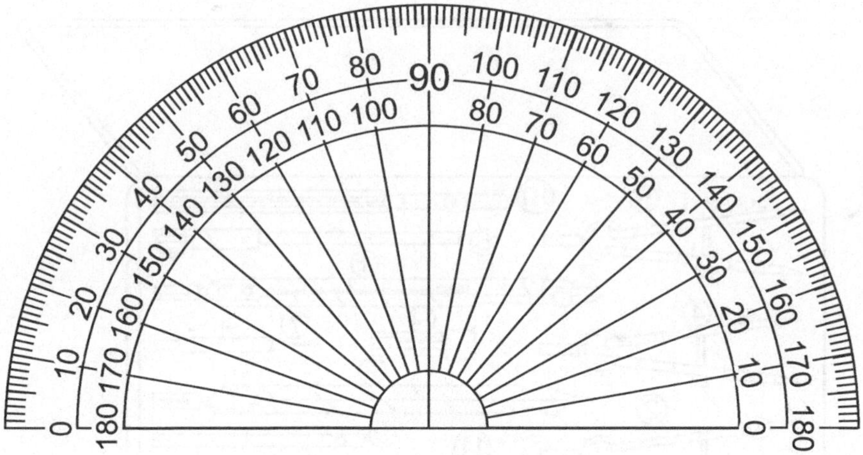

Fig.1.9: Protractor

7. Drawing Pins, Cello Tape & Clips: Shown in Fig.1.10

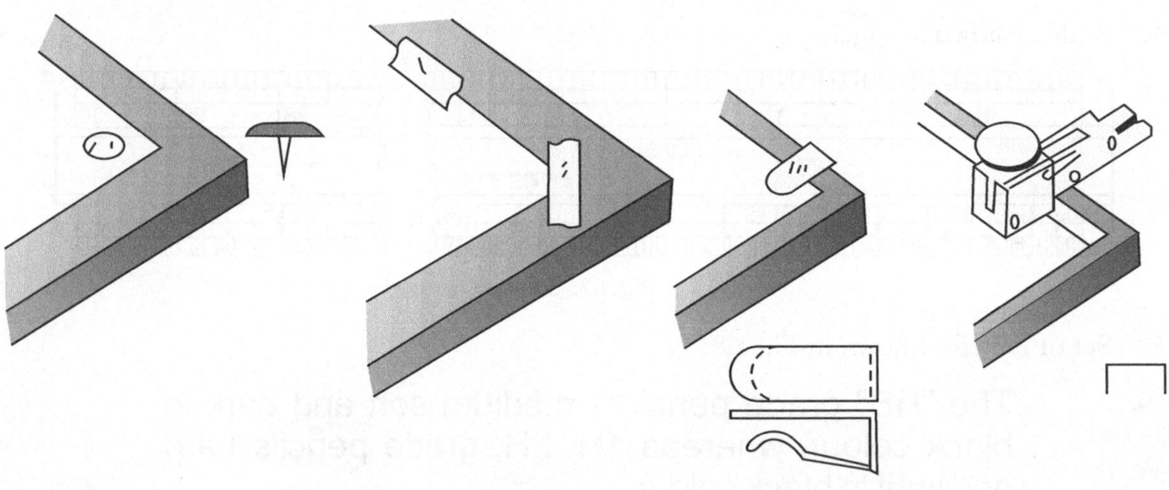

(i) Drawing pin (ii) Sellotape (iii) Spring clip (iv) Stapling machine

Fig.1.10: Drawing Pins, Cello Tape & Clips

1.4 SHEET LAYOUT

There are various standard layouts for the drawing sheet. For classroom drawings, the sheet layout A adopted. The size of AO sheet is 1189 × 841mm. The sides of all sheets are in the ratio 1: $\sqrt{2}$. The title block as per BIS is shown in fig. 1.11

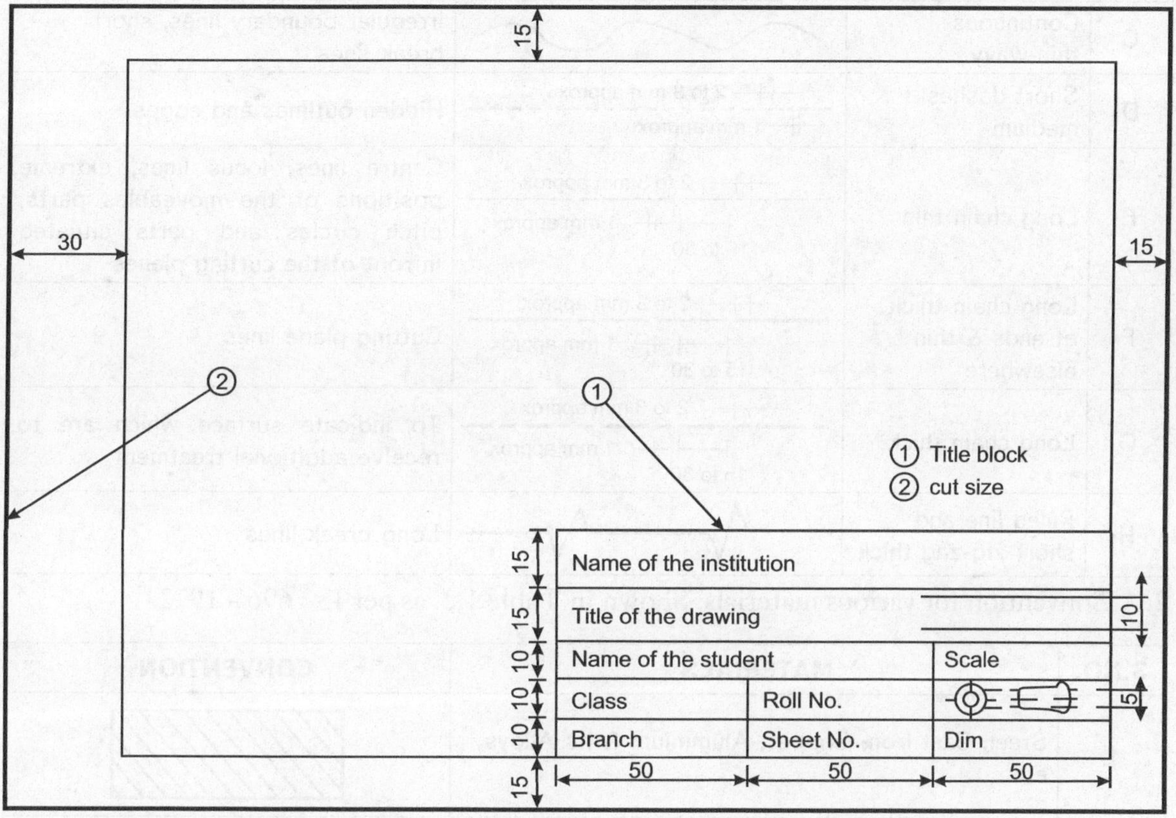

Fig.1.11: Sheet Layout (Suggested for Sheets Prepared in Classroom)

1.5 CONVENTIONS

1. Different types of lines are shown in Table.1.1.

Drawing conventions are the methods for doing things which adjust to a typical standard, for instance, specialized illustrations. Utilizing conventions save time and insure that a diagram implies a similar thing to any individual who sees it. The BSI standard for drawing is BS8888.

Description and uses of various lines (According to Indian Standard IS : 696-1972 to come up with IS : 10714-1983)

S. No.	Type of line	Illustration	Application
A	Continuous thick	————	Visible outline
B	Continuous thin	————	Dimension lines, leader lines, extension line, construction lines, outlines of adjacent parts, hatching and revolved section

C	Continuous thin-wavy	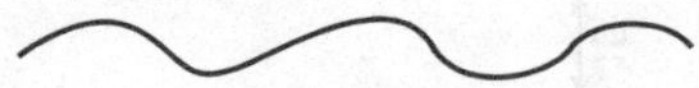	Irregular boundary lines, short break lines
D	Short dashes medium	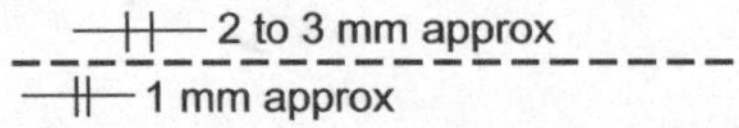	Hidden outlines and edges
E	Long chain thin	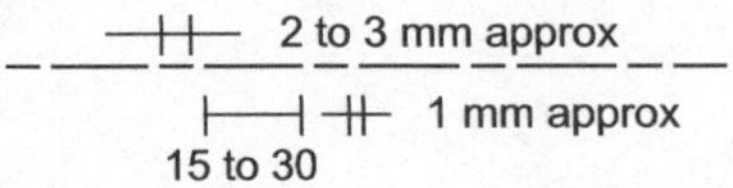	Centre lines, locus lines, extreme positions of the moveables parts, pitch circles and parts situated infront of the cutting planes
F	Long chain thick at ends & thin elsewhere	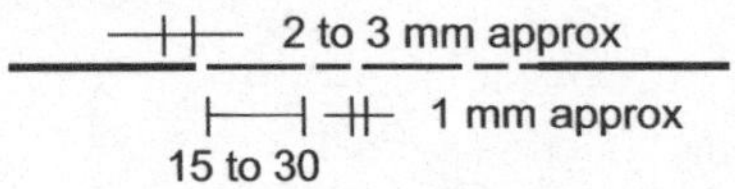	Cutting plane lines
G	Long chain thick	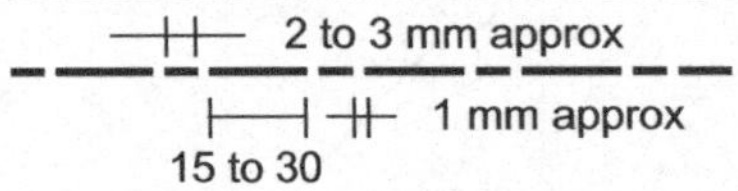	To indicate surface which are to receive additional treatment
H	Ruled line and short zig-zag thick	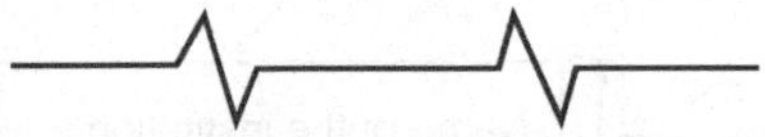	Long break lines

2. Convention for various materials: Shown in Table 1.2. as per IS : 696 - 1972

S.NO.	MATERIALS	CONVENTION
1.	Steel, Cast Iron, Copper, Aluminium & Its Alloys etc.	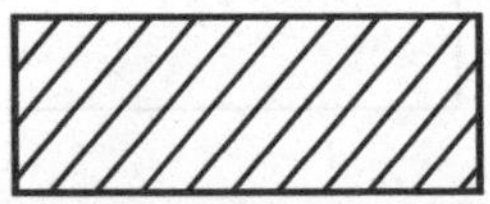
2.	Lead, Zinc, Tin, White Metal etc.	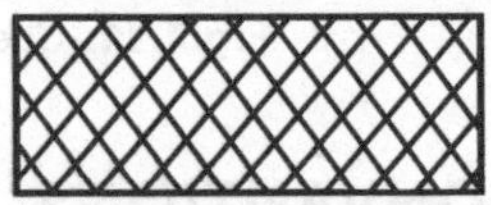
3.	Brass, Bronze, Gun Metal etc.	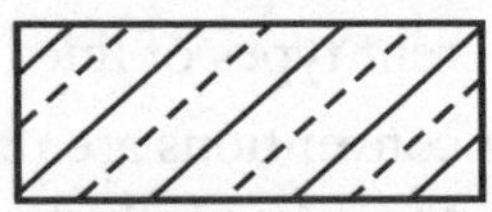
4.	Glass	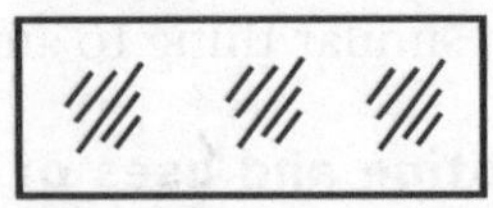
5.	Porcelain, Stone Ware, Marble, Slate etc.	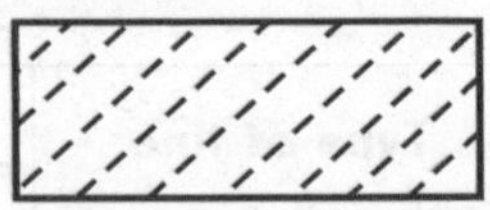
6.	Paper, Felt, Leather, Wax, Mica, Cork, Rubber	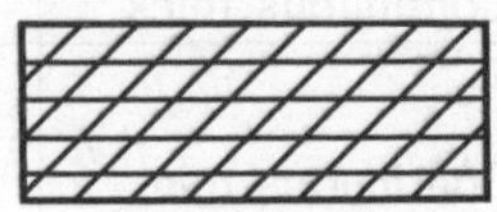

7.	Wood, Plywood etc.	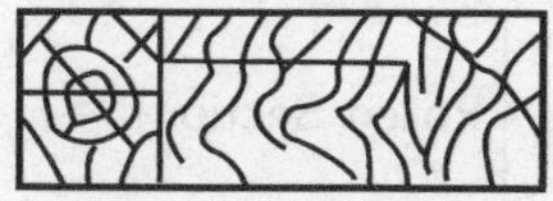
8.	Earth	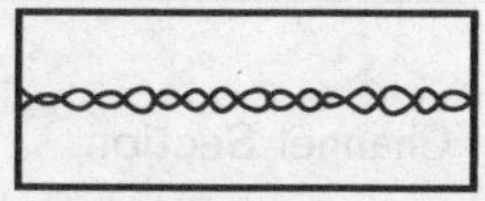
9.	Masonry, Brick Work, Fire Bricks etc.	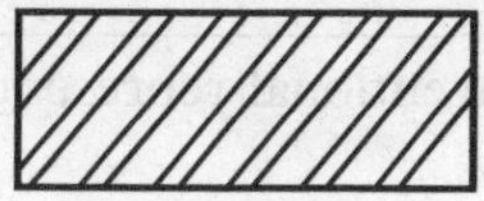
10.	Concrete	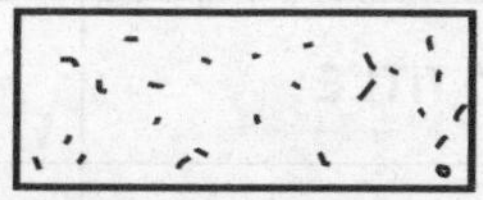
11.	Water, Oil, Petrol, Kerosene etc.	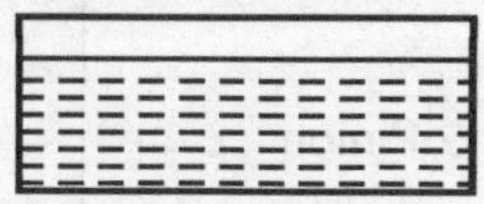

4. Conventional Breaks: Shown in Table 1.3 as per IS : 696-1972.

S.NO.	OBJECT	CONVENTION
1.	Rectangular Section	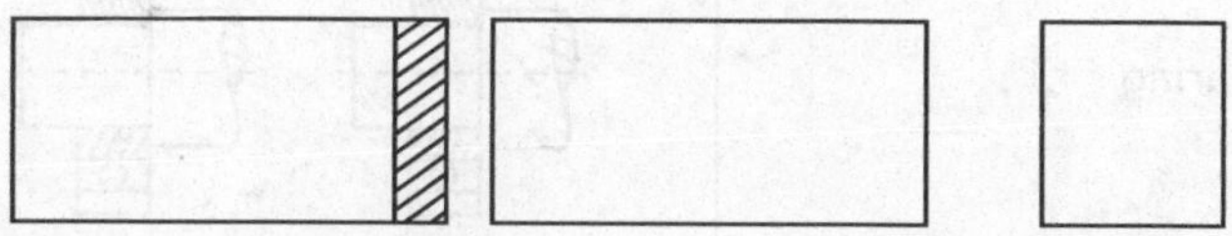
2.	Round Section	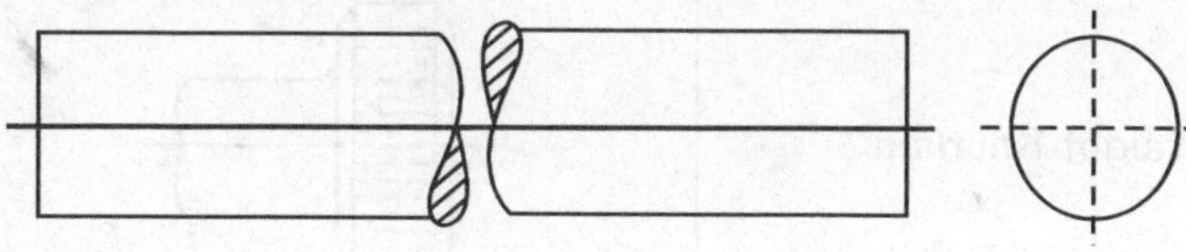
3.	Pipe or Tubing	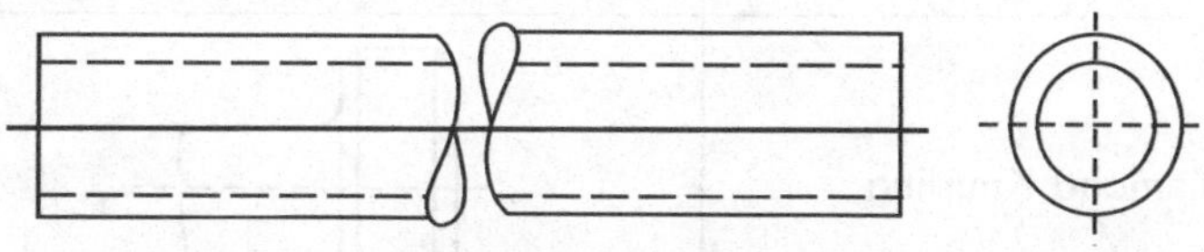
4.	Pipe or Tubing	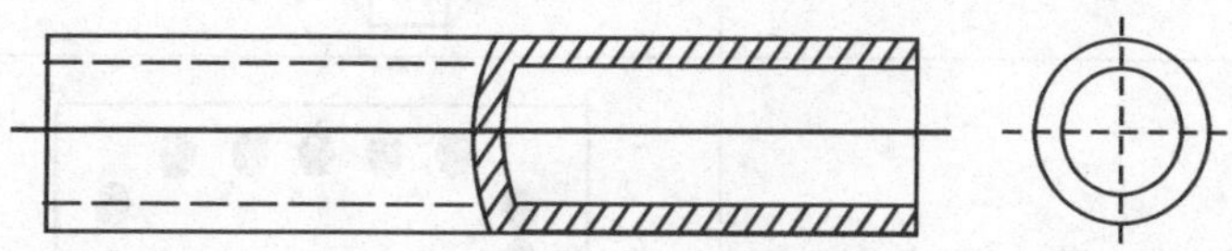
5.	Wood Rectangular Section	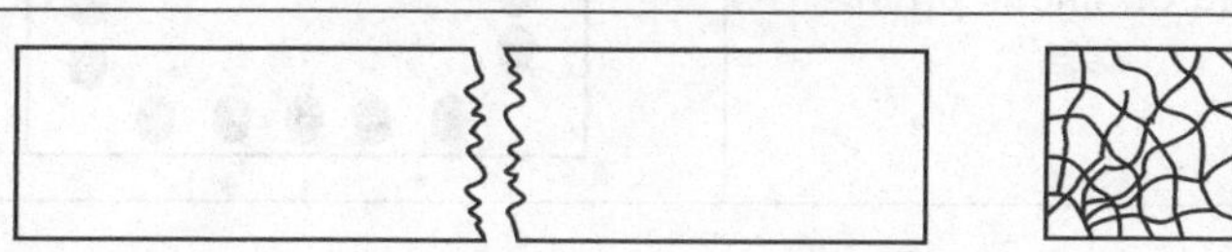

6.	Rolled Section	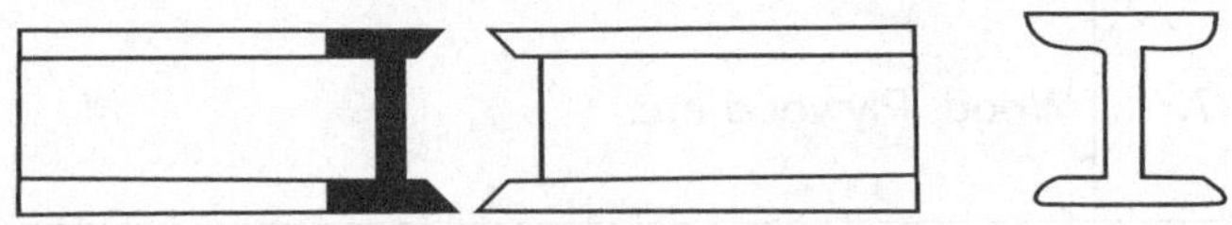
7.	Channel Section	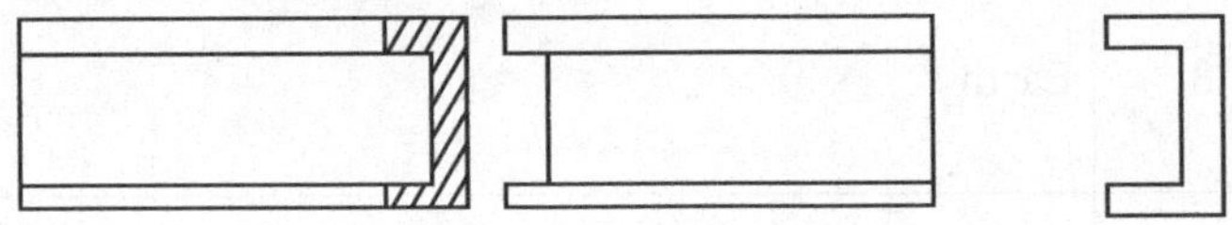

5. Conventional representation of common features: Shown in Table 1.4 as per IS : 696-1972

TITLE	ACTUAL PROJECTION/SECTION	CONVENTION
Ratchet & Pinion	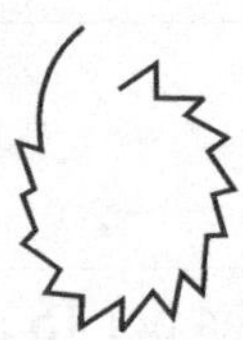	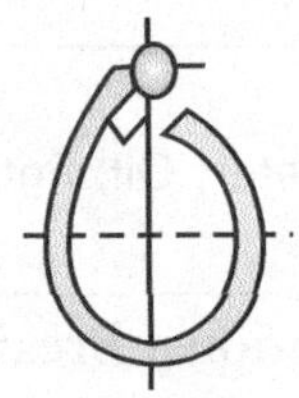
Bearing	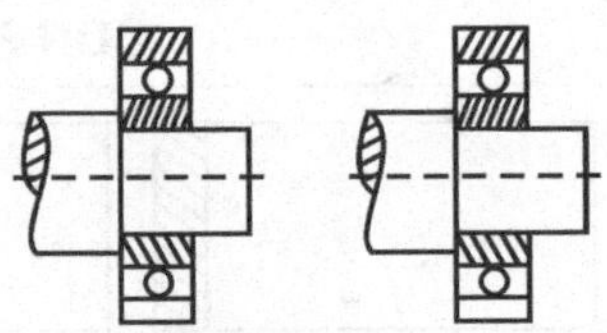	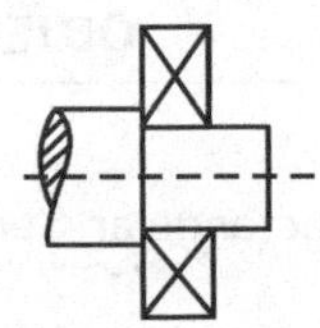
Straight Knurling	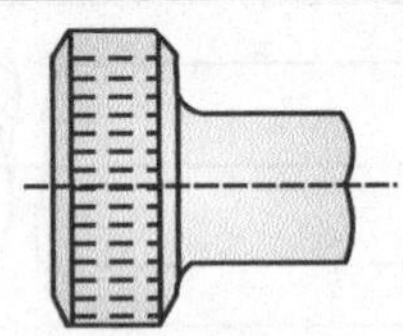	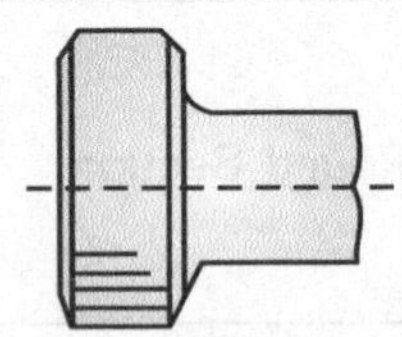
Diamond Knurling	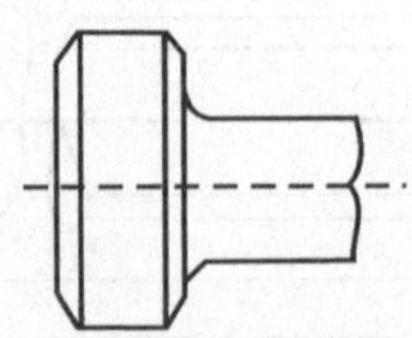	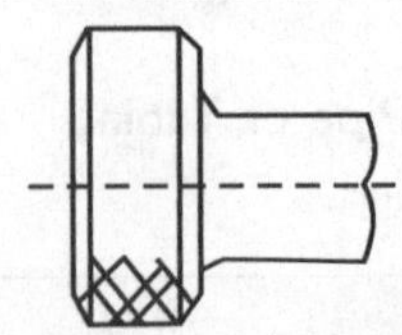
Hole on linear pitch	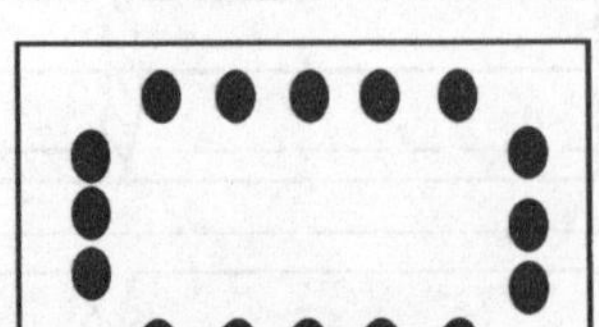	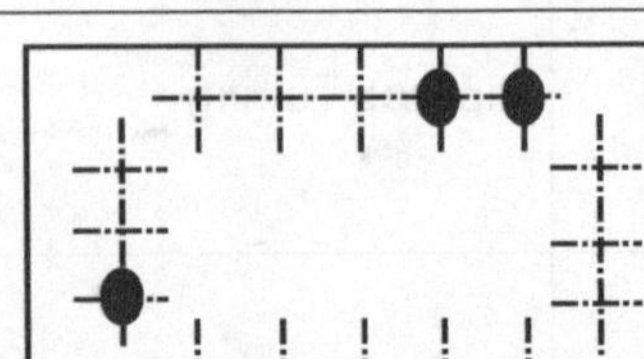

Hole on circular pitch	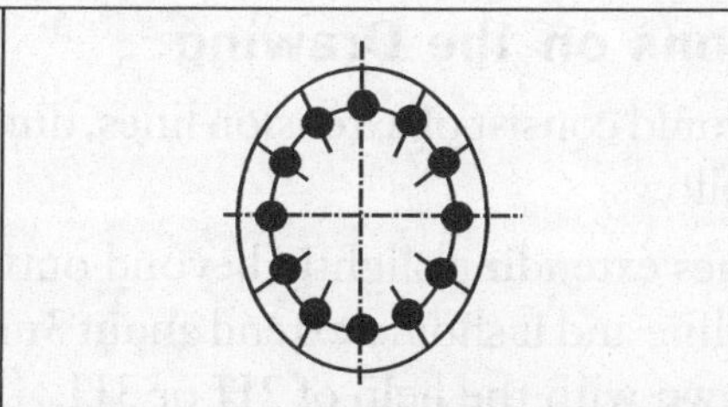	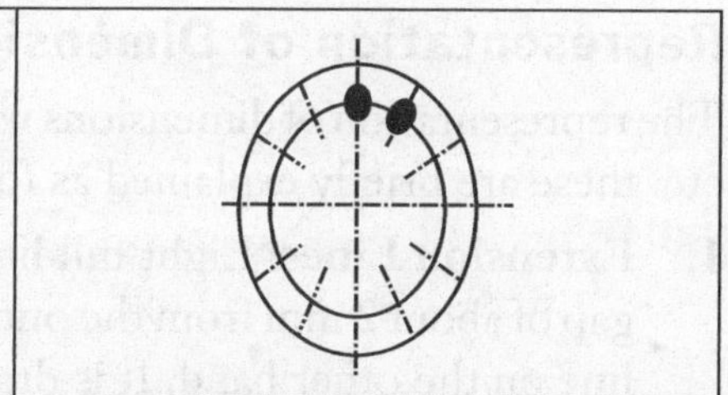
Repeated Parts	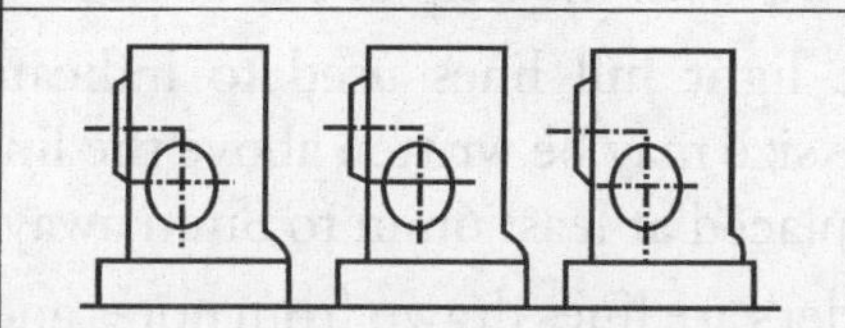	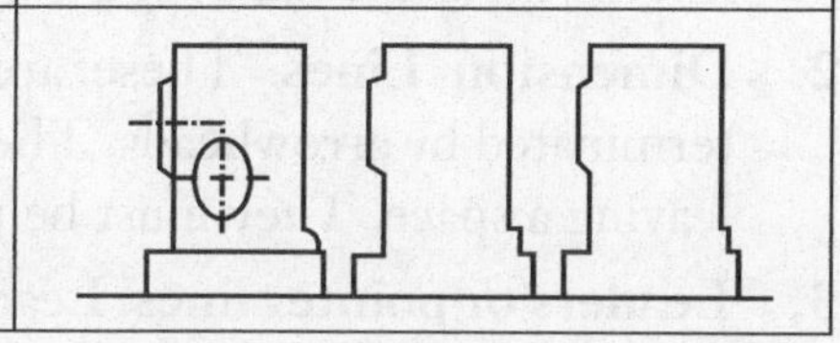

1.6 DIMENSIONING

The art of writing the various measurements on the drawing to express all sizes of an object is known as Dimensioning.

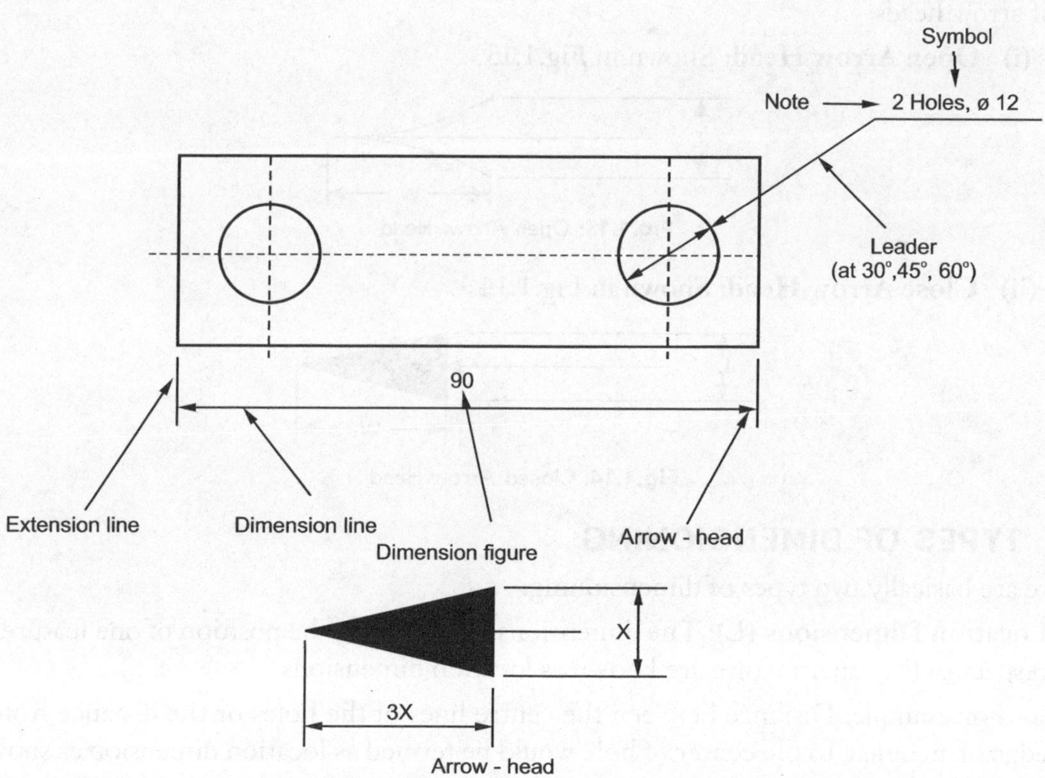

Fig.1.12: Extension Lines & Dimension Lines and arrow head

Representation of Dimensions on the Drawing

The representation of dimensions would consist of extension lines, dimension lines, arrowheads etc. these are briefly explained as follows:

1. **Extension Lines**: Light full lines extending slightly beyond outline. Extend by keeping a gap of about 2 mm from the outline and it should extend about 3mm beyond the dimension line on the other hand. It is drawn with the help of 2H or 3H.
2. **Dimension Lines**: These are light full lines used to indicate the measurement and terminated by arrowheads. The size may be written above the line or between the lines by leaving a space. They must be placed at least 6mm to 8mm away from the outlines.
3. **Leaders or pointer lines**: Leaders are lines drawn from notes and figures. They are drawn at some angle may be 30°, 45° and 60°. They are never drawn vertically or horizontally. The use of long leaders should be avoided.
4. **Arrow heads**: The arrowheads should be close filled type isosceles triangle in height to width ratio as 3:1. These are used to terminate the dimension lines. There are two types of arrow heads:

   (i) **Open Arrow Head:** Shown in Fig.1.13.

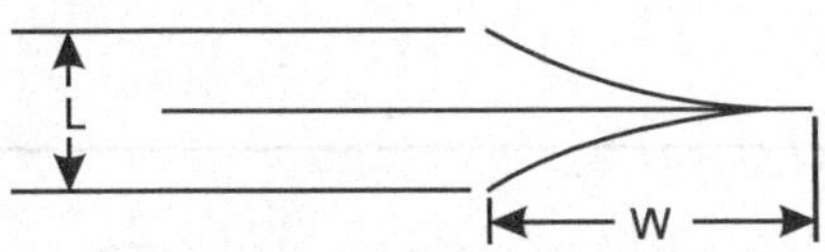

Fig.1.13: Open Arrow Head

   (ii) **Close Arrow Head:** Shown in Fig.1.14.

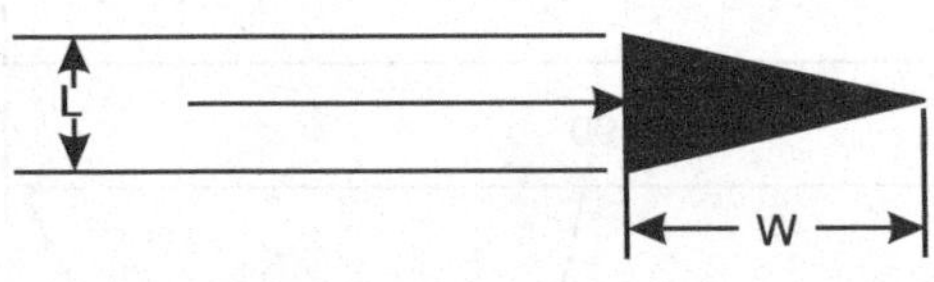

Fig.1.14: Closed Arrow Head

1.7 TYPES OF DIMENSIONING

There are basically two types of dimensioning:

1. **Location Dimensions (L)**: The dimensions which locate the position of one feature with respect to the other feature are known as location dimensions.

   For example: Distance between the centre lines of the holes or the distance from the edge of an object to the center of hole would be termed as location dimension as shown in Fig.1.15.
2. **Size Dimensions (S)**: The dimensions which indicate the various sizes of the object such as length, breadth, diameter, etc. are known as size dimensions. For example: the dimensions marked to show the sizes of various objects like length and breadth of the rectangle or the radius of a circle etc. would termed as size dimensions Fig.1.15.

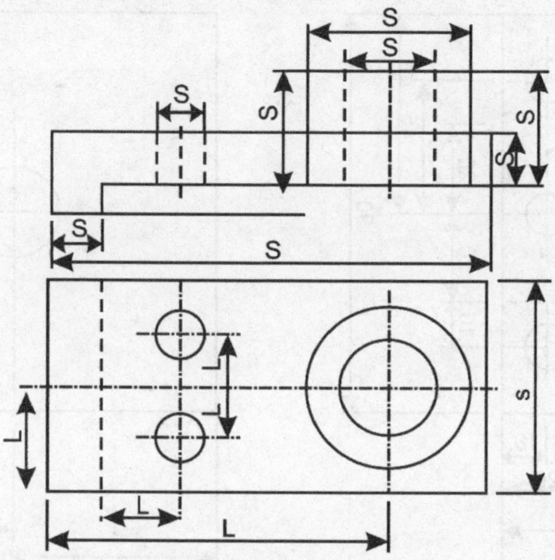

Fig.1.15: Size Dimensions & Location Dimensions

1.8 SYSTEM OF PLACING DIMENSIONS

According to B.I.S. (Bureau of Indian Standards), these two recommended systems for placing dimensions are as follows:

1. **Aligned system:** In this system of dimensioning, all the dimensions are placed so that they may be read either from the bottom or from the right hand edge of the drawing sheet. Hence all the dimensions are placed normal and above the dimension lines in the center as shown in Fig.1.16a. This system is normally used in engineering drawings.
2. **Unidirectional System:** In this system of dimensioning, all the dimensions are so placed that they may be read from the bottom edge of the drawing sheet as shown in Fig.1.16b. Hence the text of the dimension is to be fixed but their dimension line will be rotated based on the side of an object. This system is normally used on large drawings such as drawing of air-crafts, automobiles, etc.

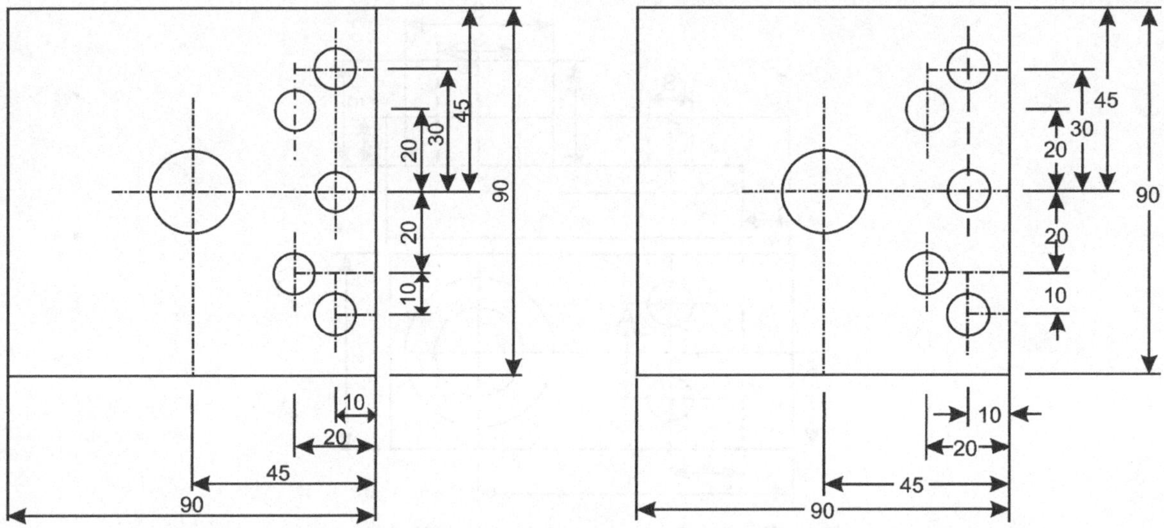

Fig.1.16: Aligned & Unidirectional System

1.8.1 Units of Dimensioning

All the dimensions are to be specified only in one unit i.e. in mm. The unit of the dimensions should not be placed along the text of the dimension but a note is to be added above the title block of the drawing sheet regarding it's unit. For example: **All dimensions are in mm.**

1.9 GENERAL RULES OF DIMENSIONING

The following general rules should be followed for dimensioning a drawing:

(i) All the dimensions necessary for the correct functioning of the part should expressed directly on the drawing.

(ii) Dimensions should be given on the view which shows the relevant features most clearly.

(iii) Dimensions marked in one view need not be repeated in another view except reference purposes as shown in Fig.1.17.

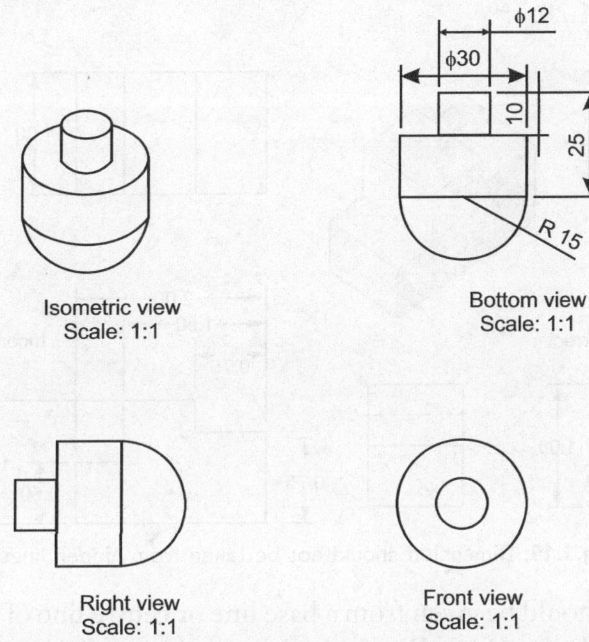

Fig.1.17: Dimension need not be repeated in another view

(iv) Dimensions should be placed outside the view, as far as possible as shown in Fig.1.18.

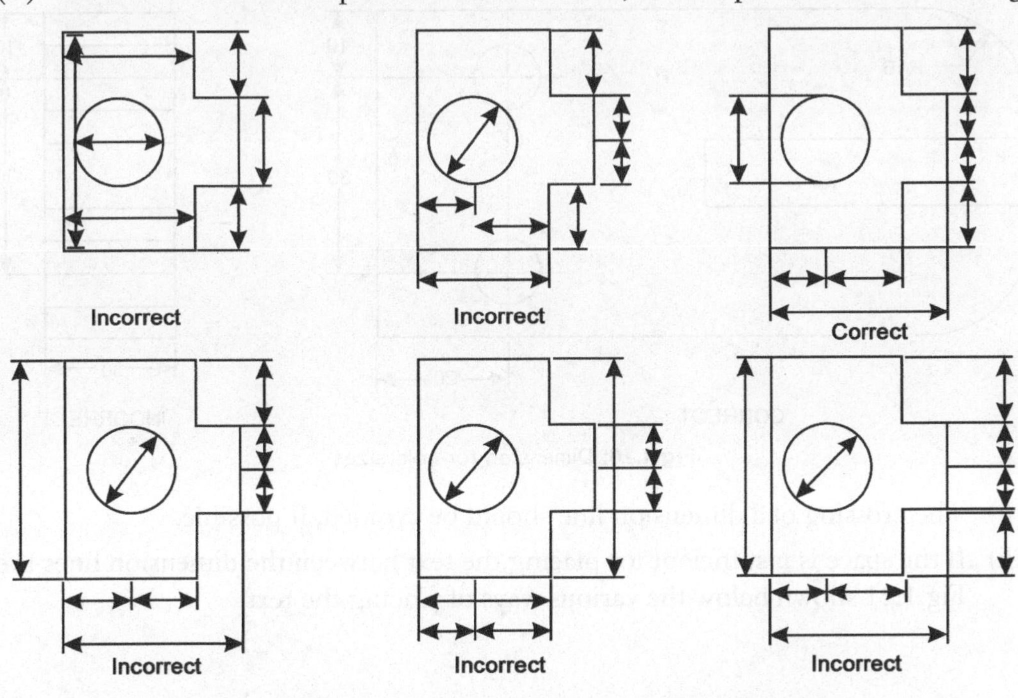

Fig.1.18: Correct & incorrect Method of Dimensioning

(v) Dimensions should be taken from visible outlines rather than from hidden lines as shown in Fig.1.20.

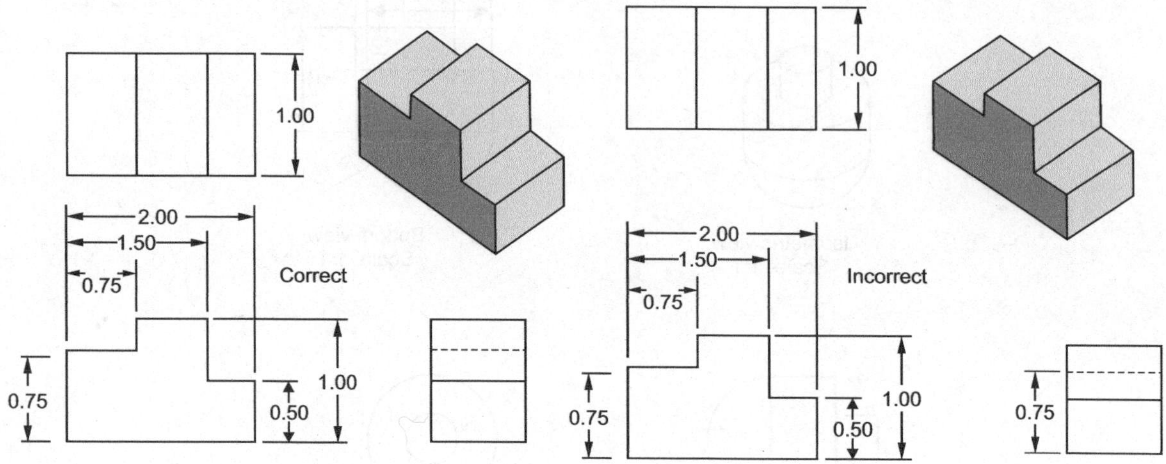

Fig.1.19: Dimension should not be taken from hidden lines

(vi) Dimensions should be given from a base line or centre line of a hole or an important hole or a finished surface. Dimensioning to a centre line should be avoided except when the centre line passes through the centre of a hole as shown in Fig.1.20.

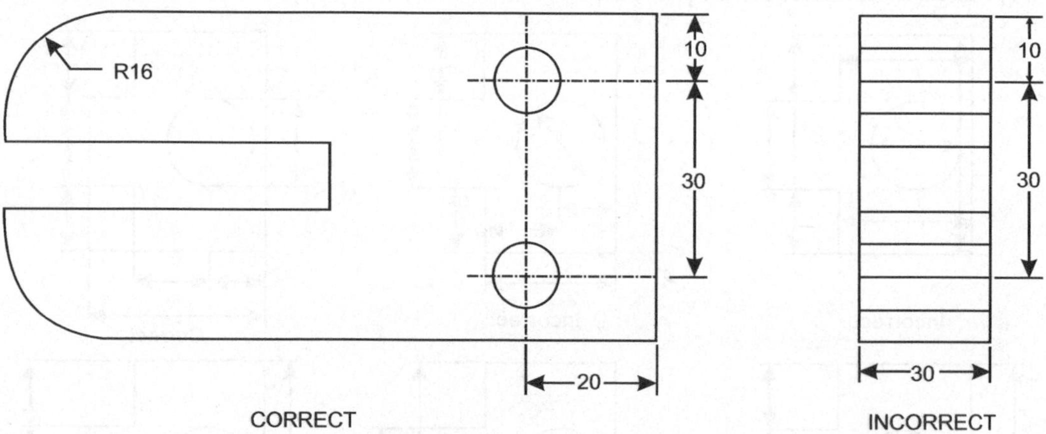

Fig.1.20: Dimension for hole sizes

(vii) The crossing of a dimension line should be avoided, if possible.

(viii) If the space is insufficient for placing the text between the dimension lines then the Fig.1.21 shown below the various ways of placing the text.

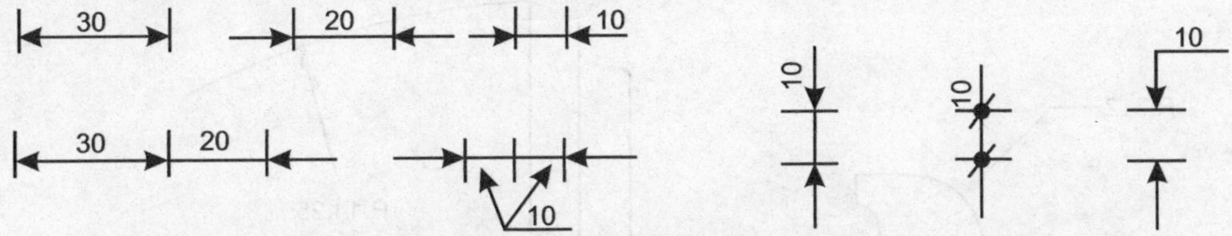

Fig.1.21: Different ways of dimensioning distances when the space is insufficient

(ix) Dimension line and extension line should not cross each other.

(x) Circles of different sizes should be dimensioned as shown in Fig.1.22. When the space for dimensioning is restricted, one of the methods should be used.

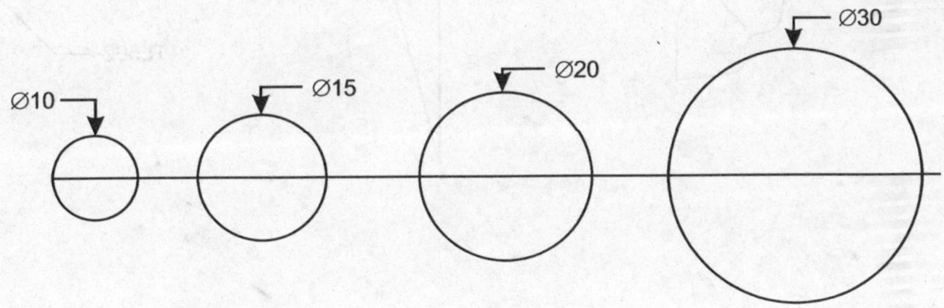

Fig.1.22: Dimensioning of circles of different sizes

(xi) Arcs of circles should be dimensioned by their respective radii. While dimensioning small radii, the arrow should be reserved as shown in Fig. Radii of arcs, the Centers of which need not be located, should be dimensioned as shown in Fig 1.23 & 1.24.

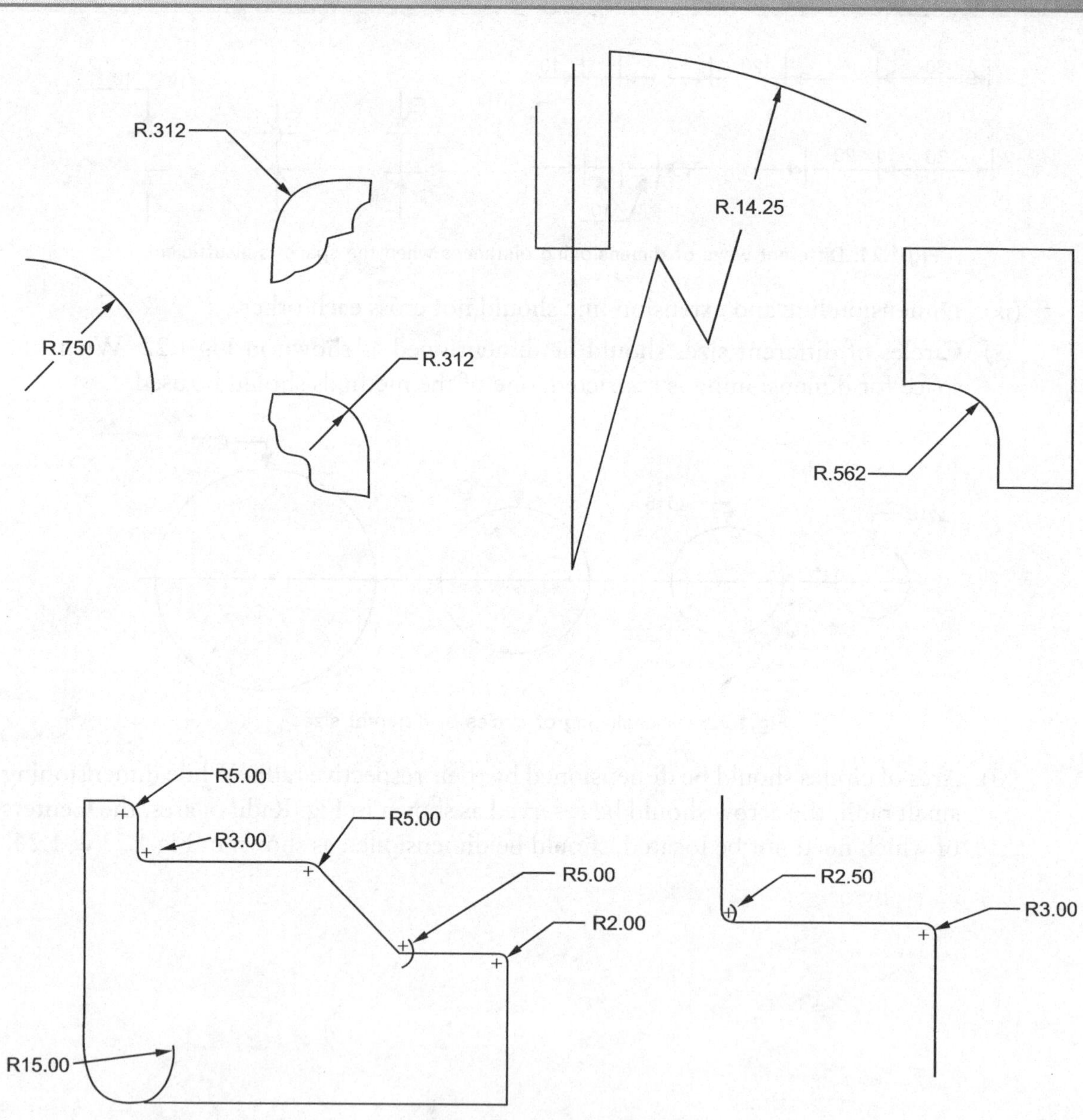

Fig.1.23: Dimensioning of radii

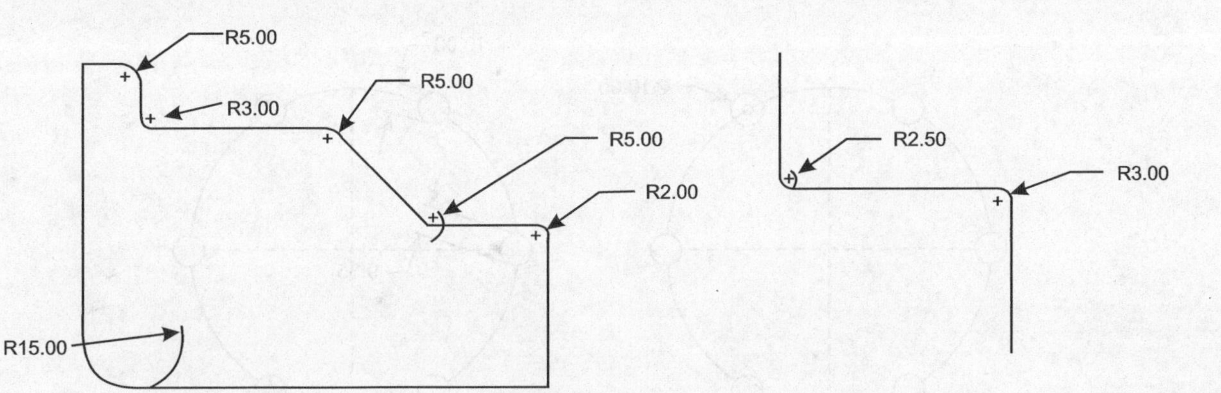

Fig.1.24: Dimensioning of radii of arc the centre which need not be located

(xii) Dimensions of angles, chords and arcs should be given as shown in Fig.1.25.

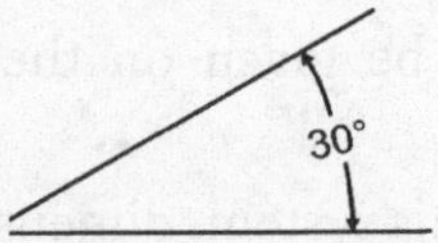

Fig.1.25: Dimensioning of angles

(xiii) Dimensions on a sectioned view should be given as shown in Fig.1.26.

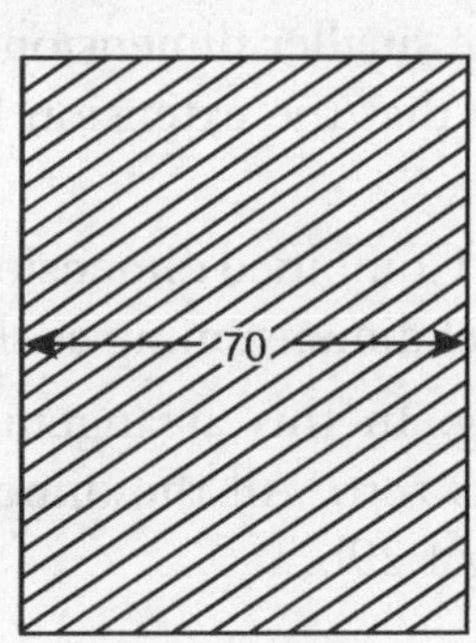

Fig.1.26: Dimensioning on a section view

(xiv) Dimensions of parts which are not drawn to scale should be underlined. However when it is required to draw the whole drawing not to scale, the abbreviation 'NTS' may be used or the column of scale be scored off.

(xv) While dimensioning an object, use of long leaders should be avoided as shown in Fig.1.27.

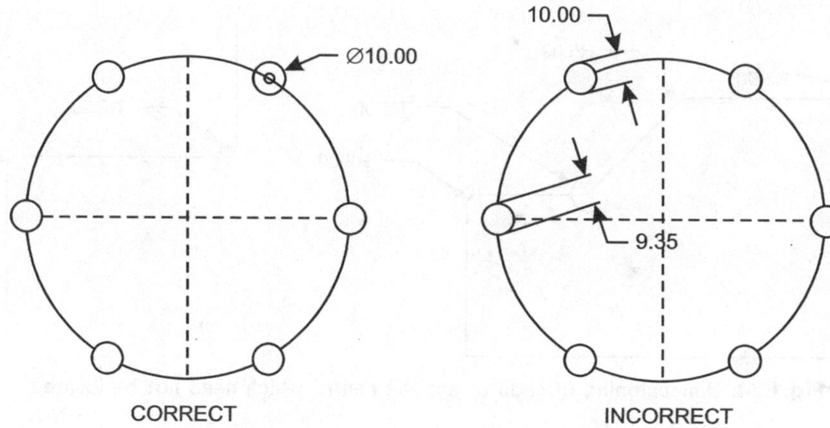

Fig.1.27: Dimensioning on number of holes

(xvi) Dimension in a series may be given on the views in any one of the following arrangements :

(*a*) *Chain Dimensioning*: In this system, dimensions are arranged in a straight line as shown in Fig.1.28a, when overall dimension is given, one of the smaller or least important dimension is generally omitted.

(*b*) *Parallel dimensioning*: In this arrangement, all the dimensions are given from a common base line. The smaller dimensions are placed nearer the view and the larger further away, so that the extension line do not cross dimension lines as shown in Fig.1.28b.

(*c*) *Combined dimensioning*: Combined dimensioning is the result of the simultaneous use of chain and parallel dimensioning as shown in Fig.1.29a.

(*d*) *Progressive dimensioning*: In this arrangement, one datum point or surface is selected which reads as zero. All the dimensions are referred to that point or surface as shown in Fig.1.29b.

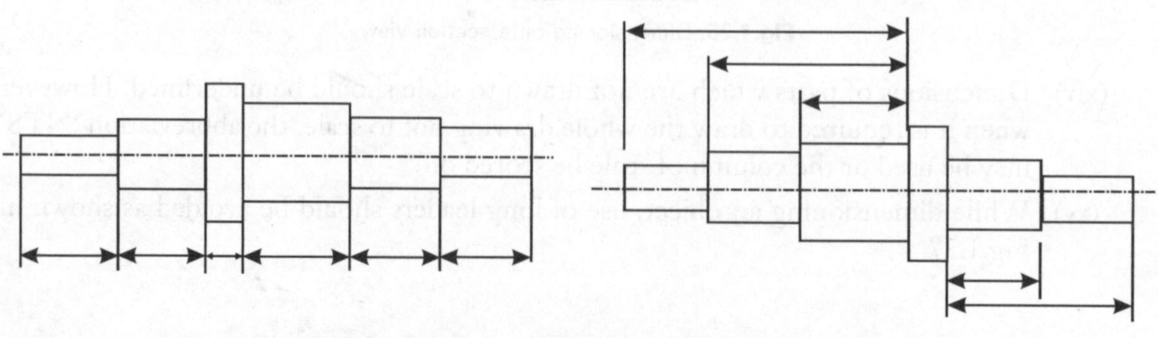

Fig.1.28: Chain Dimensioning & Parallel Dimensioning

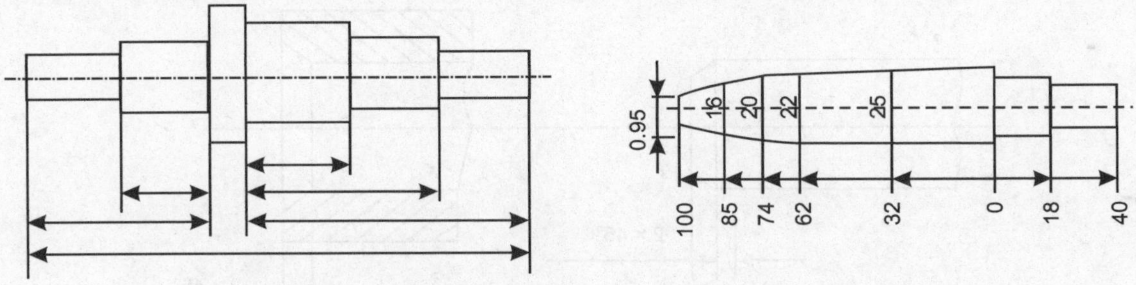

Fig.1.29: Combined Dimensioning & Progressive Dimensioning

(xvii) Never repeat the dimension which is already indicated in the drawing and understandable from geometry.

(xviii) Never repeat the same dimension in different view of the drawing. For example: length of an object indicated in the front view should not be dimensioned in the top view of the same drawing.

(xix) Dimensions of hole sizes should be given as shown in Fig 1.30.

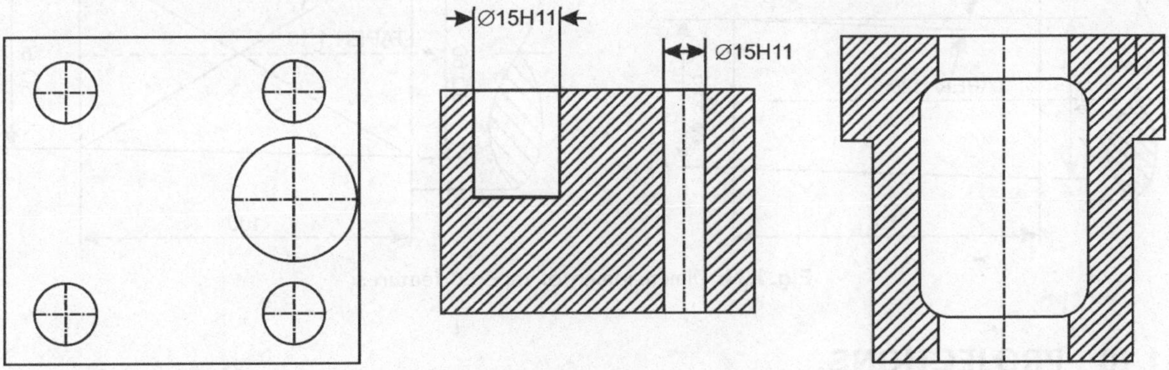

Fig.1.30: Dimensioning of Hole Sizes

(xx) The counter sinks and counter bores should be dimensioned by giving maximum diameter and the included angle as shown in Fig.1.31.

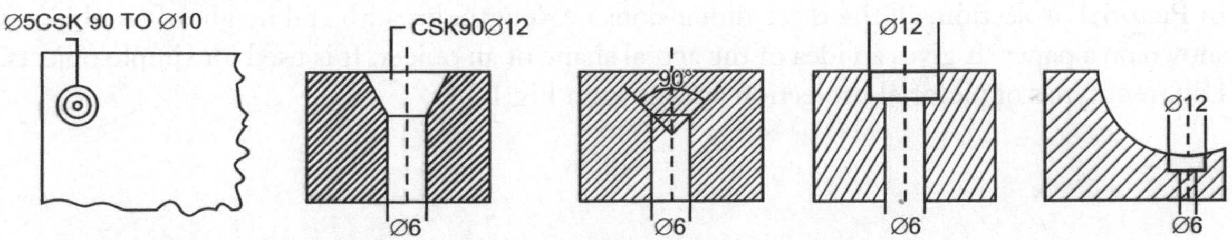

Fig.1.31: Dimensioning of countersinks & counter boress

(xxi) The chamfers should be dimensioned by the length and angle of chamfers as shown in Fig.1.32.

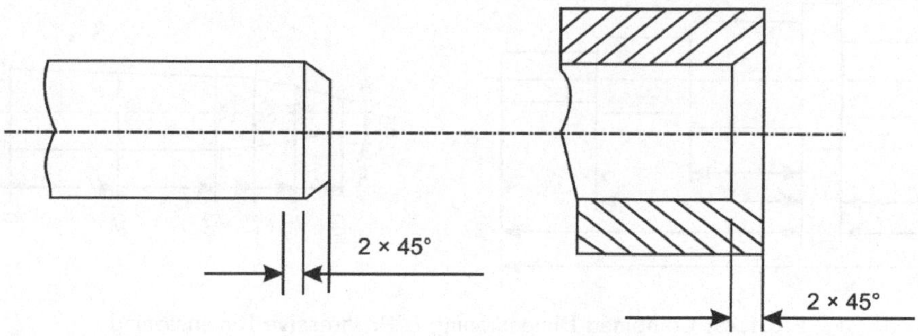

Fig.1.32: Dimensioning of chamfer

(xxii) Dimensions for specifying size and form of tapered features should be given as shown in Fig.1.34.

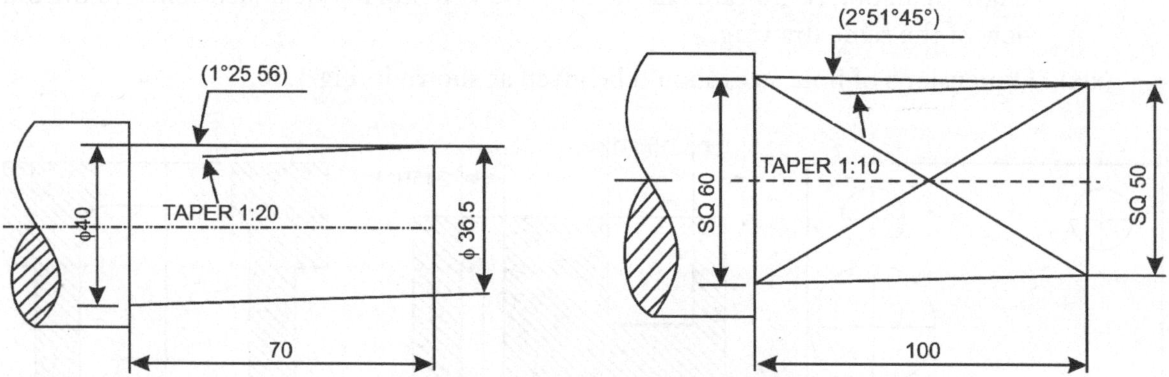

Fig.1.33: Dimensioning of tapered features

1.10 PROJECTIONS

A Projection is defined as a view imagined to be projected on a plane, known as projection plane, while projecting "rays of sight" called projectors. In the engineering, it is classified as:

(i) Pictorial Projection

In Pictorial projection, all the three dimensions i.e. length, breadth and height of an object is shown on a paper. It gives an idea of the actual shape of an object. It is used for simple objects. Different types of pictorial projection are shown n Fig.1.34.

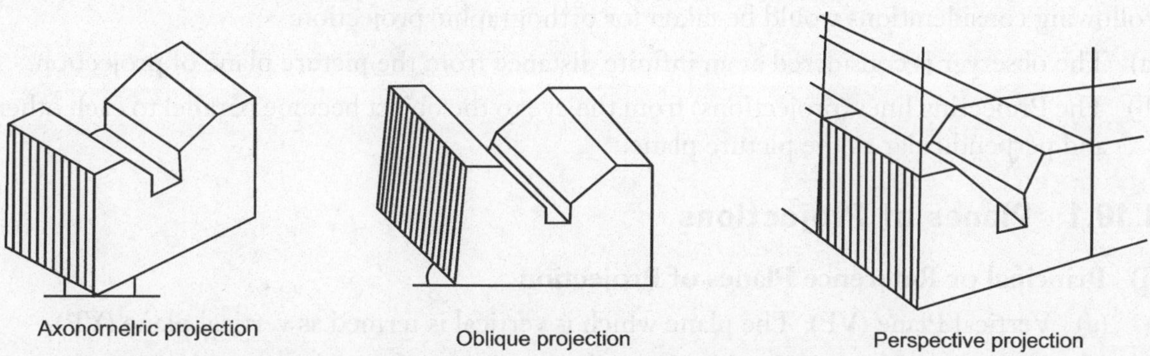

Fig.1.34: Types of pictorial projection

(ii) Orthographic Projection

The projections obtained on a plane of projection, where the projectors are parallel but perpendicular to the plane of projection is known as orthographic projections.

An object has three dimensions i.e. length, breadth and height. The problem is to represent or convert three dimensional (3D) objects into two dimensional (2D) objects on a sheet or paper as shown in Fig.1.35. The solution to this problem is orthographic projections. This method is universally used to represent complicated manufacturing and construction drawings by all engineers.

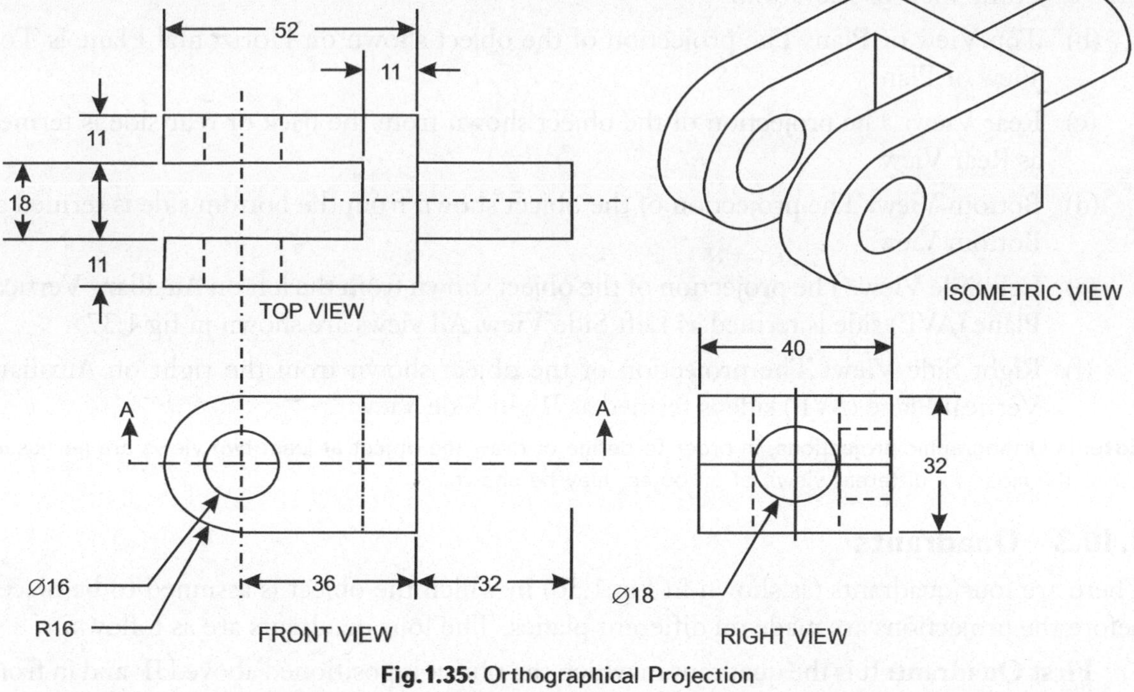

Fig.1.35: Orthographical Projection

Following considerations would be taken for orthographic projection:

(a) The observer is considered at an infinite distance from the picture plane of projection.

(b) The Projecting lines (projections) from the eye to the object become parallel to each other and perpendicular to the picture plane.

1.10.1 Planes of Projections

(i) Principal or Reference Planes of Projection

(a) Vertical Plane (VP): The plane which is vertical is termed as vertical plane (VP).

(b) Horizontal Plane (HP): the plane which is horizontal and perpendicular to vertical plane is termed as horizontal plane (HP). As both VP & HP shown in fig. 1.36

(ii) Secondary Planes of Projections

(a) Auxiliary Plane (AP): Any other plane, placed at any angle to the two principal planes is termed as Auxiliary Plane (AP).

(b) Profile Plane (PP): The plane which is perpendicular to the two principal planes is termed as Profile Plane (PP) or Auxiliary Vertical Plane (AVP).

1.10.2 Views

(a) Front View or Elevation:The projection of the object shown on Vertical Plane is Front View or Elevation.

(b) Top View or Plan: The projection of the object shown on Horizontal Plane is Top View or Plan.

(c) Rear View: The projection of the object shown from the back or rear side is termed as Rear View.

(d) Bottom View: The projection of the object shown from the bottom side is termed as Bottom View.

(e) Left Side View: The projection of the object shown from the left on Auxiliary Vertical Plane (AVP) side is termed as Left Side View. All views are shown in fig 1.37

(f) Right Side View: The projection of the object shown from the right on Auxiliary Vertical Plane (AVP) side is termed as Right Side View.

Note: In Orthographic projections, in order to define or draw the object at least two views are necessary but at the most six different views of an object may be shown.

1.10.3 Quadrants

There are four quadrants (as shown in Fig.1.36) in which the object is assumed to be placed before the projections are made on different planes. The four quadrants are as follows:

1. **First Quadrant:** It is the quadrant in which the object is positioned above HP and in front of VP.

2. **Second Quadrant:** It is the quadrant in which the object is positioned above HP and behind of VP.
3. **Third Quadrant:** It is the quadrant in which the object is positioned below HP and behind of VP.
4. **Fourth Quadrant:** It is the quadrant in which the object is positioned below HP and in front of VP.

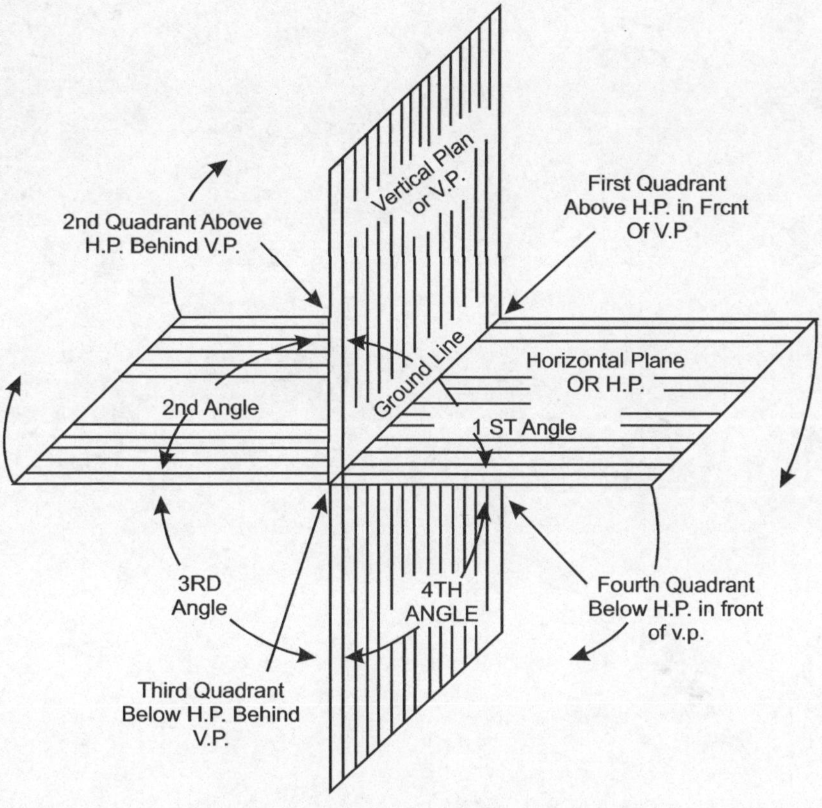

Fig.1.36: Four Quadrants

1.10.4 Methods of Projections

There are four methods of projection which are as follows:

1. First angle projection
2. Second angle projection
3. Third angle projection
4. Fourth angle projection

Note: Second angle & Fourth angle projection method are not used because after rotating the H.P. in clockwise direction, elevation and plan overlap with each other and no separate details can be viewed.

1. First Angle Projection

In this method of projection, the object is assumed to be positioned or situated in first quadrant. This method is used in India and European countries. According to Bureau of Indian Standard (BIS), the conventional symbol of first angle projection method is as shown n Fig.1.37:

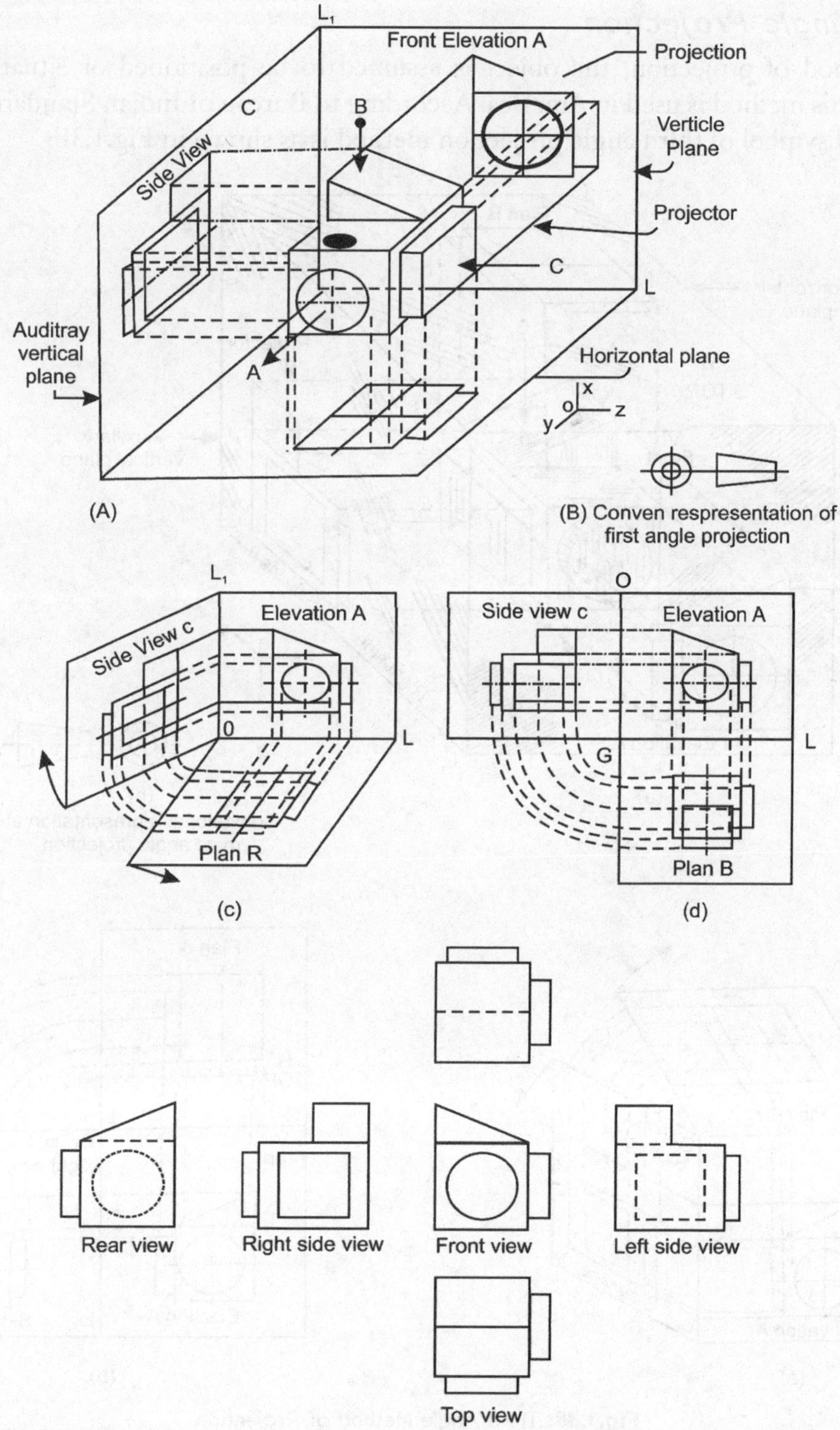

Fig.1.37: First Angle Method of Projection

2. Third Angle Projection

In this method of projection, the object is assumed to be positioned or situated in third quadrant. This method is used in America. According to Bureau of Indian Standard (BIS), the conventional symbol of third angle projection method is as shown in Fig.1.38:

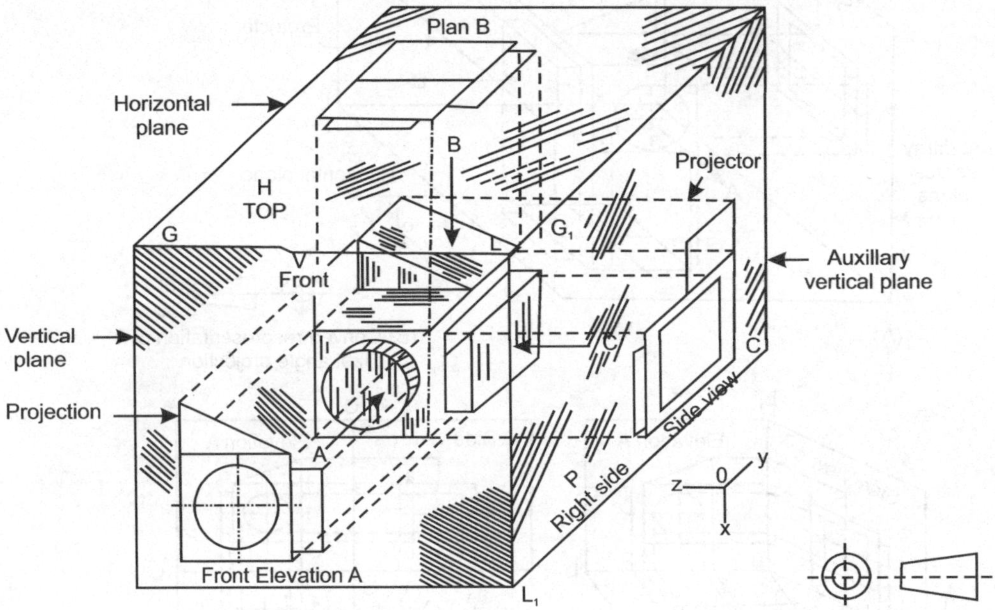

(a)

(b)

Convetional representation at mind angle projection

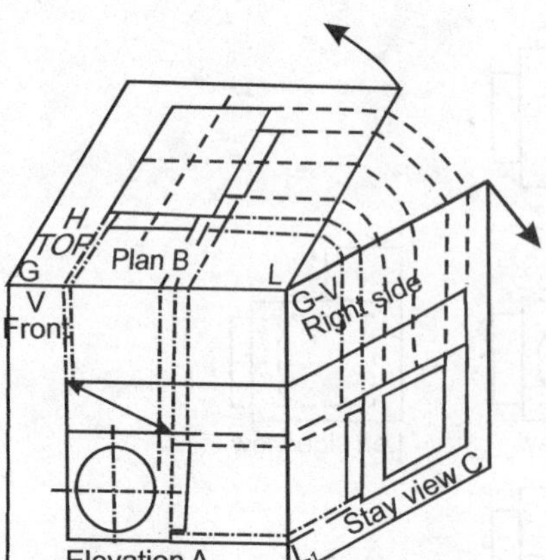

(a)

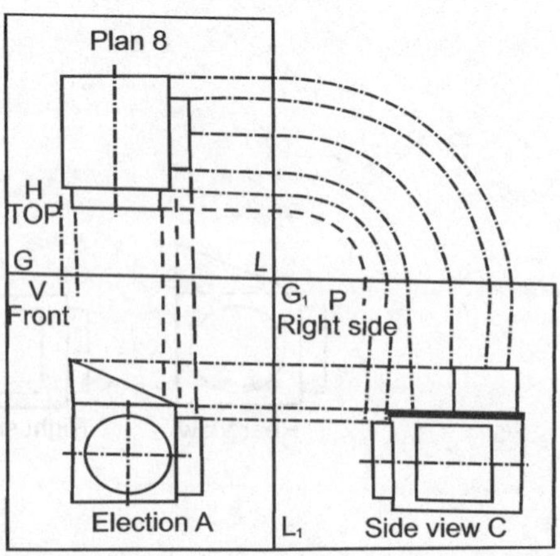

(b)

Fig.1.38: Third Angle Method of Projection

Comparison of First Angle Projection and Third Angle Projection

S. No.	First angle projection	Third angle projection
a.	The object is placed in the 1st quadrant.	The objects placed in the 3rd quadrant.
b.	Observer is assumed at infinite distance from the object in RHS of the quadrant.	Observer is assumed at infinite distance from the object in LHS of the quadrant.
c.	The object is placed in between the observer and the plane of projection.	The plane of projection comes between the eye of the observer and the object.
d.	The planes need not be transparent.	The planes are assumed to be transparent.
e.	Elevation is projected on VP, plan on HP and side view on auxiliary vertical plane (AVP) which are at right angles to both HP & VP.	Elevation is projected on VP, plan on HP and side views on auxiliary vertical plane (AVP) which are at right angles to both HP & VP.
f.	Now rotation of planes would be carried out in order to place all the view in one plane of drawing sheet.	Rotation of plane is carried out.
g.	VP is kept fixed and rotation of HP in clockwise direction resulting that plan comes below the elevation.	VP is kept fixed and rotation of HP in ant-clockwise direction resulting that plan comes above the elevation.
h.	Keeping VP fixed, rotation of AVP is carried out in such that the side view will not coincide with elevation. As a result LHS view comes on RHS of elevation.	Keeping VP fixed, rotation of AVP is carried out in such that the side view will not coincide with the elevation. As a result LHS view comes on the same side.
i.	This method has been recommended by Bureau of Indian Standard and some countries of Europe.	This method is used in America.
j.	The symbol according to Bureau of Indian Standard (BIS) as follows: 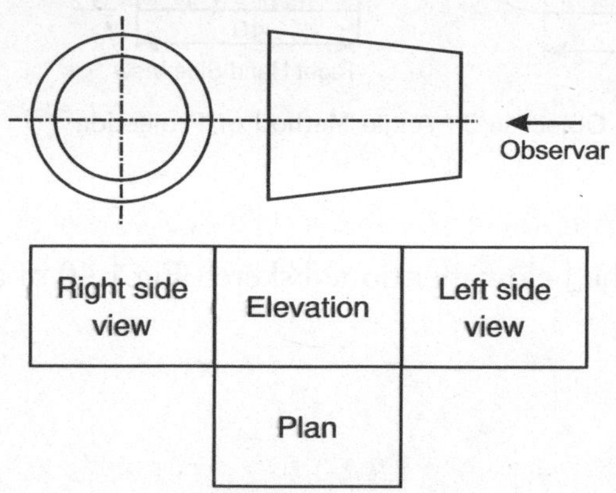	The symbol is as follows: 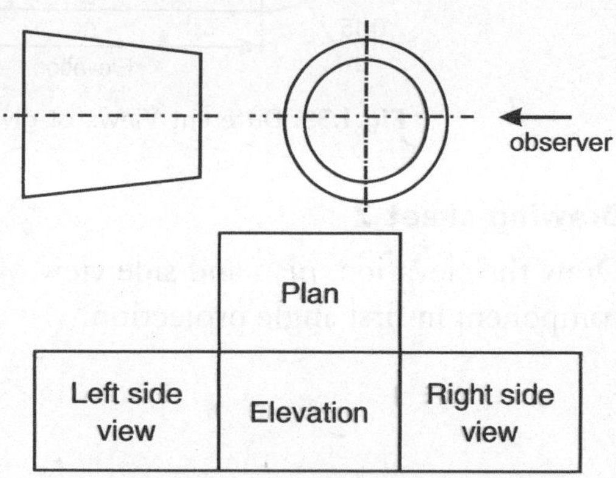

Problems

Drawing sheet 1

Draw the elevation, plan and side view of the below mentioned sketch Fig.1.39 of a machine component in third angle projection.

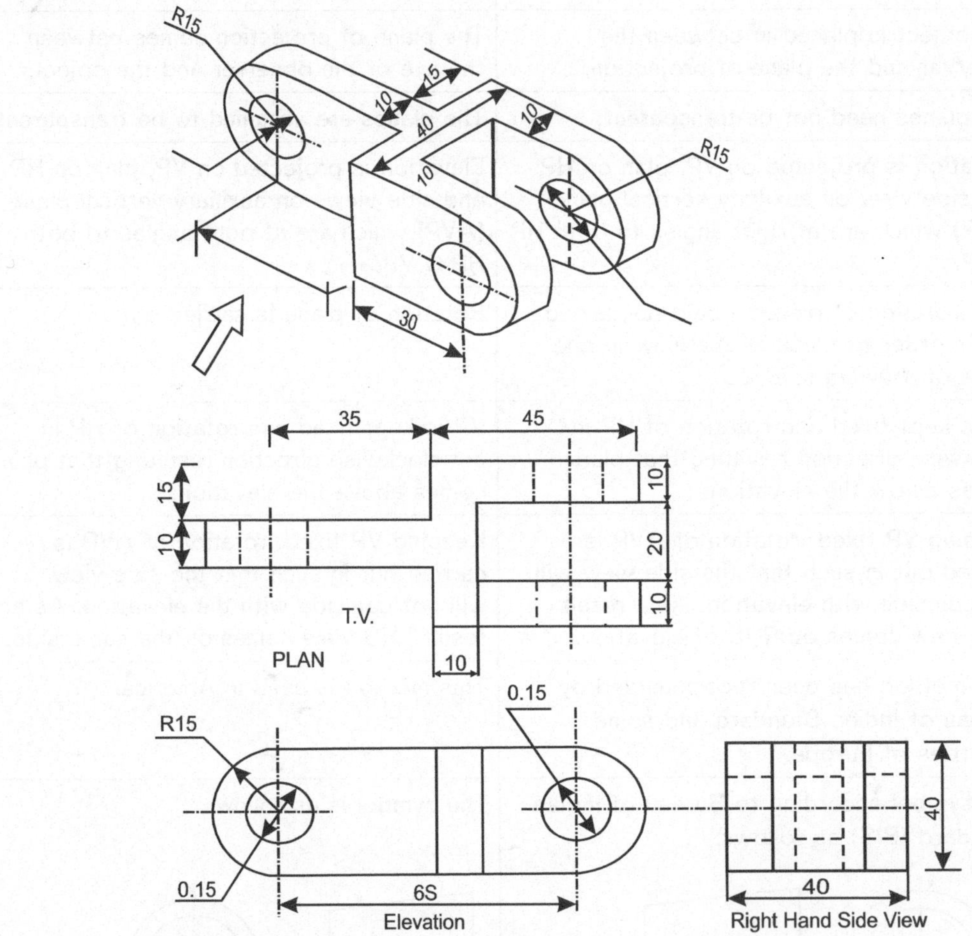

Fig.1.39: Different Views of given Object in 3rd Angle Method of Projection

Drawing sheet 2

Draw the elevation, plan and side view of the below mentioned sketch Fig.1.40 of a machine component in first angle projection.

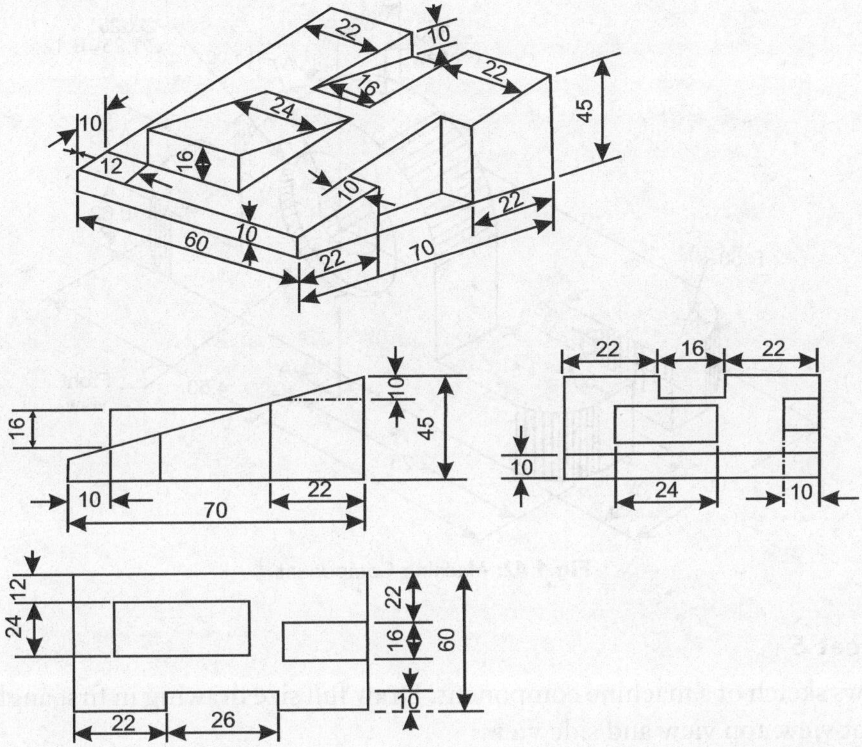

Fig.1.40: Different Views of given Object in 1st Angle Method of Projection

Drawing sheet 3

Draw the three different views of the following objects as shown in the Fig.1.41 given below taking the direction of front view as indicated by arrow.

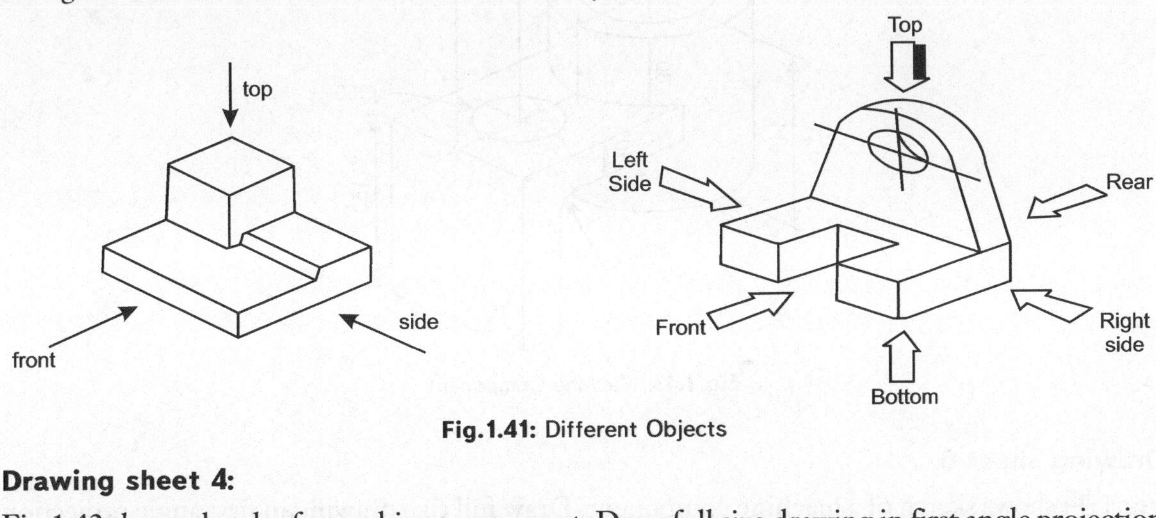

Fig.1.41: Different Objects

Drawing sheet 4:

Fig.1.42 shows sketch of a machine component. Draw full size drawing in first angle projection showing front view, top view and side view.

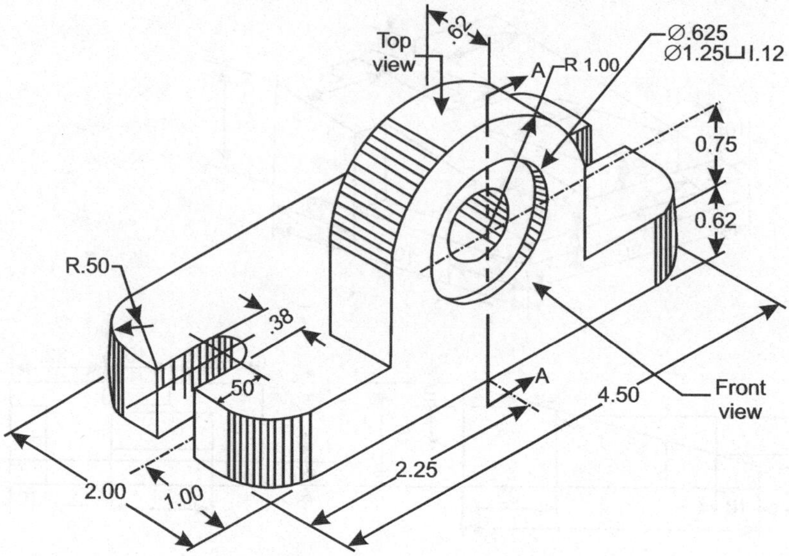

Fig.1.42: Machine Component

Drawing sheet 5

Fig.1.43 shows sketch of a machine component. Draw full size drawing in first angle projection showing front view, top view and side view.

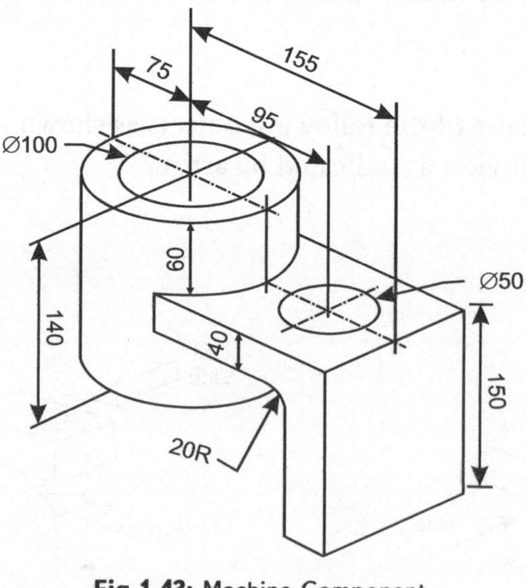

Fig.1.43: Machine Component

Drawing sheet 6

Fig.1.44 shows sketch of a machine component. Draw full size drawing in first angle projection showing front view, top view and side view.

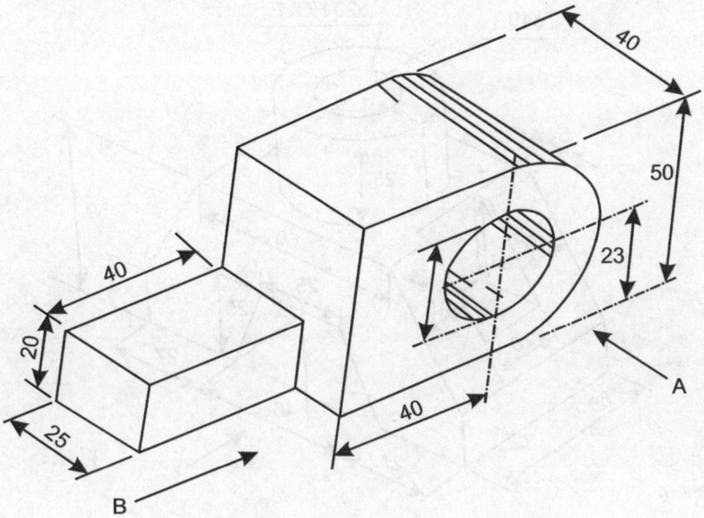

Fig.1.44: Machine Component

Drawing sheet 7

Fig.1.45 shows sketch of the machine components. Draw full size drawing in first angle projection showing front view, top view and side view.

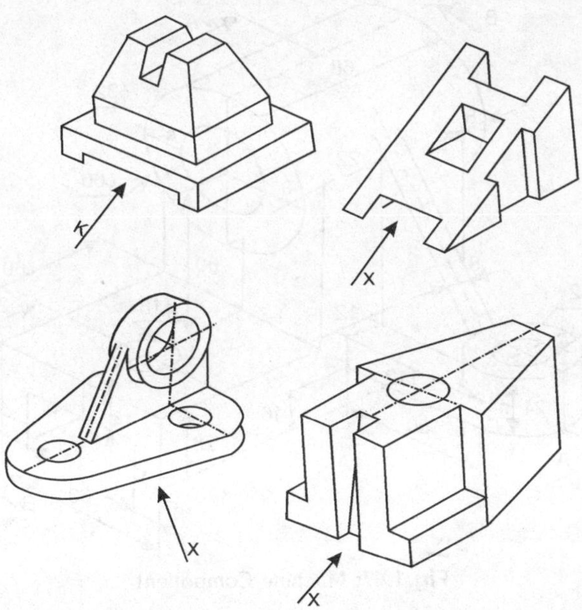

Fig.1.45: Machine Components

Drawing sheet 8

Fig.1.46 shows sketch of a machine component. Draw full size drawing in first angle projection showing front view, top view and side view.

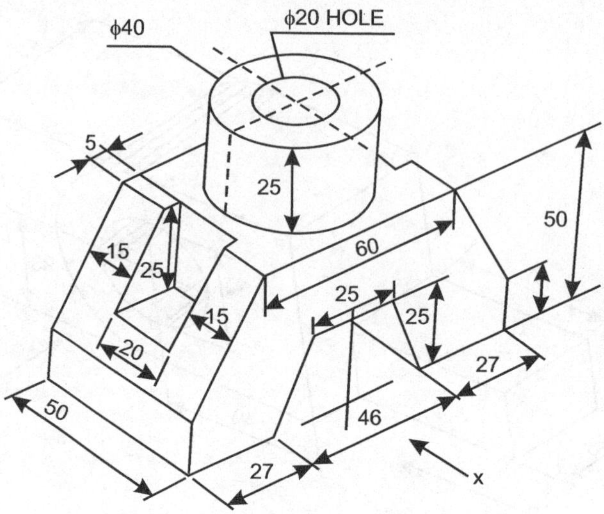

Fig.1.46: Machine Component

Drawing sheet 9

Fig.1.47 shows sketch of a machine component. Draw full size drawing in first angle projection showing front view, top view and side view.

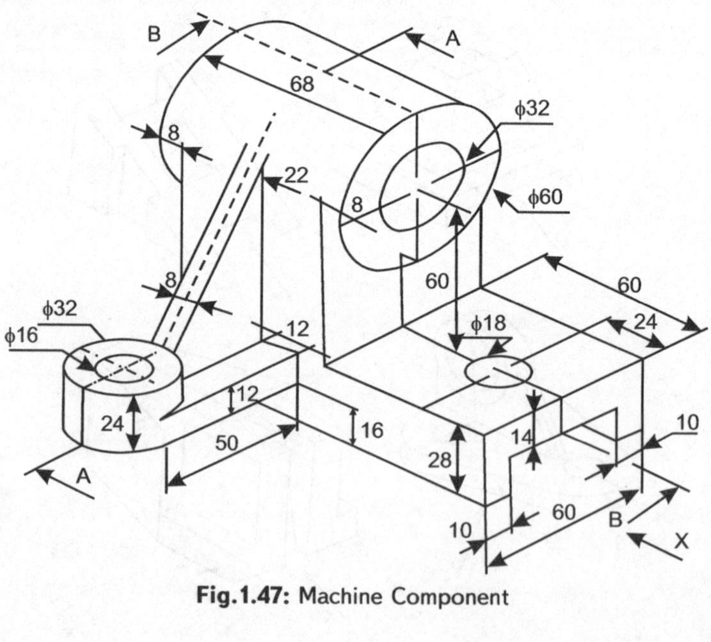

Fig.1.47: Machine Component

Viva Voce Questions

1. What are the various conventions of lines?
2. What is the importance of dimensioning?
3. What are the different systems of dimensioning?
4. What are the different types of dimensioning?
5. What are the various rules of dimensioning?
6. What do you mean by principal planes of projection?
7. What is difference between plan and elevation?
8. What is the need of orthographic projection?
9. Differentiate between first angle and third angle projection methods?
10. Why the drawing is not drawn in second and fourth angle projection methods?
11. Draw the symbol of first angle projection method.
12. Draw the symbol of third angle projection method.

2

SECTIONAL VIEWS

When there are too many hidden details, the orthographic views become obscure and cannot be read easily due to a network of dashed lines. In such cases, the views are drawn by assuming the object to be cut down by an imaginary plane. Such views are known Sectional Views and the concerned imaginary plane is called a Cutting Plane or a Section Plane. The nearer part after cutting is assumed to be removed and the remaining view (elevation, plan or side view) as the case may be is drawn. This method shows the interior details of an object.

Sectioning or hatching lines are used as a convention to represent sectional views. The thin lines at some angle (usually 45°) are drawn over the portion to be sectioned by cutting plane. The cutting plane is represented by thick long line at the ends and thin long and short lines at the centre. Arrow heads with capital letters such as X-Y etc. are marked at the two ends of cutting plane line. The cutting plane of one view does not affect the other view. In other words, after getting one sectioned view, the other views are drawn as if the entire object exists as a whole.

Sectioning can be done by using two methods:

2.1 FULL SECTIONING

When the entire object is assumed to be cut into two equal halves by cutting plane and the front half is removed, it is said to be in full section.

Full sectional views are shown in Fig. 2.1.

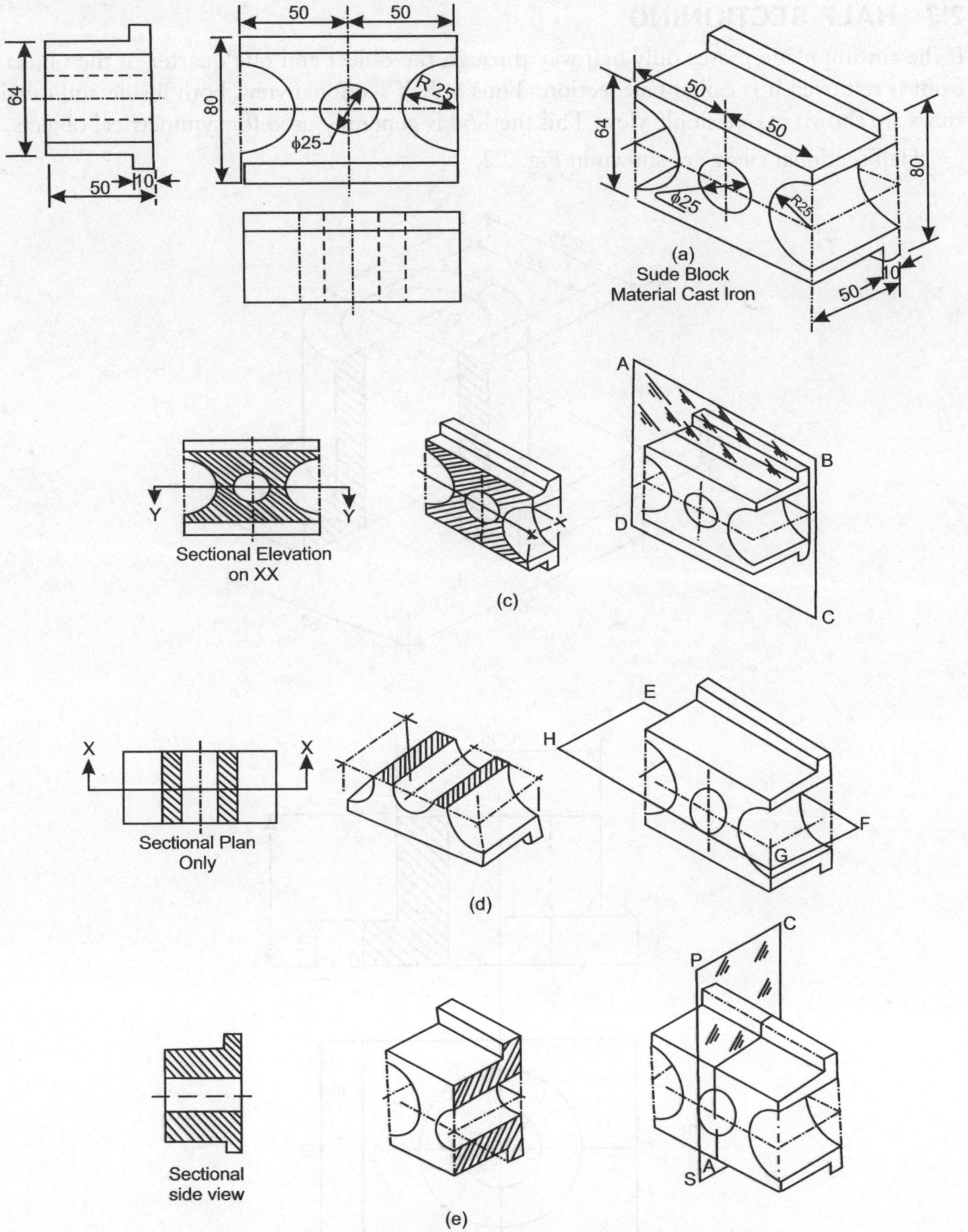

Fig.2.1: Full Sectional Views

2.2 HALF SECTIONING

If the cutting plane passes only half way through the object and one quarter of the object in front is removed it is called half section. Thus in half sectional view, both inside and outside views are shown in one single view. This method is generally used for symmetrical objects.

Half sectional views are shown in Fig. 2.2.

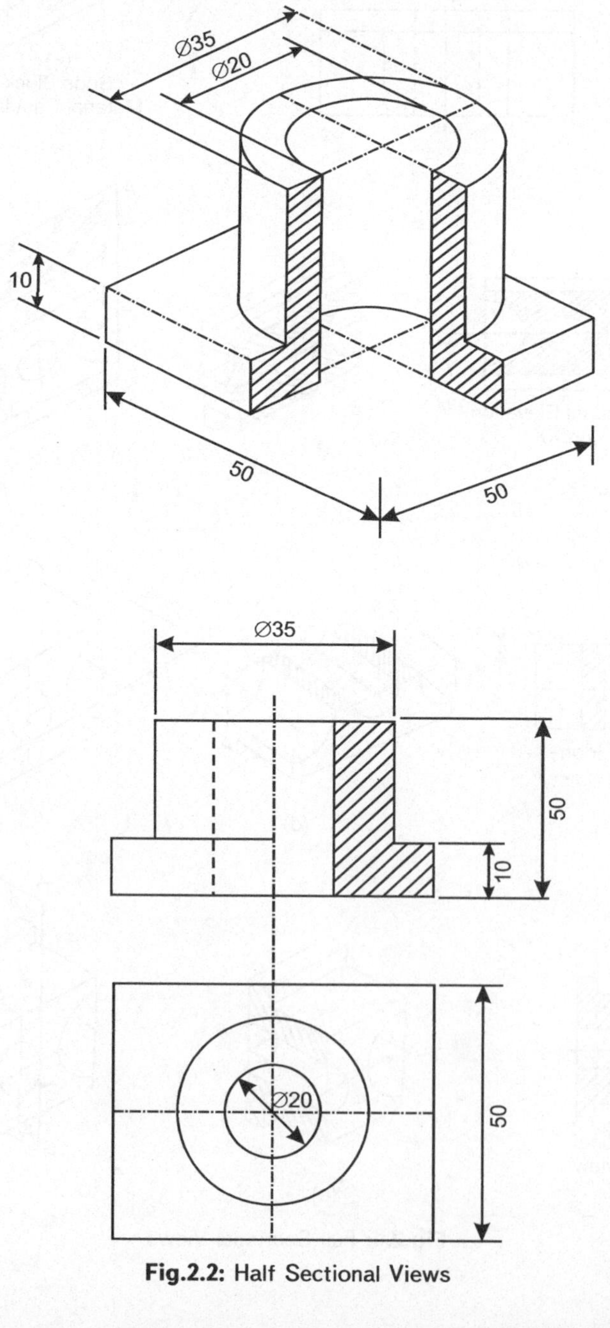

Fig.2.2: Half Sectional Views

2.3 SOME IMPORTANT SECTIONS

Some important sections used in drawing are as follows:

(a) **Broken or Partial Section:** It is required to be shown for a small detail in long objects instead of showing a full section or half section. Partial section suffices which is limited by a short break line. A broken or partial section is shown in Fig. 2.3.

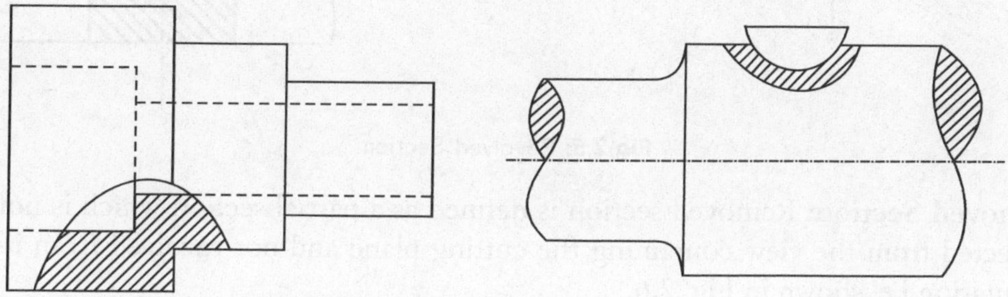

Fig.2.3: Broken or Partial Section

(b) **Offset Section:** It is required to show the maximum detail of an object through offset cutting plane which cannot be shown by full or half section. An offset section is shown in Fig. 2.4.

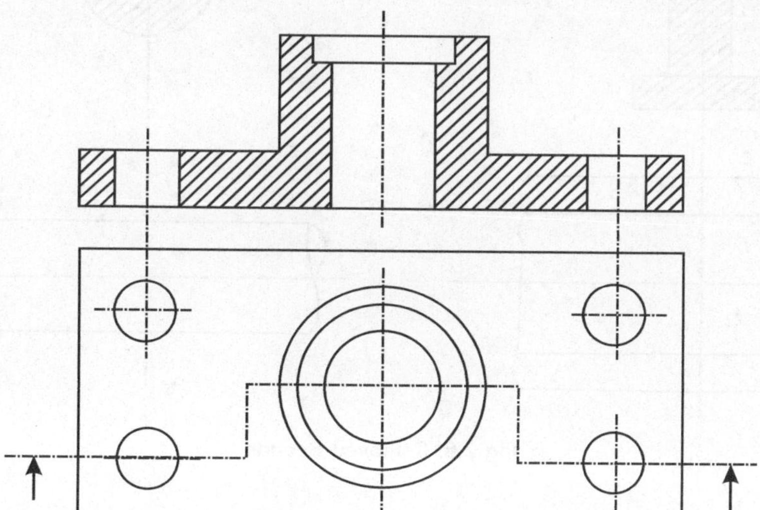

Fig.2.4: Offset Section

(c) **Revolved Section:** It is required to show the cross section of elongated objects such as spokes, ribs, arms etc. on its longitudinal view. As shown in Fig. 2.5 an imaginary plane is made to pass perpendicular to the centre line of the object and then the resulting section is revolved at right angles to its axis and shown there. A revolved section is shown in Fig. 2.5.

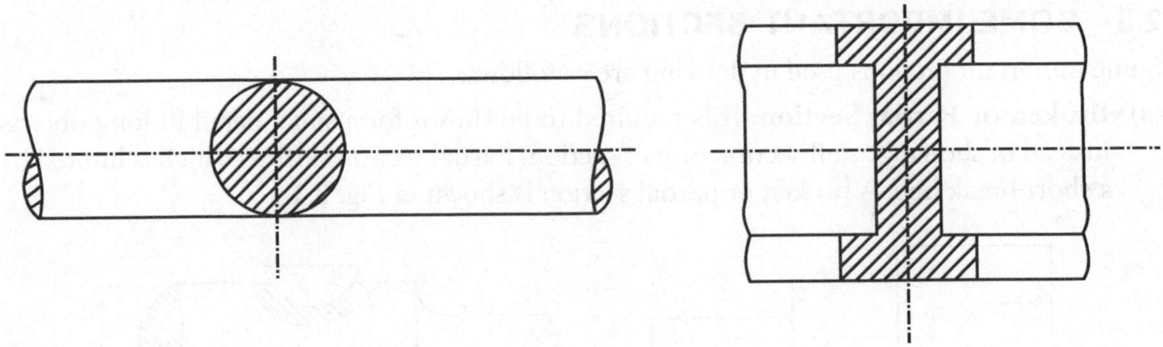

Fig.2.5: Revolved Section

(d) Removed Section: Removed section is defined as a partial section which is not directly projected from the view containing the cutting plane and not revolved from its normal orientation i.e. shown in Fig. 2.6.

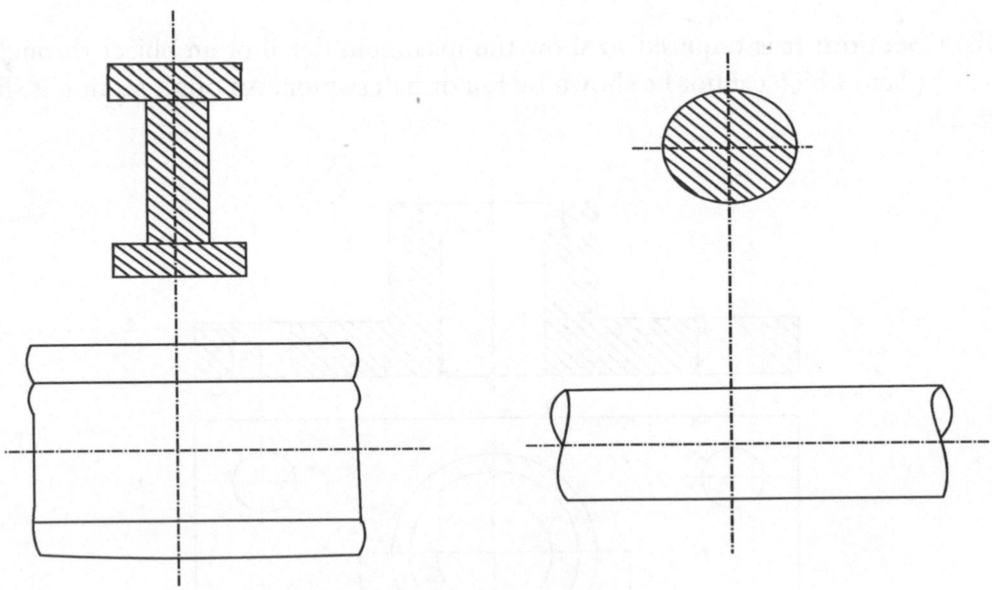

Fig.2.6: Removed Section

(e) **Outline Section:** Large surfaces are sectioned around the edges as shown in Fig. 2.7.

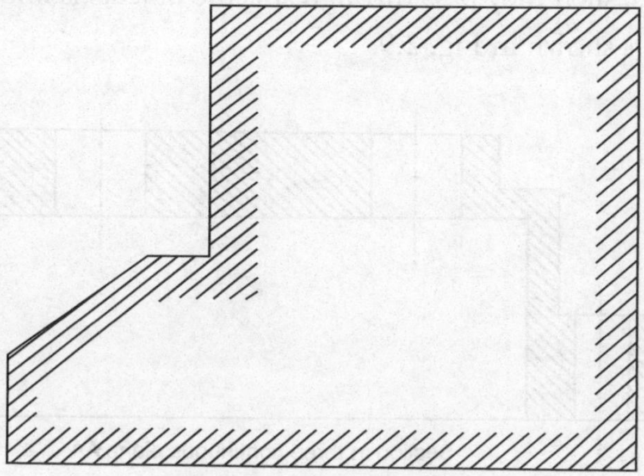

Fig.2.7: Outline Section

(f) **Auxiliary Section:** A section i.e. projected on a plane other than one of the regular planes. A rectangular object is in normal position for regular multi- view orthographic projection when each of its faces is parallel to one regular plane of projection and perpendicular to the other two.

An auxiliary section is shown in Fig. 2.8.

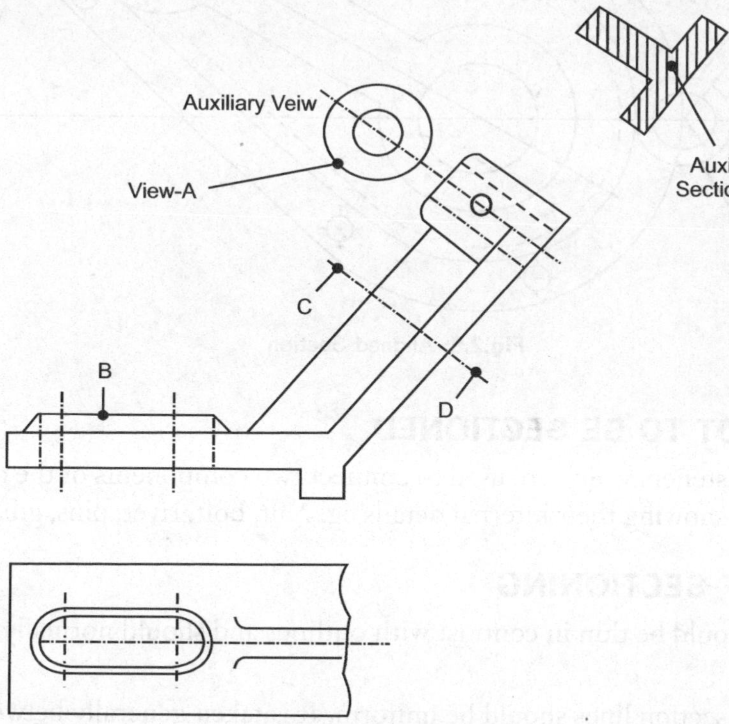

Fig.2.8: Auxiliary Section

(g) Aligned Section: A section i.e. generated by cutting through the entire object along two parallel work planes, such they pass through specific objects is known as aligned section. An aligned section is shown in Fig. 2.9.

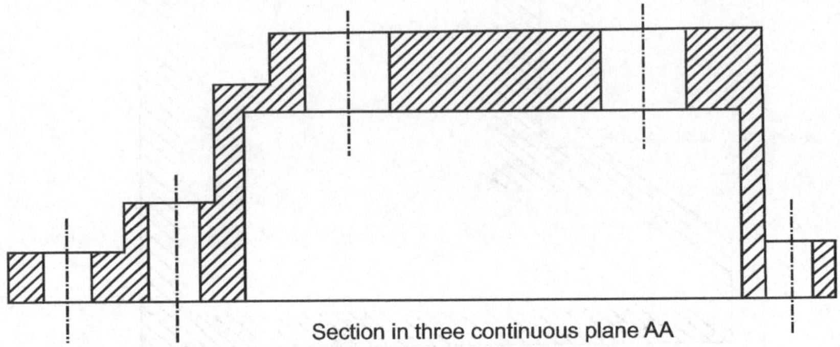

Section in three continuous plane AA

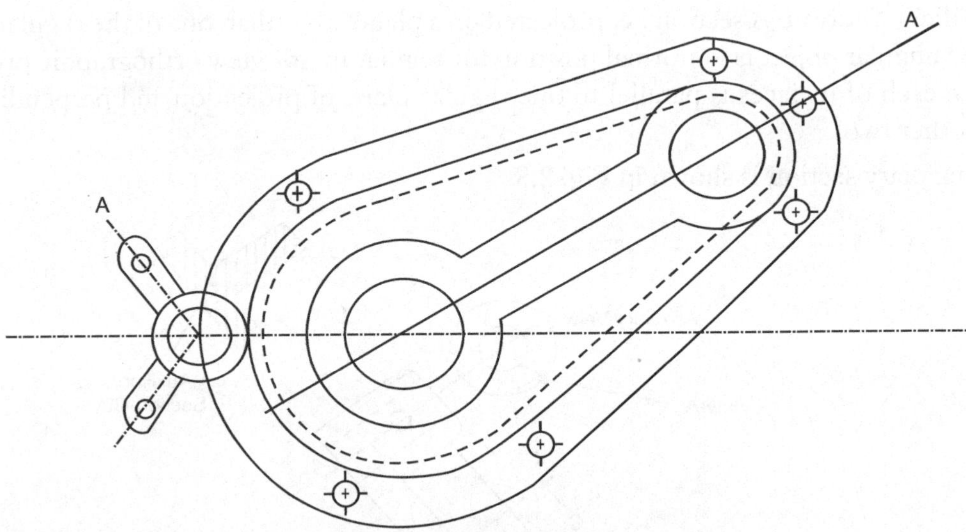

Fig.2.9: Aligned Section

2.4 PARTS NOT TO BE SECTIONED

All the temporary fasteners which are used to connect two components of the drawing are not to be hatched while showing their internal details eg. Nut, bolt, rivet, pins, gib, web, shaft etc.

2.5 RULES OF SECTIONING

1. Section lines should be thin in contrast with outlines and should normally be drawn at 45 degree.
2. The spacing of section lines should be uniform. It is taken generally between 1 to 3mm.

3. No sectional area can ever be bounded by dashed lines. All sectional areas in a view of a single piece must be sectioned in the same direction.
4. Two adjacent parts in an assembly drawing are hatched in opposite directions.
5. Dimensions for a section should be placed outside the section, if possible.

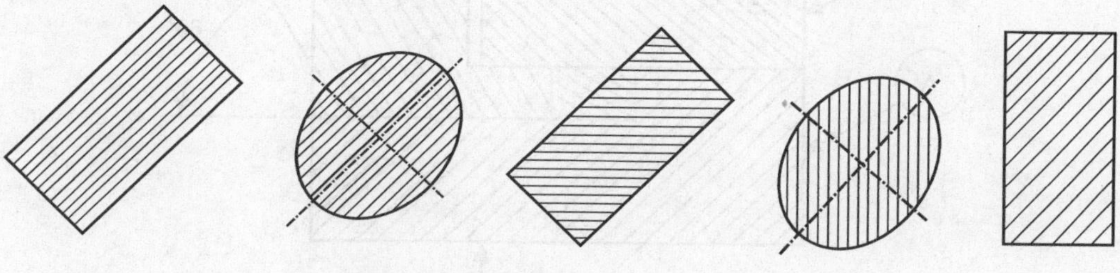

Fig.2.10: Section lines in odd shapes

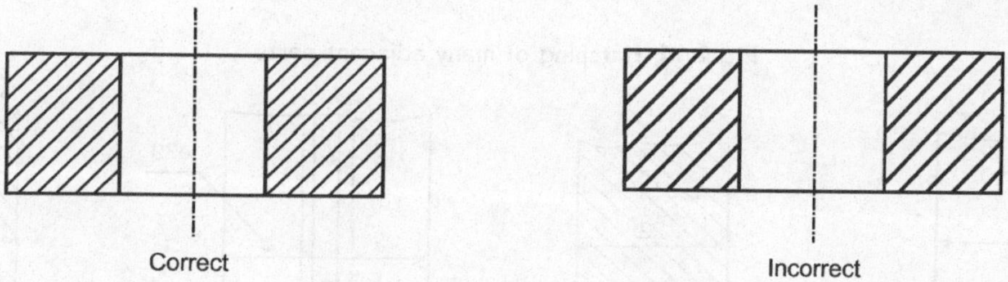

Fig.2.11: Spacing of section lines

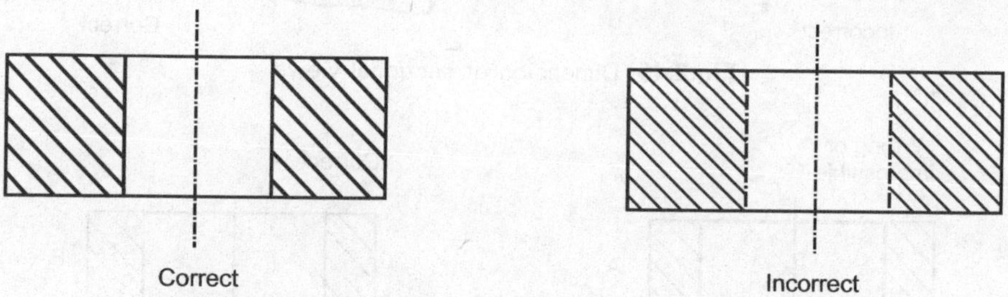

Fig.2.12: Sectioned areas cannot be bounded by dashed lines

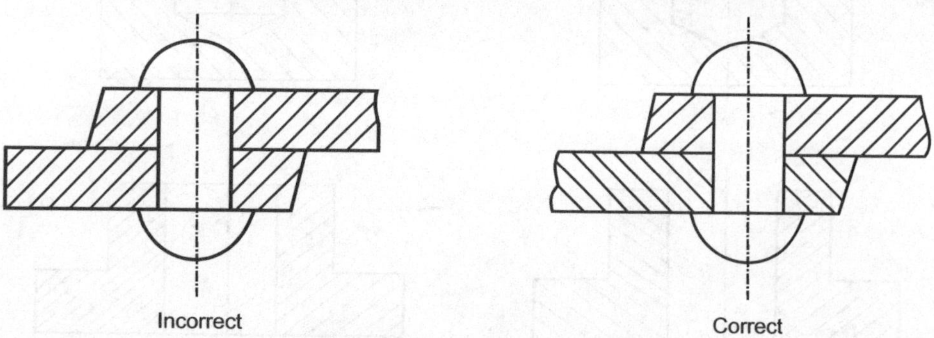

Fig.2.13: Hatching of adjacent parts

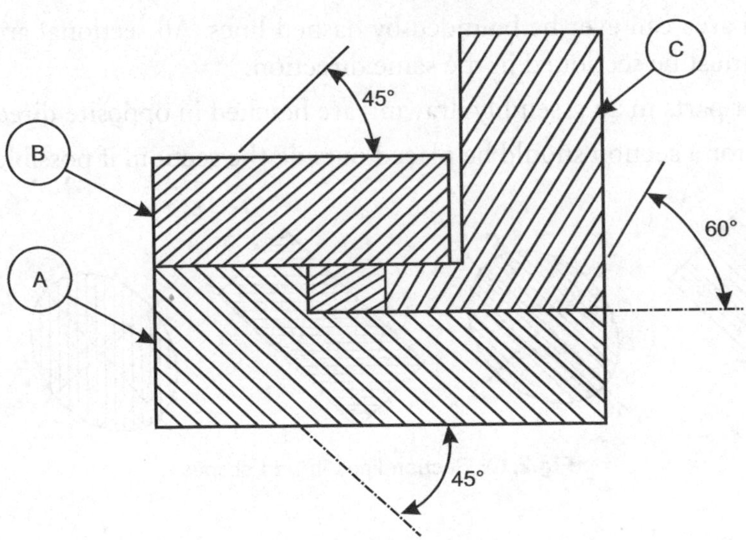

Fig.2.14: Hatching of many adjacent parts

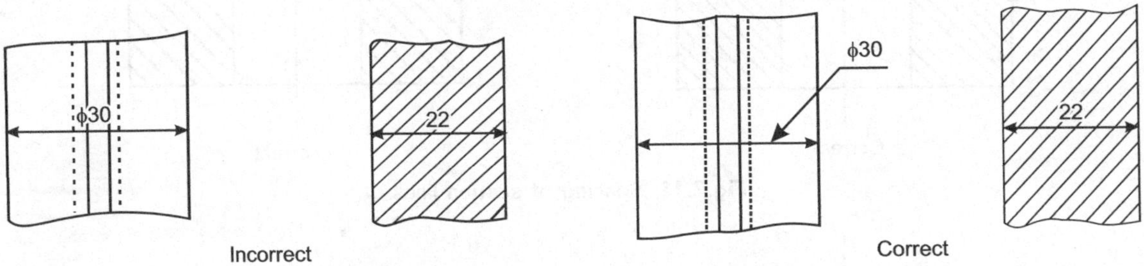

Fig.2.15: Dimension of sectional views

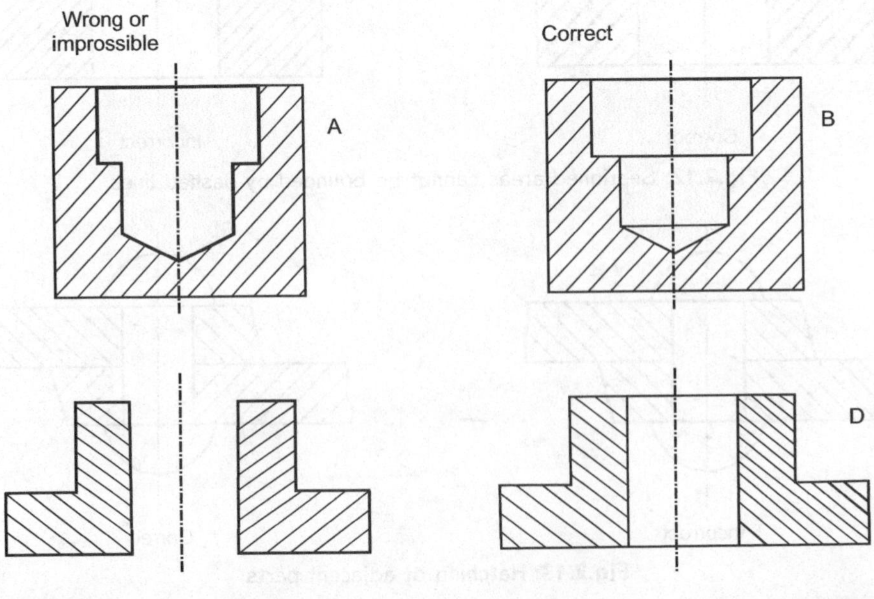

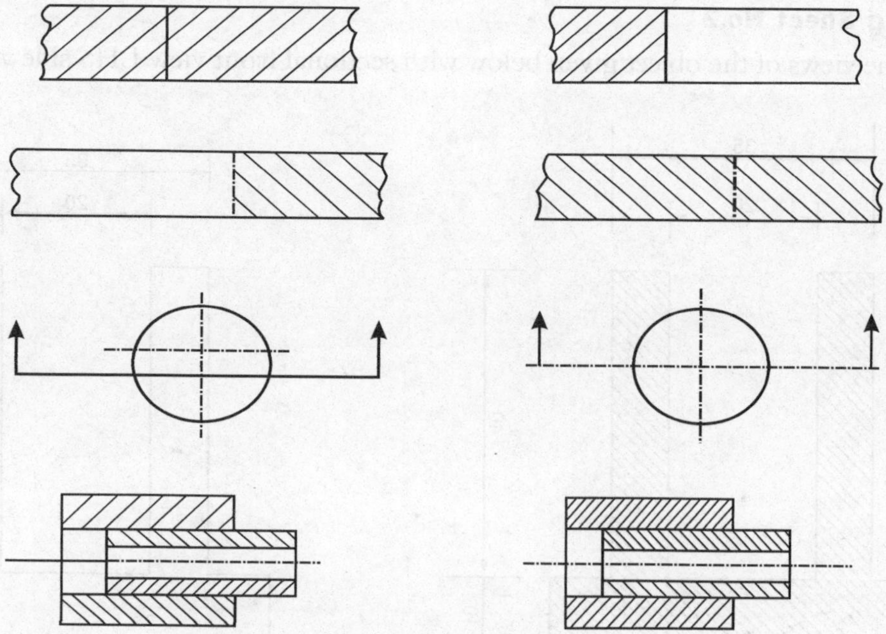

Fig.2.16: Common mistakes in sectioning

Problems

Drawing Sheet No.1

Draw full sectional elevation as shown the location of cutting plane A-A in Fig. 2.17 And also draw its plan and left hand side view.

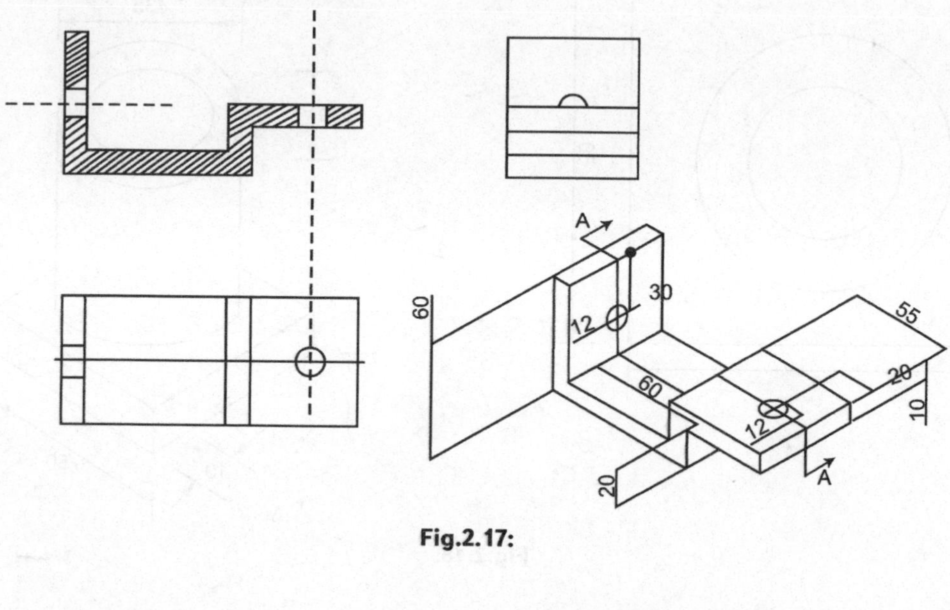

Fig.2.17:

Drawing Sheet No.2

Draw the views of the object given below with sectional front view LHS side view plan.

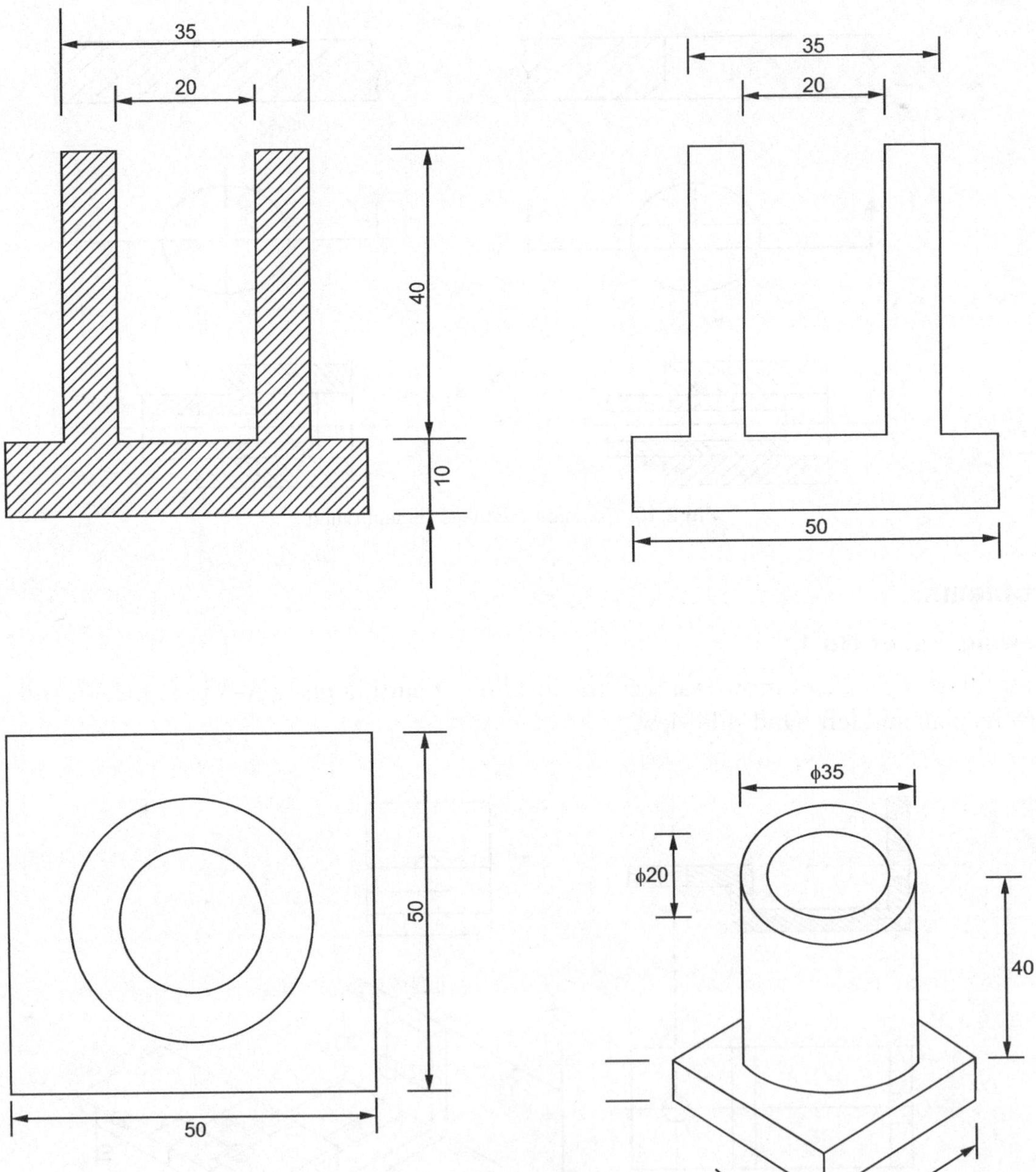

Fig.2.18:

Drawing Sheet No.3

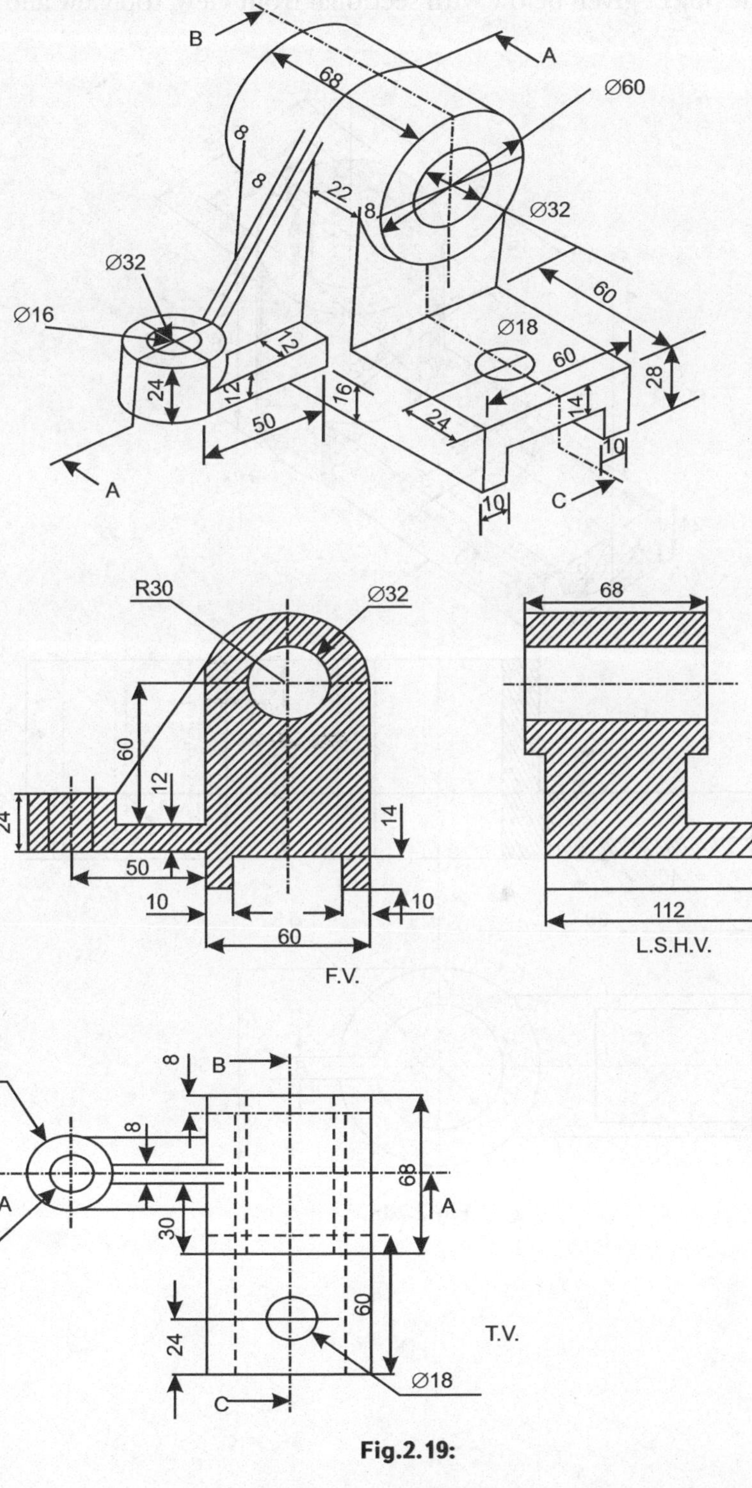

Fig.2.19:

Drawing Sheet No.4

Draw the views of the object given below with sectional front view, top view and sectional side view.

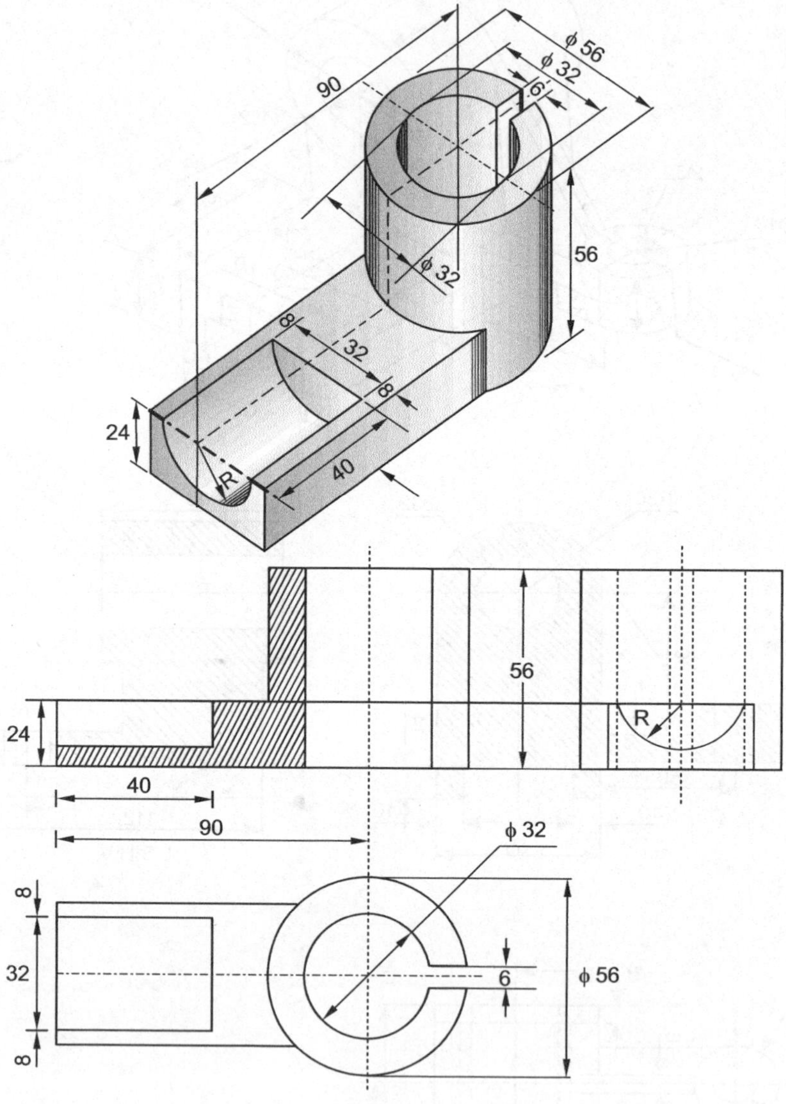

Fig.2.20:

Drawing Sheet No.5

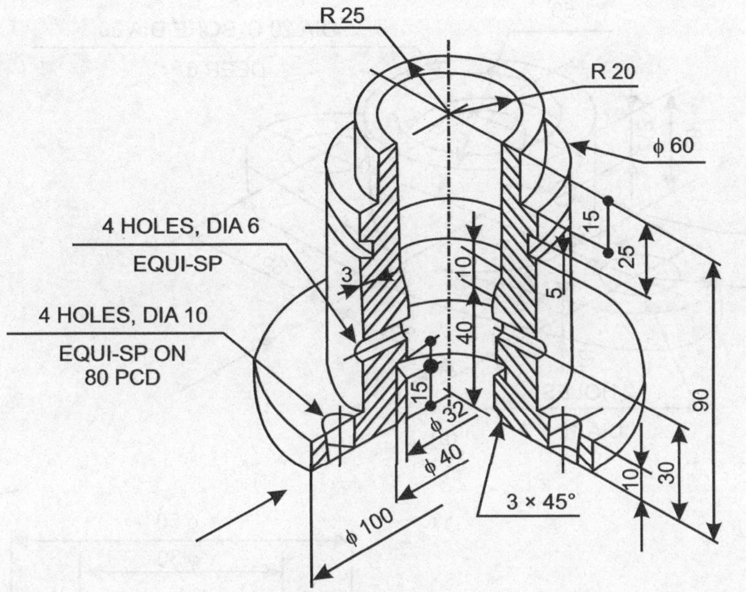

Fig.2.21:

Drawing Sheet No.6

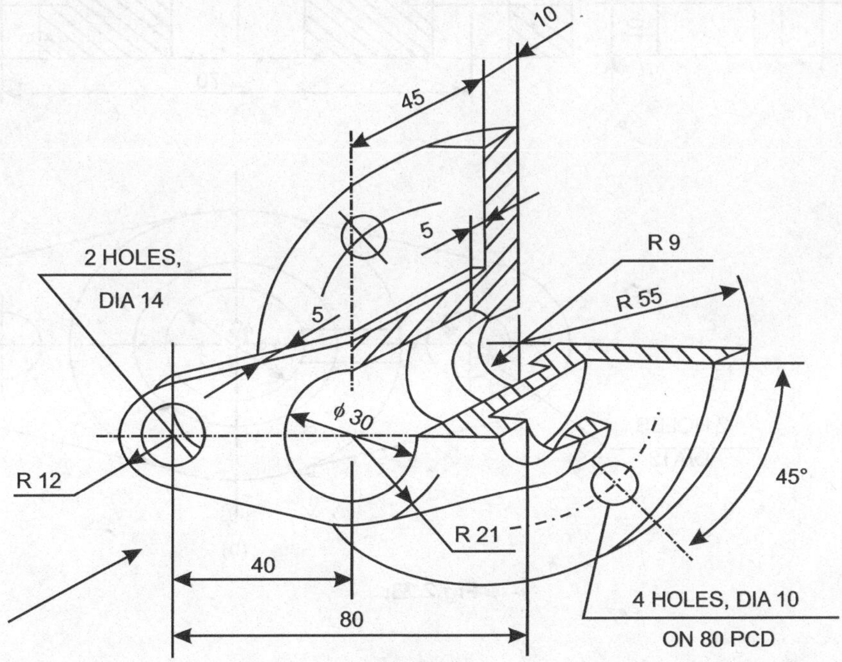

Fig.2.22:

Drawing Sheet No.7

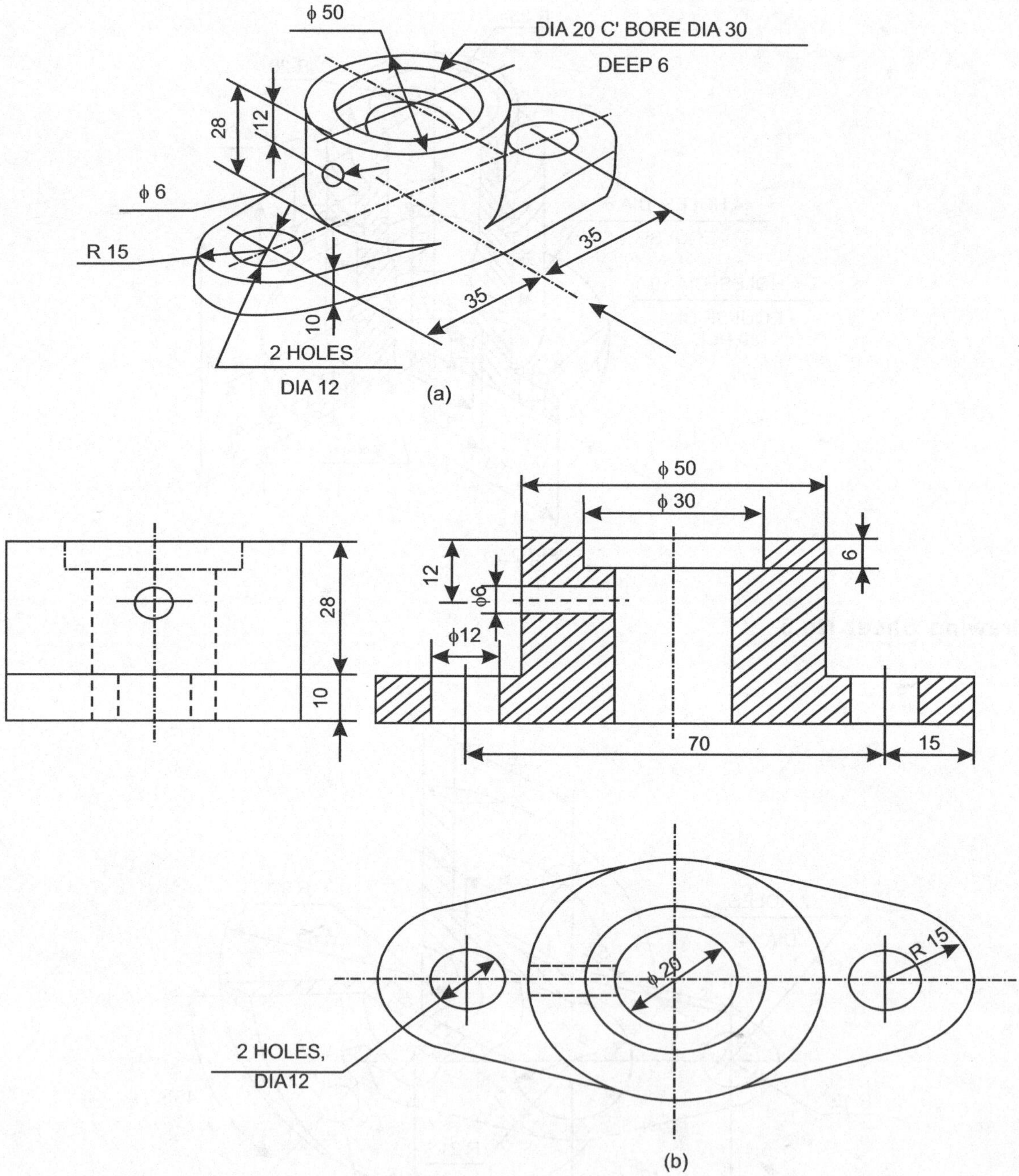

Fig.2.23:

Viva Voce Questions

1. Can section lines (hatching lines) be bounded by dashed lines?
2. Why the edge produced by the cutting plane is not shown as solid line in half sections?
3. What is offset section?
4. What is broken section?
5. When should the ribs and webs shown sectioned and when not?
6. What is revolved section and when this is used?
7. What is difference between a regular section (full, half, or offset) and revolved or removed section?
8. A wheel has five arms and it is sectioned. How the arm which is not sectioned must be projected?
9. What is meant by revolution of features in sectioning?

3

RIVETS AND RIVETED JOINTS

3.1 FASTENING

In engineering practice fastenings are used to join together parts in machines or structures.

(a) **Temporary Fastening:** Temporary fastening can be unfasten easily without breaking anything e.g. bolts & nuts, studs and nuts, keys, cotters, pins, etc.

(b) **Permanent Fastening:** Permanent fastening has to be broken to separate the two joining parts e.g. soldering, brazing, welding, riveting.

3.2 RIVET

A rivet is made of round wrought iron or steel bar with cup or other shaped head on one side formed by dies. A rivet specified by the diameter of shank, length and types of head. Rivets are used in structural work like roof trusses, bridges, ship building, and aircraft work and in pressure vessels like boilers, air receivers and hydraulic tanks.

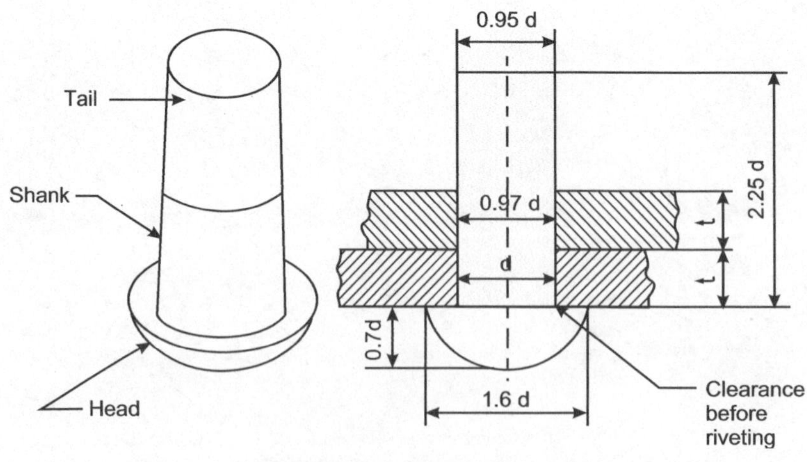

Fig.3.1: Snap Head Rivet

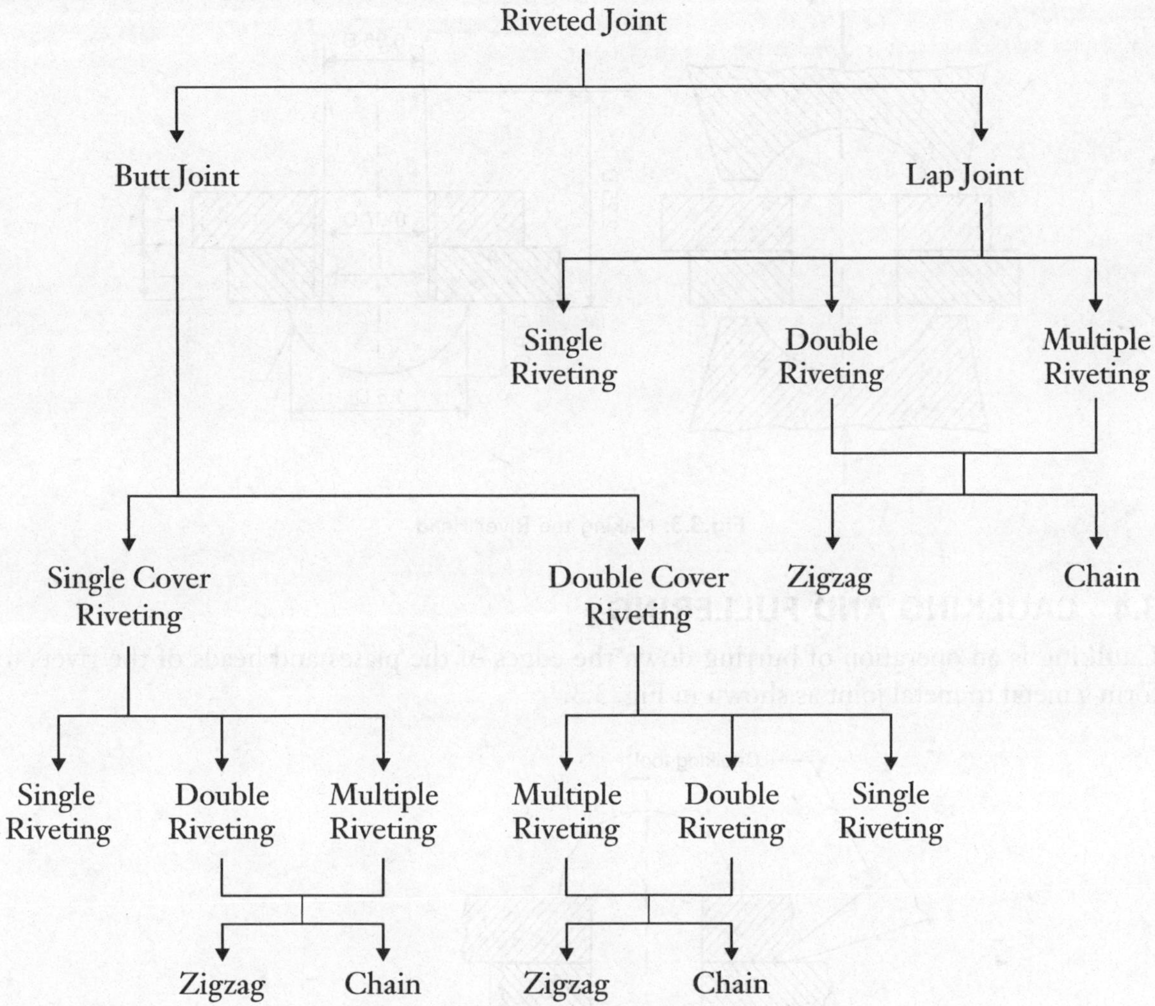

Fig.3.2: Classification of Riveted Joints

3.3 RIVETING

The process of joining two or more plates by means of rivets is called riveting.

The rivet is inserted pride down from the bottom of the plate and then the tail is hammered against the riveting die of the same curvature to make the identical shape of the tail end. This is the process of riveting.

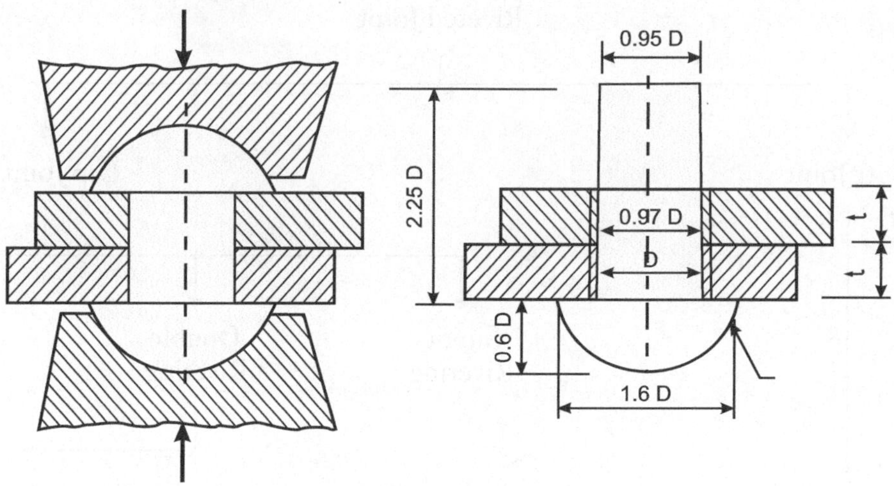

Fig.3.3: Making the Rivet Head

3.4 CAULKING AND FULLERING

Caulking is an operation of burring down the edges of the plates and heads of the rivets to form a metal to metal joint as shown in Fig. 3.3.

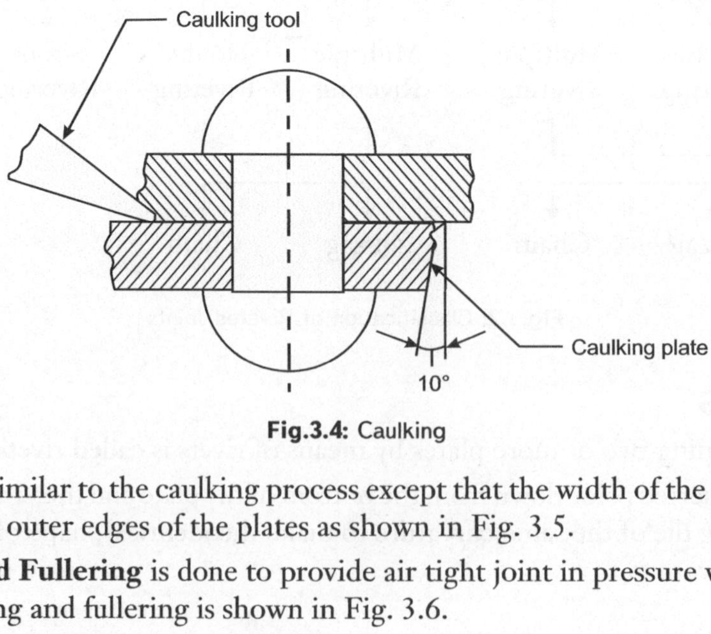

Fig.3.4: Caulking

Fullering is similar to the caulking process except that the width of the tool is equal to the width of pevelled outer edges of the plates as shown in Fig. 3.5.

Caulking and Fullering is done to provide air tight joint in pressure vessels like boilers. Combined caulking and fullering is shown in Fig. 3.6.

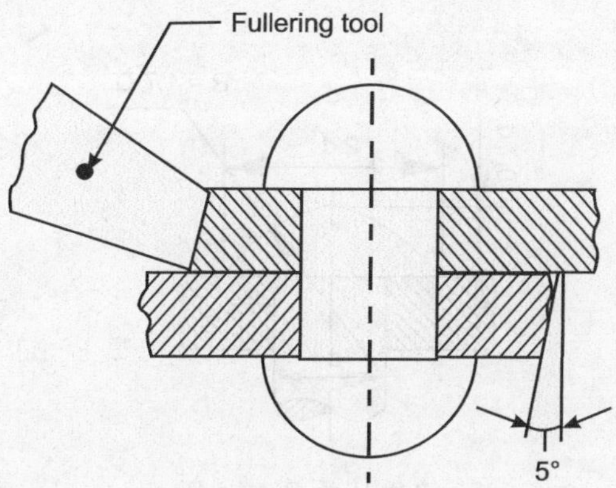

Fig.3.5: Fullering

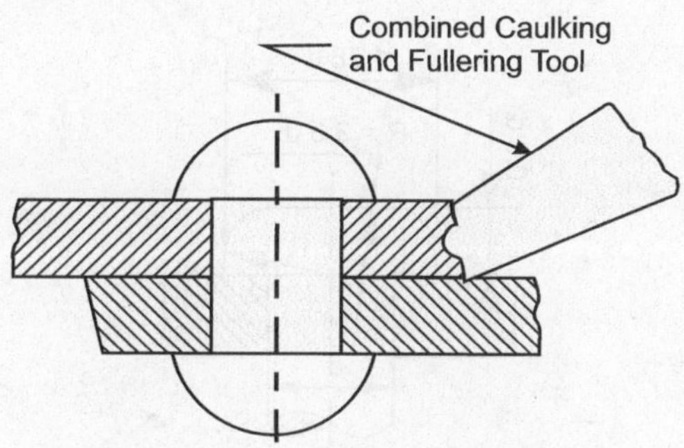

Fig.3.6: Combined Caulking & Fullering

3.5 DIFFERENT TYPES OF RIVET HEAD

1. Snap Head

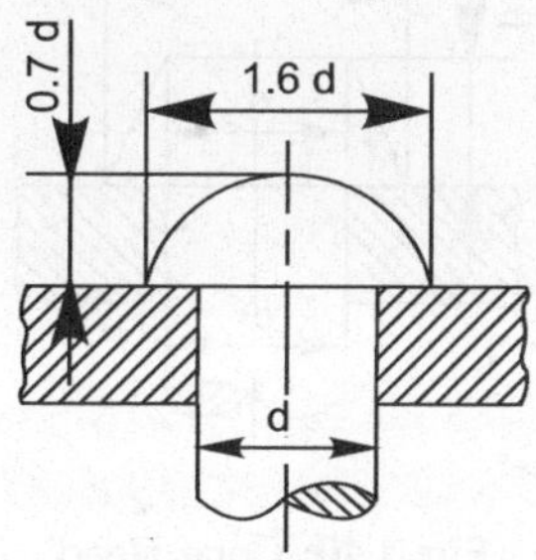

Fig.3.7: Snap Head

2. High Button Head

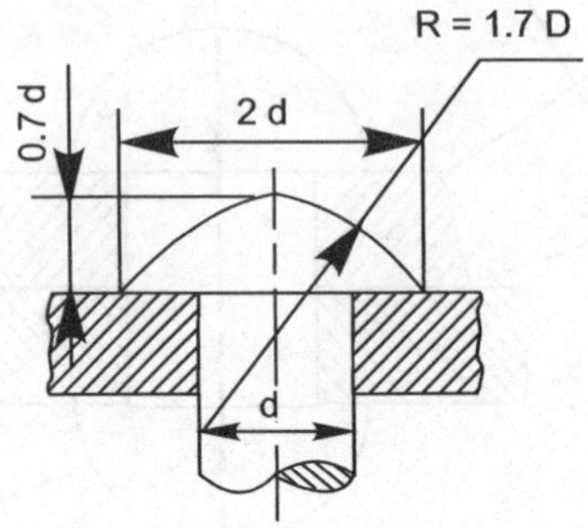

Fig.3.8: High Button Head

3. Pan Head

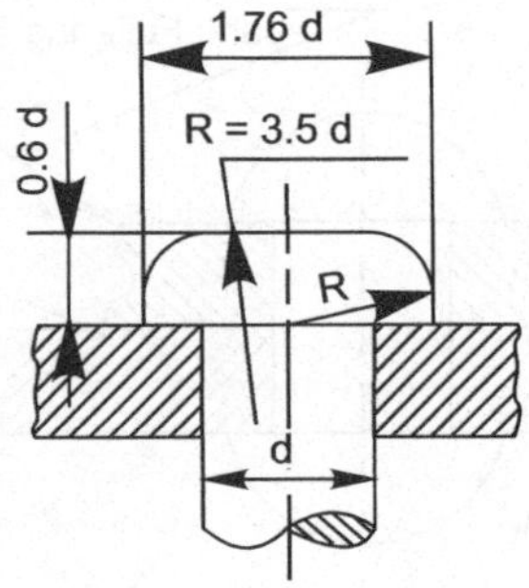

Fig.3.9: Pan Head

4. Cone Head

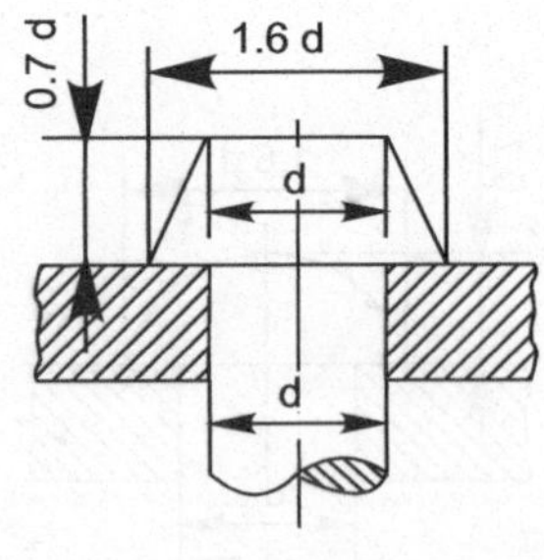

Fig.3.10: Cone Head

5. Round Top Countersunk Head

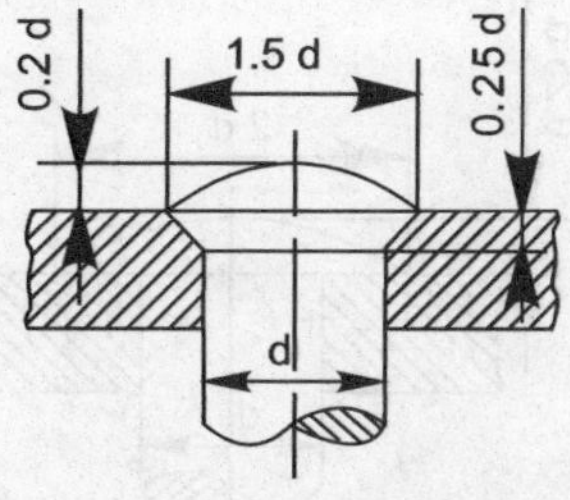

Fig.3.11: Round Top Countersunk Head

6. Flush Countersunk Head

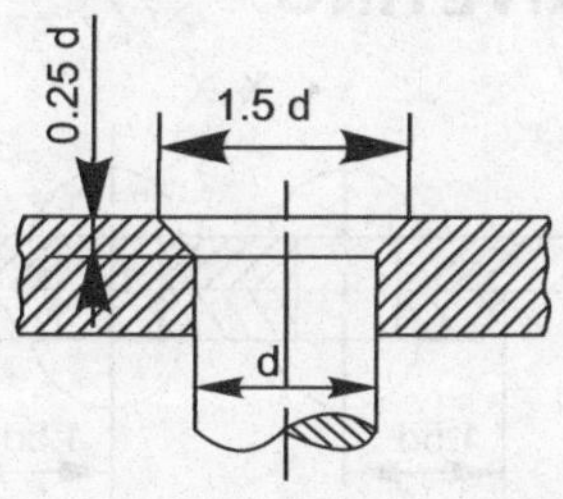

Fig.3.12: Flush Countersunk Head

7. Flat Head

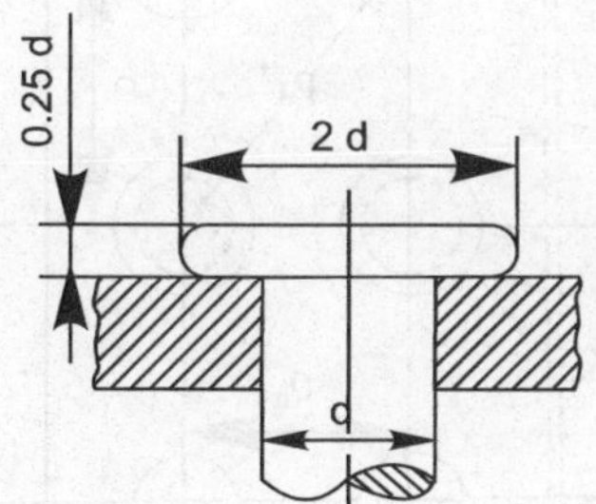

Fig.3.13: Flat Head

8. Truss Head

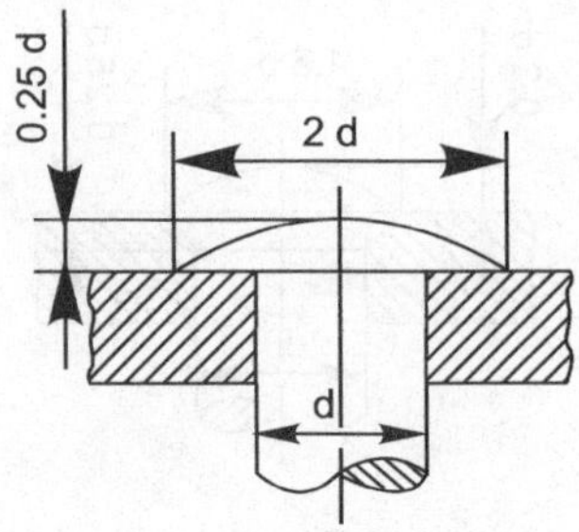

Fig.3.14: Truss Head

3.6 TERMINOLOGY OF RIVETING

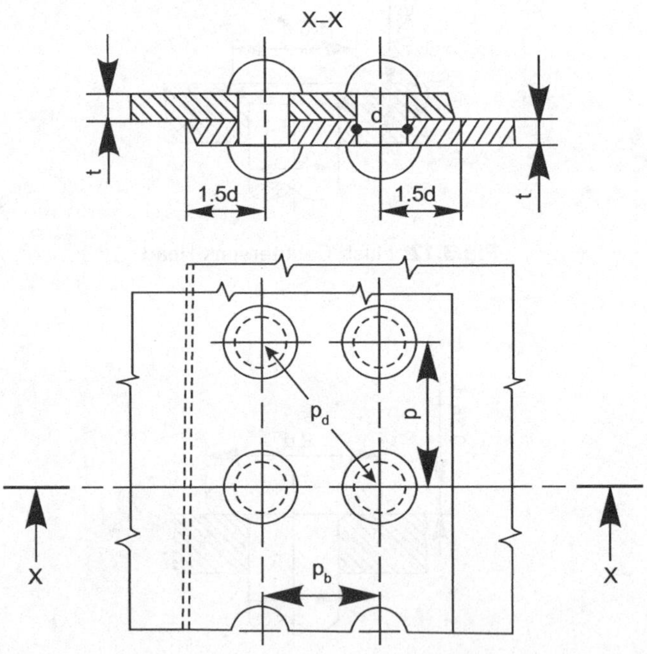

Fig.3.15: Terminology of Riveted Joint

1. **Pitch (P):** Pitch is the distance from the Centre of one rivet to the Centre of next rivet in the same row measured parallel.
2. **Diagonal Pitch (Pd):** Diagonal pitch is the distance from the Centre of one rivet to the Centre of the next rivet in the adjoining row.
3. **Back Pitch (Pb):** Back pitch is the distance between rows of rivets measured perpendicular to the seas.
4. **Overlap:** In lap joints the overlap of two plates (minimum 3) is known as overlap.

5. **Chain Riveting:** If the rivets on the same plates are arranged directly opposite each other it is known as chain-riveting.
6. **Zigzag riveting:** If the rivets on one plate are arranged zigzag, i.e. rivets in one row are placed facing between in the two rivets of other row, it is called zigzag riveting.
7. **Margin (m):** The distance between the edge of the plate and rivet hole is called margin. It is generally equal to 1.5d.

3.7 RIVETED JOINTS

1. **Lap Joint:** In lap joint, one plate overlaps the other. All the rivets pass through both plates.

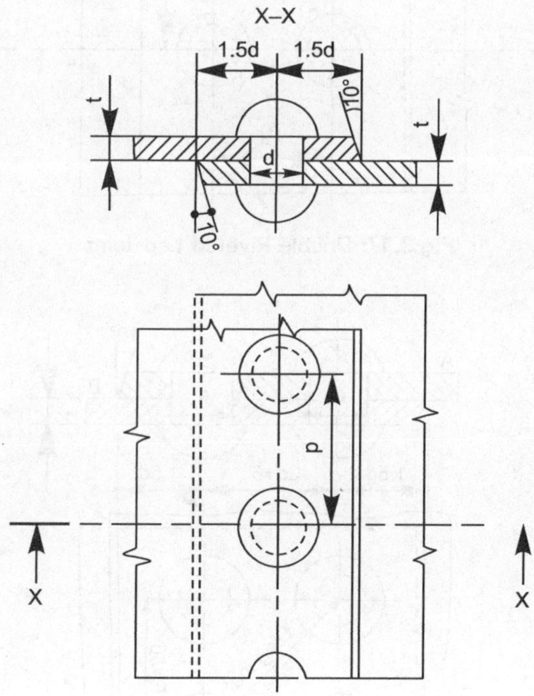

Fig.3.16: Single Riveted Lap Joint

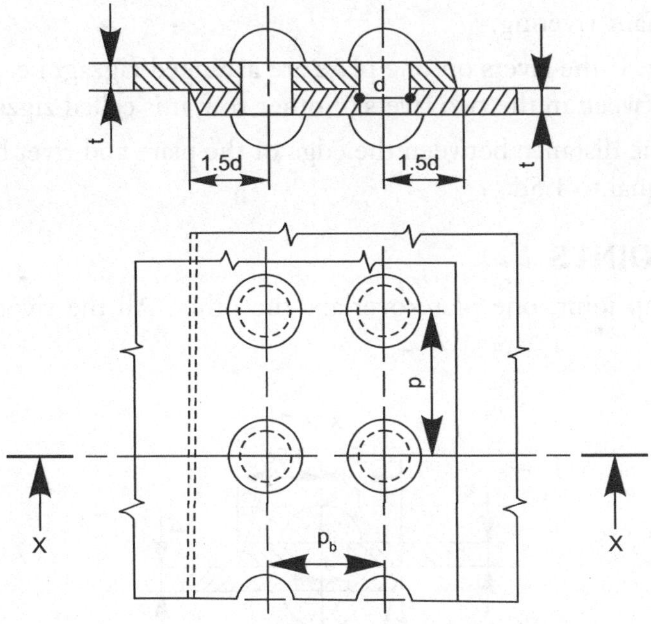

Fig.3.17: Double Riveted Lap Joint

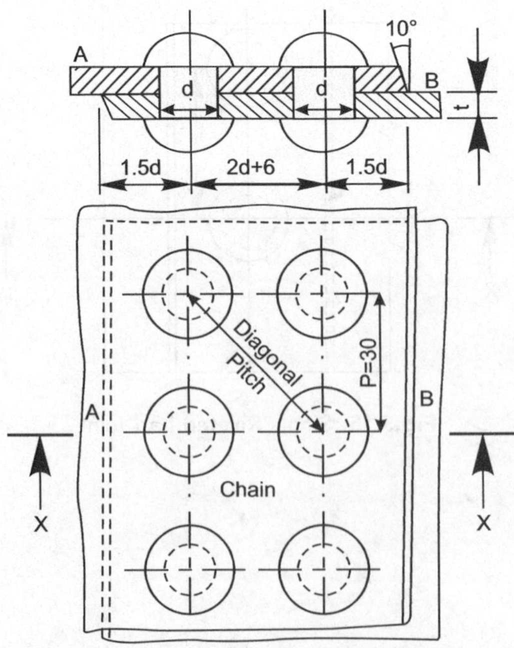

Fig.3.18: Double Riveted Lap Joint with Chain Riveting

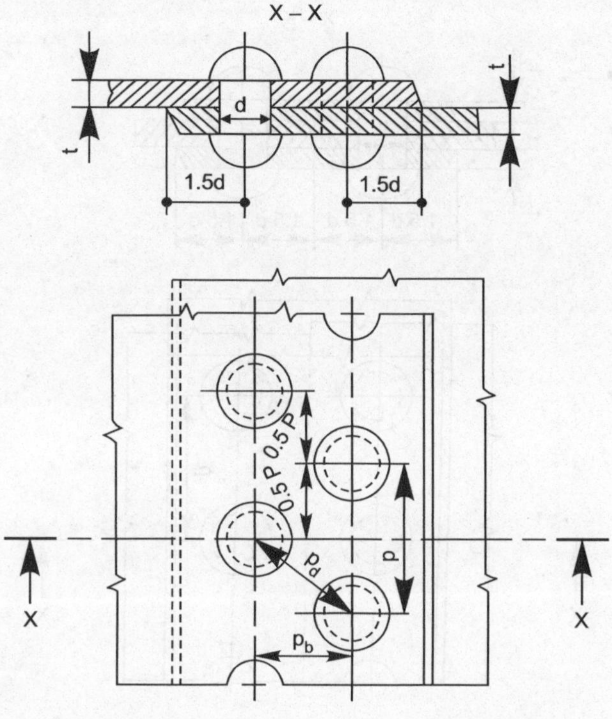

Fig.3.19: Double Riveted Lap Joint with Zigzag Riveting

2. **Butt Joint:** In butt joint, the ends of the main plates butt up against other and may be considered as lying in the same plane. One or two strap or cover plates are placed over the joint and riveted to each plate.

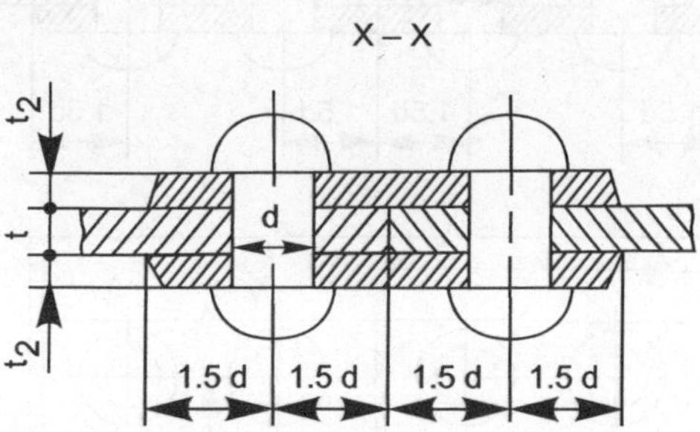

Fig.3.20: Double Strap Butt Joint

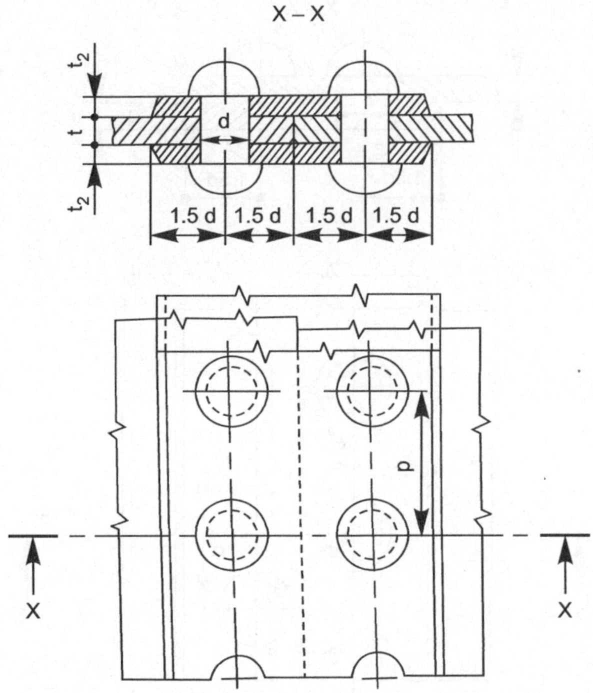

Fig.3.21: Single Riveted Double Strap Butt Joint

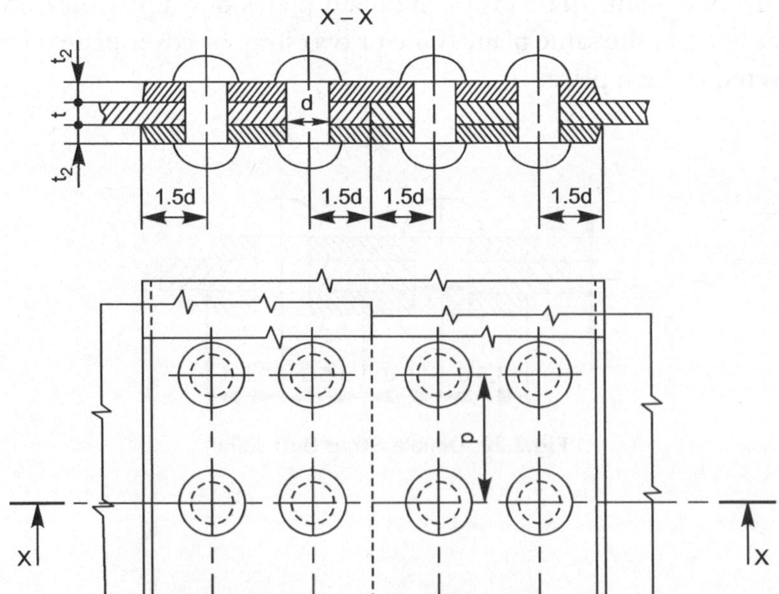

Fig.3.22: Double Riveted Butt Joint Double Cover Plate Chain Riveting

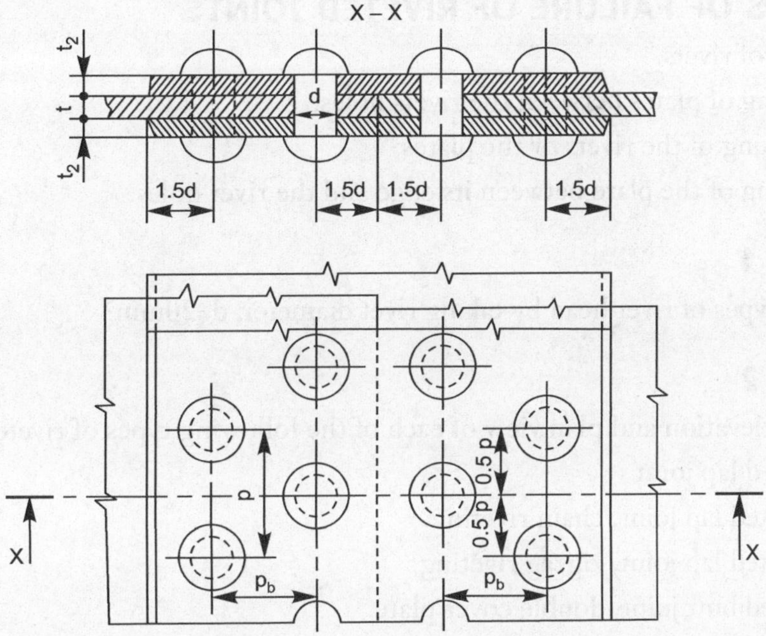

Fig.3.23: Double Riveted Butt Joint Double Cover Plate Zigzag Riveting

3.8 EMPIRICAL PROPORTIONS FOR RIVETING

d = $6\sqrt{t}$ or $3\sqrt{t} + 10$ mm

p = 3d

m = 1.5d

Thickness of Cover Plate

t_1 = 1.125t, if Single Cover Plate

t_2 = 0.625t, if Double Cover Plate

Notations

d = Diameter of the Shank of Rivet

t = Thickness of Plate

m = Margin

t_1, t_2 = Thickness of Cover Plates

P = Pitch i.e. Perpendicular distance between rows of Rivets

P_d = Back Pitch in chain Riveting = 2d + 6 mm

P_b = Back Pitch in zigzag Riveting = 2d

Table 3.1 Standard Table for Selecting Diameter with Input to Thickness

Thickness of Plate, t mm	8	9	10	11	12	14	16	18	20	22
Diameter of Finished Rivet, d mm	17	18	19	20	21	22	24	25	27	28

3.9 CAUSES OF FAILURE OF RIVETED JOINTS

1. By shearing of rivets.
2. By the tearing of plates between the rivets holes.
3. By the crushing of the rivets or the plates.
4. By the tearing of the plate between its edge and the rivet holes.

Problem No. 1

Draw different types of rivet head by taking rivet diameter, d=20mm?

Problem No. 2

Draw sectional elevation and plan view of each of the following types of riveted joints:

(a) Single riveted lap joint.
(b) Double riveted lap joint, chain riveting.
(c) Double riveted lap joint, zigzag riveting.
(d) Single riveted butt joint, double cover plate.
(e) Double riveted double cover plate, zigzag riveting.
(f) Double riveted double cover plate, chain riveting.

Viva Voce Questions

1. Name the commonly used materials for rivets.
2. Define the following:
   (a) Ppitch, (b) Row pitch, (c) Diagonal pitch and (d) Margin
3. How are riveted joints made air-tight?
4. Name the different type of rivet heads as recommended by BIS : SP-46 : 1988.
5. What is a structural joint?
6. How are boiler joints classified?
7. Differentiate between:
   (a) Lap joint and butt joint, (b) Chain riveting and zig-zag riveting?
8. What is the function of a cover plate in riveted joints?
9. What are the different application of rivet?
10. What is caulking and fullering?
11. What is the difference between lap & butt joint?
12. Explain margin, back pitch, diagonal pitch.
13. What are the merits & demerits of rivets?

4

SCREW THREADS AND FASTENERS

4.1 SCREW THREADS

The helical grooves cut on the surface of a cylindrical piece for temporary fastening of parts or power transmission is known as screw threads.

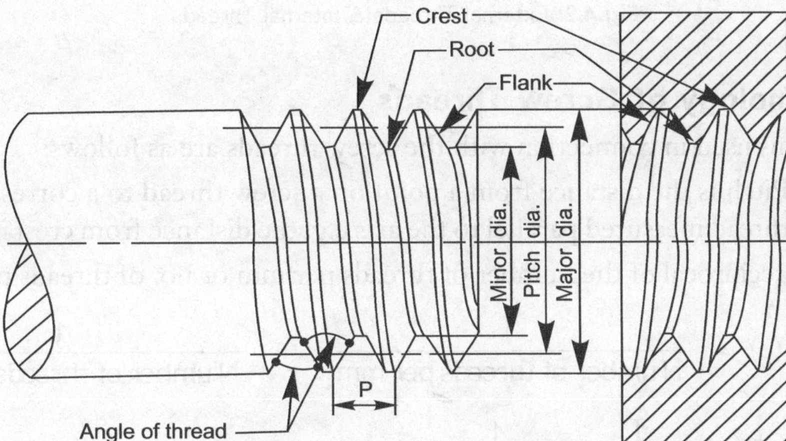

Fig.4.1: Screw Thread Nomenclature

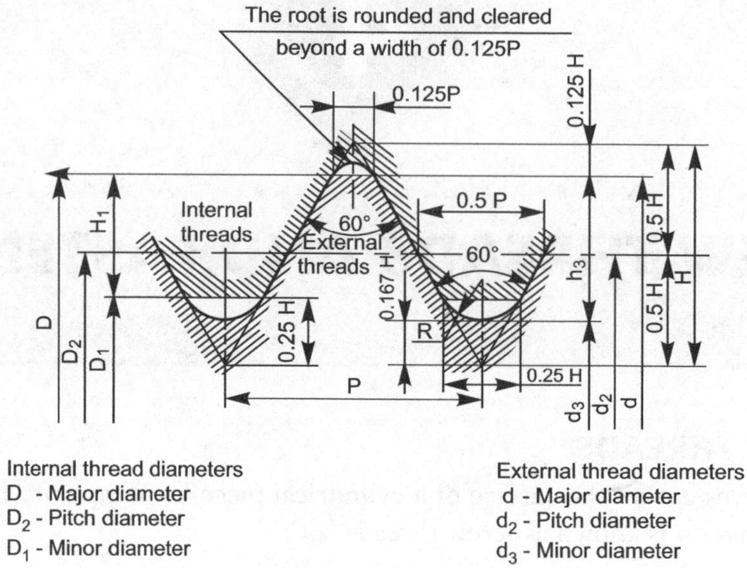

Fig.4.2: External Threads & Internal Threads

4.1.1 Terminology of Screw Threads

The various terms used in connection with the screw threads are as follows:

1. **Pitch (p) :** Pitch is the distance from a point on a screw thread to a corresponding point on the next thread measured parallel to the axis e.g. the distance from crest or root to root. Pitch is the reciprocal of the number of threads per mm or no. of threads per inch.

$$\text{Pitch (p)} = \frac{1}{\text{Number of threads per mm}} = \frac{1}{\text{Number of threads per inch}}$$

$$P = \frac{1}{\text{t.p.mm}} = \frac{1}{\text{t.p.i}}$$

2. **Lead:** Load is the linear distance moved by a nut or bolt in the axial direction in one complete revolution. In single start threads, the lead is equal to the pitch. In multi start threads load is equal to number of starts multiplied by pitch.

   Thus, Lead = No. of starts x pitch

3. **Crest:** It is the outermost portion which joins the two sides of a thread.
4. **Root:** It is the innermost portion which joins the adjacent sides of a thread.
5. **Angle of Thread:** It is the angle between the two sides of thread measured in an axial planes
6. **Depth of the Thread:** It is the distance between the crest and root of a thread measured perpendicular to the axis.

7. **Nominal Diameter:** It is the diameter of the cylindrical piece on which the threads are cut. The screw is specified by this diameter.
8. **Major Diameter:** It is the largest diameter of a screw thread. It is also known as outside or crest diameter.
9. **Minor Diameter:** It is the smallest diameter of a screw thread. It is also known as root or outside or core diameter.
10. **Pitch Diameter:** It is the diameter of an imaginary cylinder passing through the width of the threads at which the threads and the width of the gap are equal.
11. **Slope:** It is the axial distance through which a thread is tilted on the front view. The slope of a thread is equal to half the itch or load on single start threads.
12. **External Threads:** Threads on the outer surface of a cylinder are called external threads, such as threads in case of bolt.

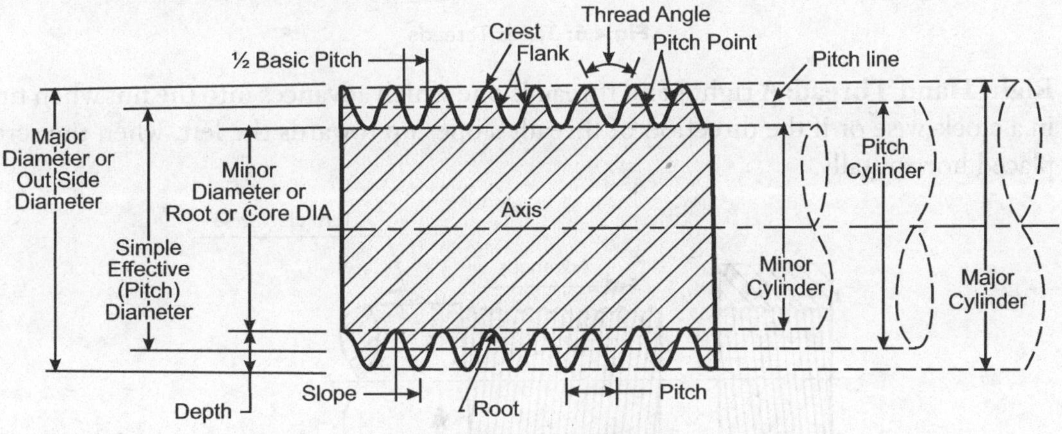

Fig.4.3: External Threads

13. **Internal Threads:** Threads on the inner surface of a cylinder are called internal threads, such as threads in case of nut.

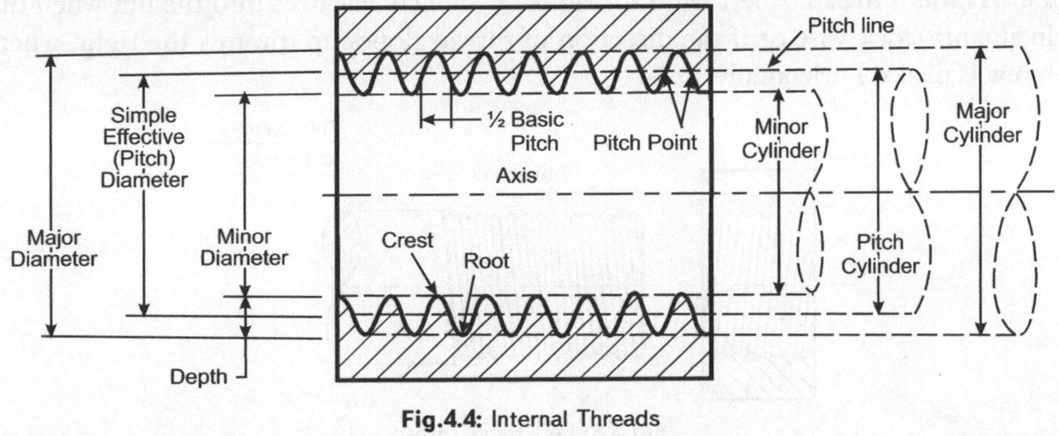

Fig.4.4: Internal Threads

14. Straight or Cylindrical Threads: Threads formed on a cylinder are called straight or cylindrical threads.

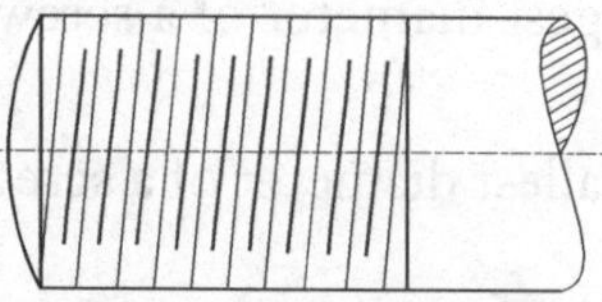

Fig.4.5: Straight Threads

15. Taper Threads: Threads formed on a cone shaped rod are called taped threads (Fig. 5.3)

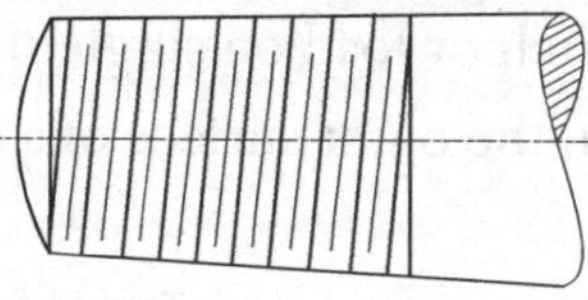

Fig.4.6: Taper Threads

16. Right Hand Thread: A right hand thread is one which advances into the nut when turned in a clock-wise or if the direction of threads slopes up towards the left, when the screw is placed horizontally.

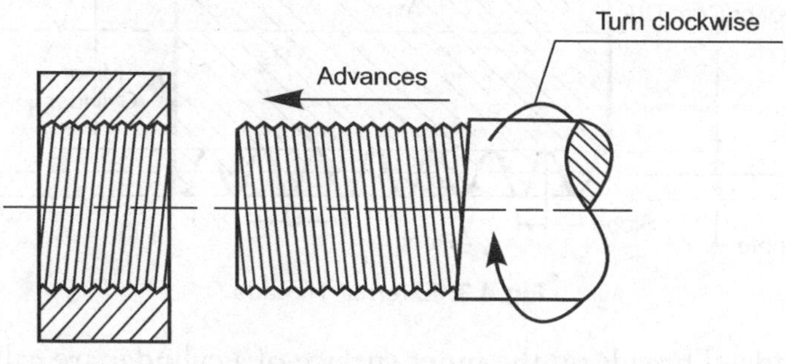

Fig.4.7: Right Hand Thread

17. Left Hand Thread: A left hand thread is one which advances into the nut when turned in an anti-clock-wise or if the direction of thread slopes up towards the right, when the screw is placed horizontally.

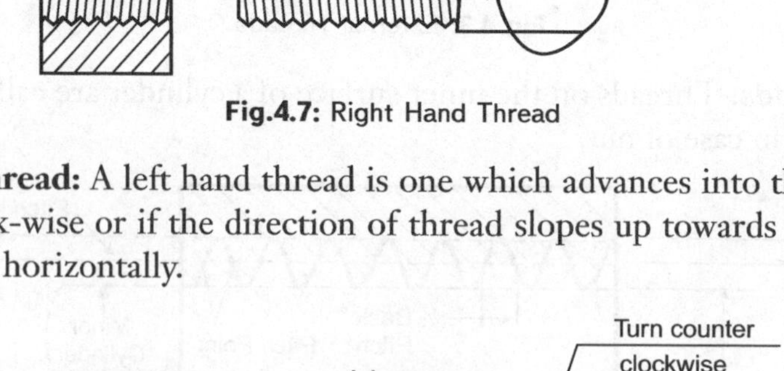

Fig.4.8: Left Hand Thread

18. **Single Start Threads:** When only one helix forming the threads, run on a surface is called a single start thread. It is also called single start threads, because only one starting point is seen on the beginning of the threaded portion. In a single start threads, the pitch is equal to the load. Threads are always start unless or otherwise specified.

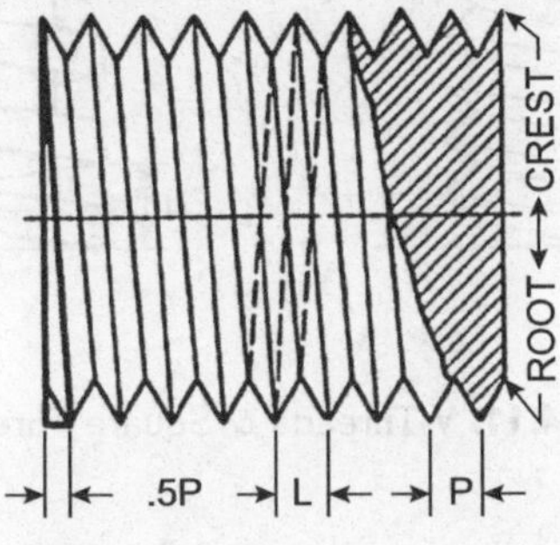

Fig.4.9: Single Start Thread

19. **Multiple Start Threads:** When two or more helices forming the threads, run side by side on the cylindrical surface, it is called multiple start threads. It is also called multiple start threads, because two or more than two starting points are seen on the beginning of the threaded portion.

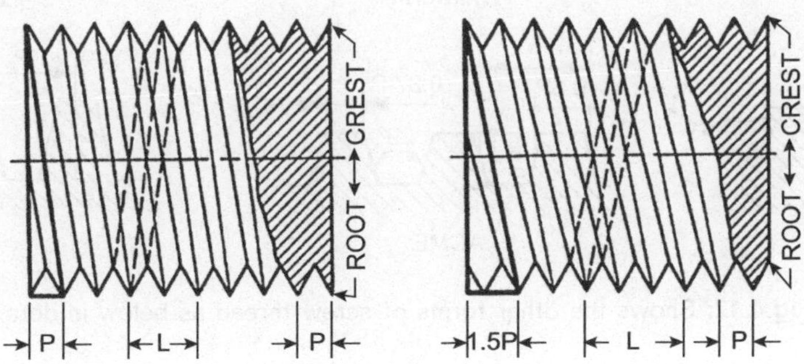

Fig.4.10: Multi Start Thread

In double start threads, the load is twice the pitch; in triple start threads, load is three times the pitch and so on.

Uses of Multiple Threads: Multiple threads are used wherever quick motion is required and application of great force is not allowed e.g. on fountain pens, bottles, tooth-paste caps, valves etc. to impart quick action in opening and closing.

4.1.2 Forms of Screw Thread

There are two main types of screw thread forms:

(a) V type used mainly for fastening and adjusting purposes and

(b) Square type, used for transmitting power.

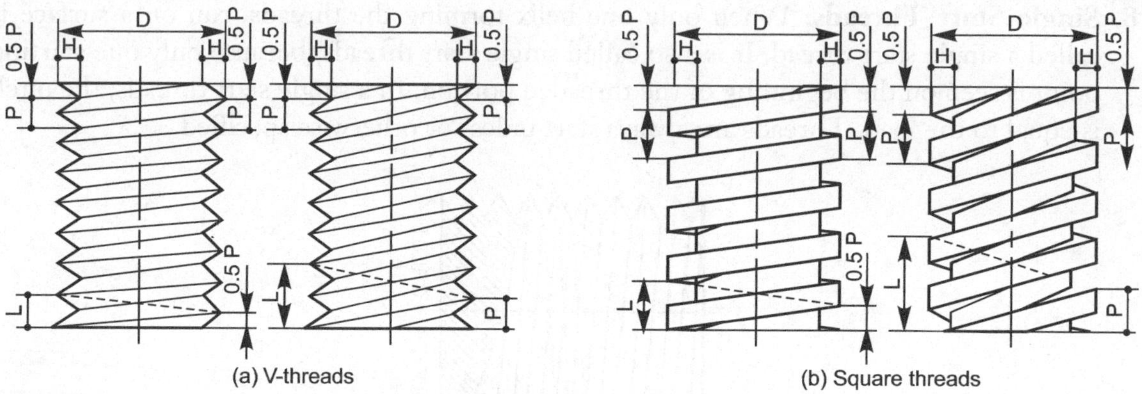

Fig.4.11: V-Threads & Square Threads

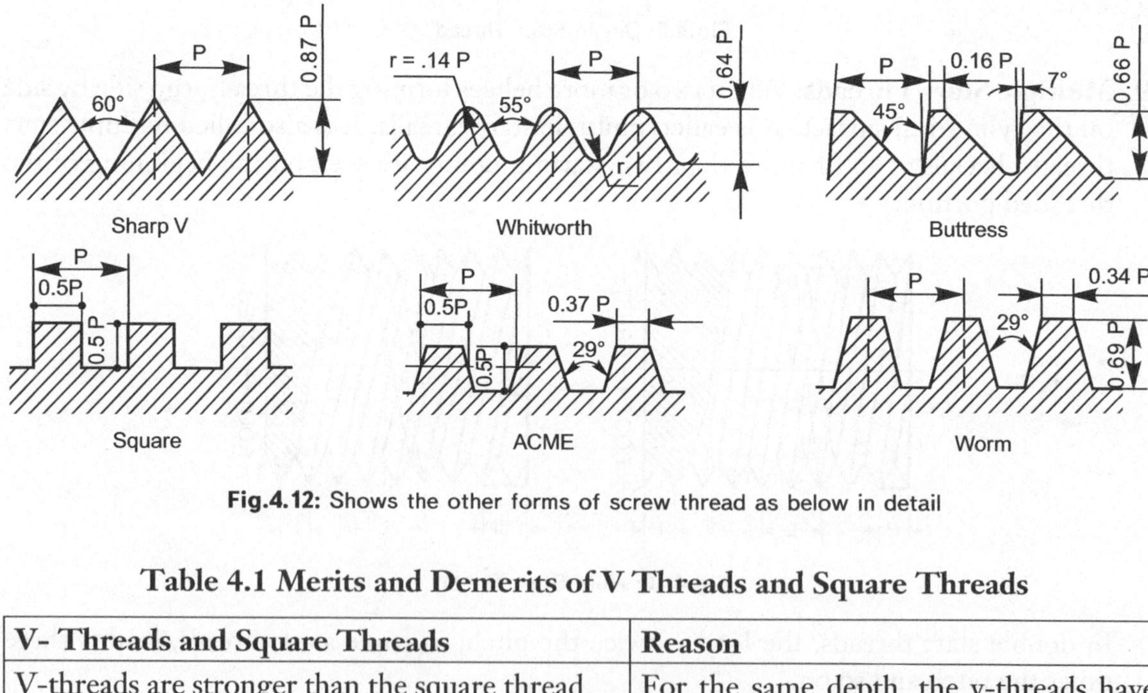

Fig.4.12: Shows the other forms of screw thread as below in detail

Table 4.1 Merits and Demerits of V Threads and Square Threads

V- Threads and Square Threads	Reason
V-threads are stronger than the square thread	For the same depth, the v-threads have twice the amount of frictional resistance at the root of the thread than a square thread
V-threads are best salted for fastening purposes as in bolts and nuts, studs and nuts, set-screws etc.	V-threads offer greater frictional resistance to motion than square threads

Square threads are used for transmission of power or motion from one part to another as in the case of bench-vice, valve spindles, lead screw of a lathe, screw jacks etc.	Square threads offer less frictional resistance to motion than v-threads

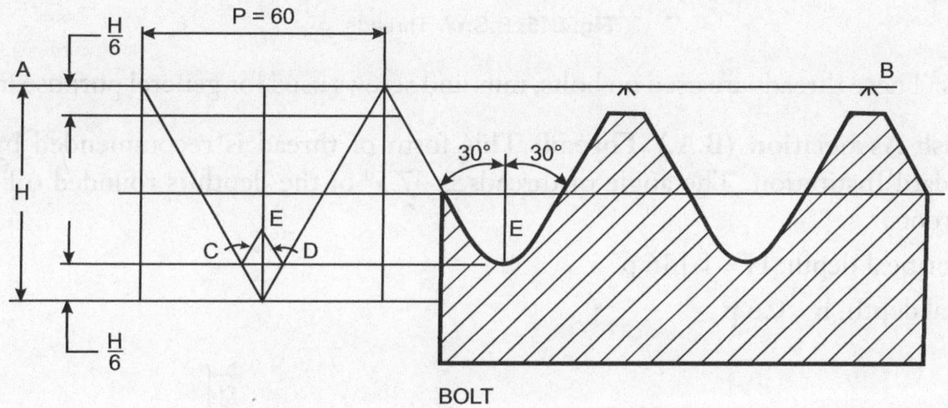

Fig.4.13: ISO Metric External Thread

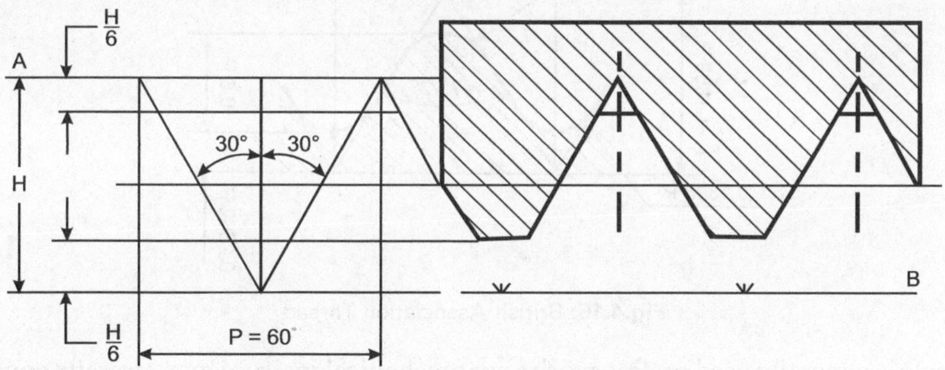

Fig.4.14: ISO Metric Internal Thread

4.2 DIFFERENT TYPES OF SCREW THREADS

(i) **British Standard Whitworth (B.S.W.) Thread:** This form of thread is used as a standard thread in Britain. It is the modified form of "v" thread having angle of threads 55^0 and 0.167 of the depth of the full "v" is rounded off at the crests and roots.

Pitch (p) = 1/(t.p.i.)

Theoritical depth, H = 0.96 p

Actual depth, h = 0.64p

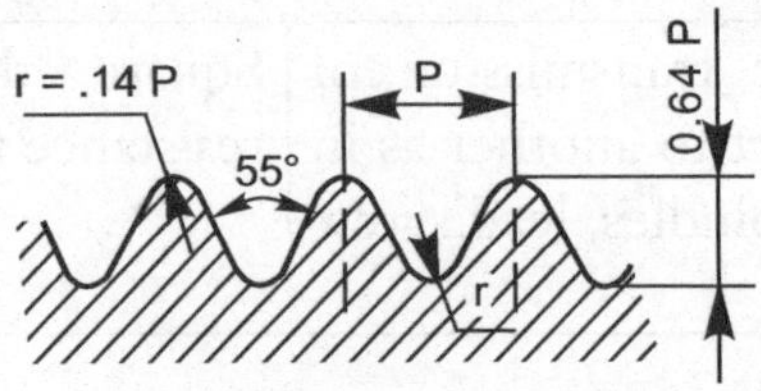

Fig.4.15: B.S.W. Threads

Uses: These threads are used on bolts, nuts and screws used for general purpose fastening.

(ii) British Association (B.A.) Thread: This form of thread is recommended by British Standard Institution. The angle of threads is 47.5^0 of the depth is rounded off at crests and roots.

Theoritical depth, H = 1.136 p

Actual depth, h = 0.6 p

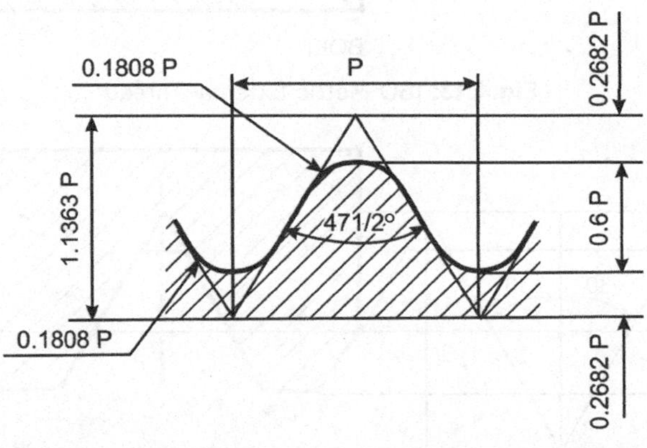

Fig.4.16: British Association Thread

Uses: It is generally used on fine work as in mechanical instruments, aircrafts construction etc.

(iii) American National or Seller Thread: This form of thread is adopted as a standard form in America. The angle between the sides of threads is 60^0. The crests and roots are flattened up to 0.125 of the depth.

Theoritical depth, H = 0.866 p

Actual depth, h = ¾ H = 0.649 p

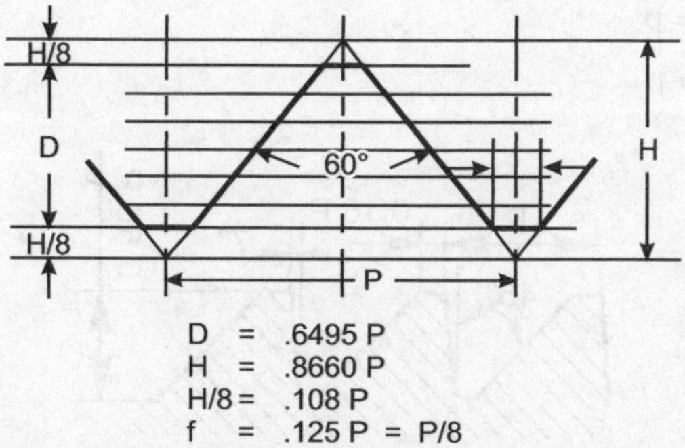

Fig.4.17: Seller Thread/American National Thread

Uses: It is mostly used on fasteners for making adjustments.

(iv) ISO Metric Thread: The basic profile of the ISO metric screw thread is a v-form thread. In ISO metric screw threads the angle is 60^0.

Theoritical depth, H = 0.866025 p

Actual depth, h = 0.54127 p

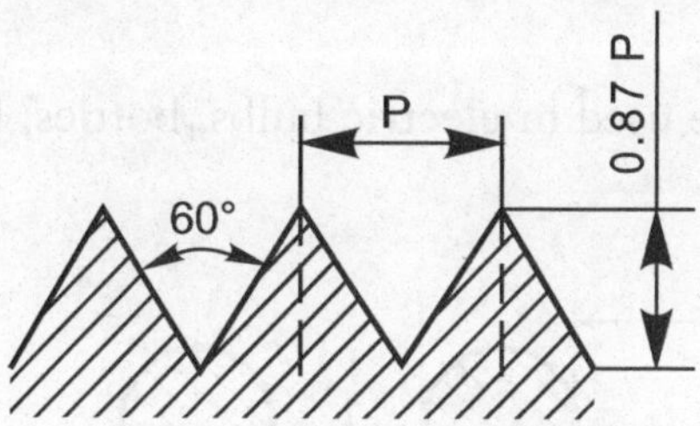

Fig.4.18: ISO Metric Thread

(v) Acme Thread: It is a modification of square thread. It is stronger at the root but its inclined flank give rise to some frictional resistance. It is generally used in load screws, heavy power transmission.

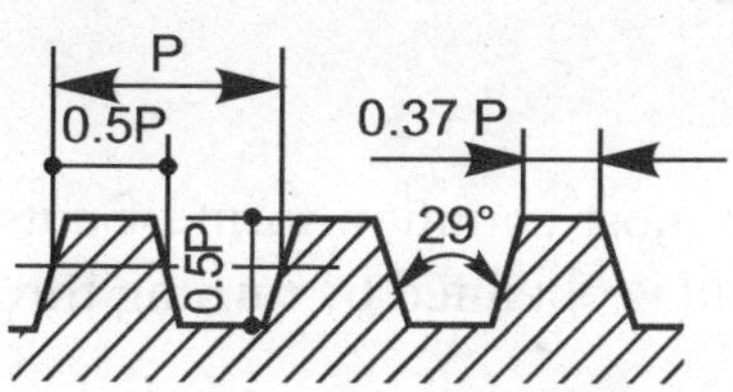

Fig.4.19: Acme Thread

(vi) Buttress Thread: It is combined form of v and square threads. One side of the thread is perpendicular to the axis of the thread and the other inclined at 45^0. Sharp edges at crest and the root are flattened to 0.125 of the depth.

Theoritical depth, H = p

Actual depth, h = 0.75 p

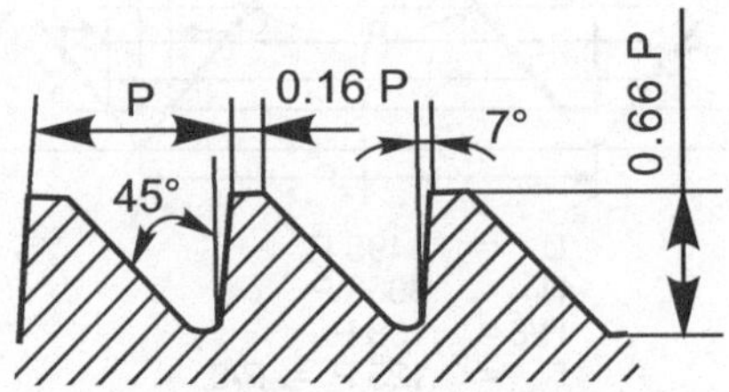

Fig.4.20: Buttress Thread

Uses: It is used for power transmission in one direction only as in breach locks of large guns, jacks, in air plane propellers, carpenter's vices etc.

(vii)Knuckle Thread: It is the modified form of the square threads. It is semi-circular at the crest and root. In this, radius is equal to 0.25 p and working depth of the thread is 0.5 p. It is a strong thread suitable for rough and ready work. It is usually rolled from sheet metal but sometimes crested.

Depth = 0.5 p

Uses: Knuckle threads are used in electric bulbs, bottles, fire hydrants, railway, couplers etc.

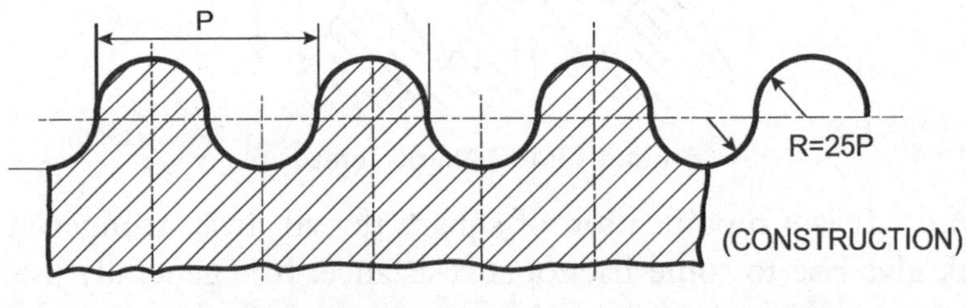

Fig.4.21: Knuckle Thread

4.3 NUTS

A nut has internal threads. The most common form of nuts is hexagonal, for screwing it is turned by spanner and a new hold is obtained by turning through 45°.

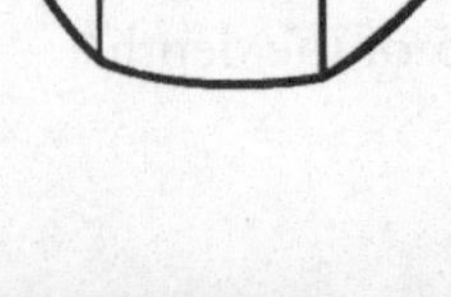

Fig.4.22: Nut

4.3.1 Hexagonal Nut

The upper corners of the hexagonal prism are leveled off or chamfered at 30° to 45° the nut. The chamfering is generally conical.

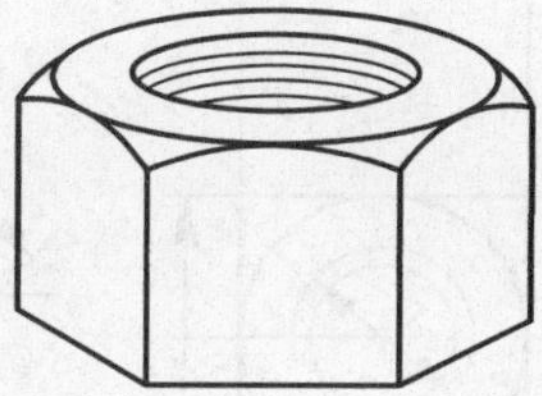

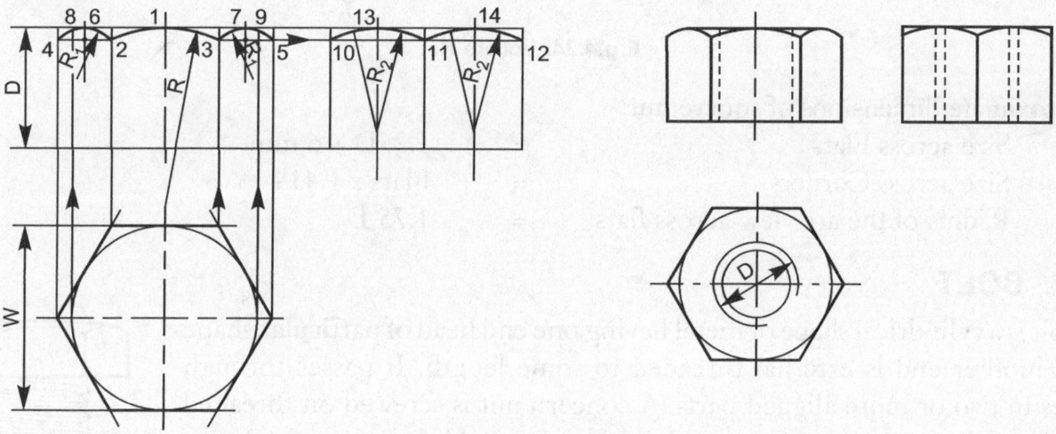

Fig.4.23: Hexagonal Nut

Approximate dimensions of hexagonal nut:

Let D = Dia. Of the screwed hole in hexagonal nut and outside or nominal diameter of bolt.

Size across Flats = 1.25D + 6 mm
Height of Nut = 0.8 D to D
Chamfer of front corners = flats x 1.55
Chamfer at top = 30^0 to base of nut
Radius of front chamfer = 0.9 D to D

4.3.2 Square Nut

In this nut the distance across flats is the same as in the hexagonal nut.

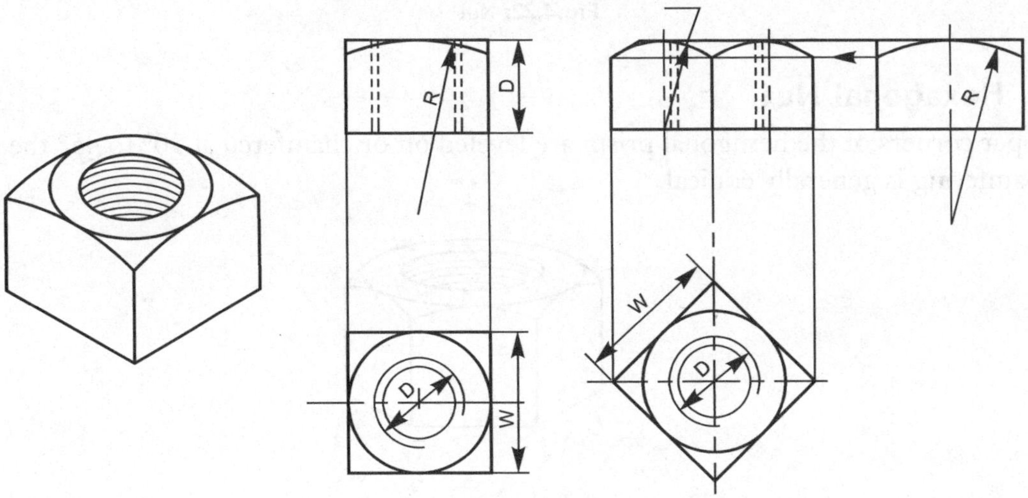

Fig.4.24: Square Nut

Approximate dimensions of square nut:

Size across Flats	=	1.25D + 6 mm
Size across Corners	=	Flats x 1.414
Radius of the arc view across flats	=	1.75 D

4.4 BOLT

A bolt is a cylindrical shape of metal having one end head of particular shape and another end is external threaded to some length. It passes through holes in two or more aligned parts. A concern nut is screwed on threaded end from the other side of part and tightened to hold the parts together.

It is used for temporary fastening purpose. Generally hexagonal headed and square headed bolt are in use.

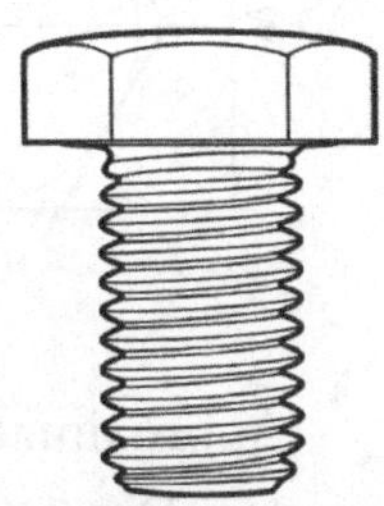

Fig.4.25: Bolt

4.4.1 Hexagonal Bolt

The shape of head of bolt is hexagonal and that is why the name given to this type of bolt is hexagonal bolt. This is the most common form of bolt and widely used in machines and engineering works to tighten two or more parts together.

Properties of the Hexagonal Bolt:

Assume D is the nominal diameter of bolt, then

Width across flat (w)	= 1.5 D + 3 mm
Thickness of Head (t)	= 0.8 D
Angle of chamfer (θ)	= 30° to the base of the head
Radius of the chamfer (R)	= 1.5 D

Length of Bolt (L)	= 3D to 20D	
Length of threaded part (L_1)	= 2D + 5mm	40 to 80 mm Dia.
	= 2D + 10mm	81 to 200mm Dia.
	= 2D + 20mm	above 200mm Dia.

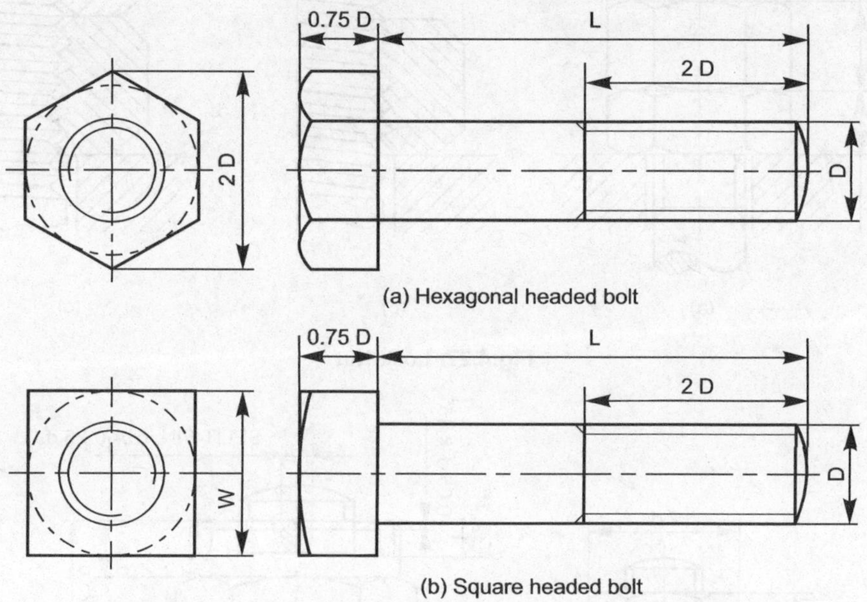

Fig.4.26: Hexagonal Headed Bolt & Square Headed Bolt

4.5 LOCKING DEVICES

When a bolted machine part is subjected to vibration and rotation the nut tends to get loose or slacken back, and may cause to be very harmful and dangerous to the machinery. For Example the cross head of connecting rod of engines. The devices used to prevent loose or slacking tendency of nuts and to keep in right position are called locking devices. Many locking devices for nuts are as follows:

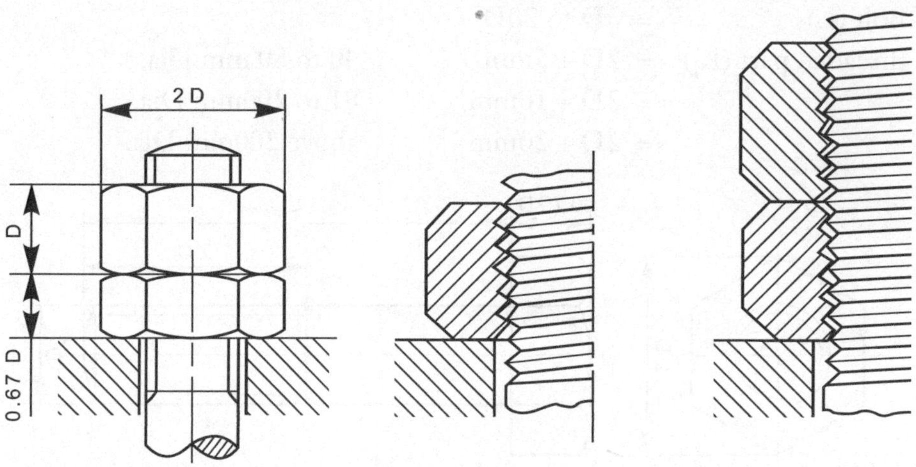

(a) (b) (c)

Fig.4.27: Lock Nut

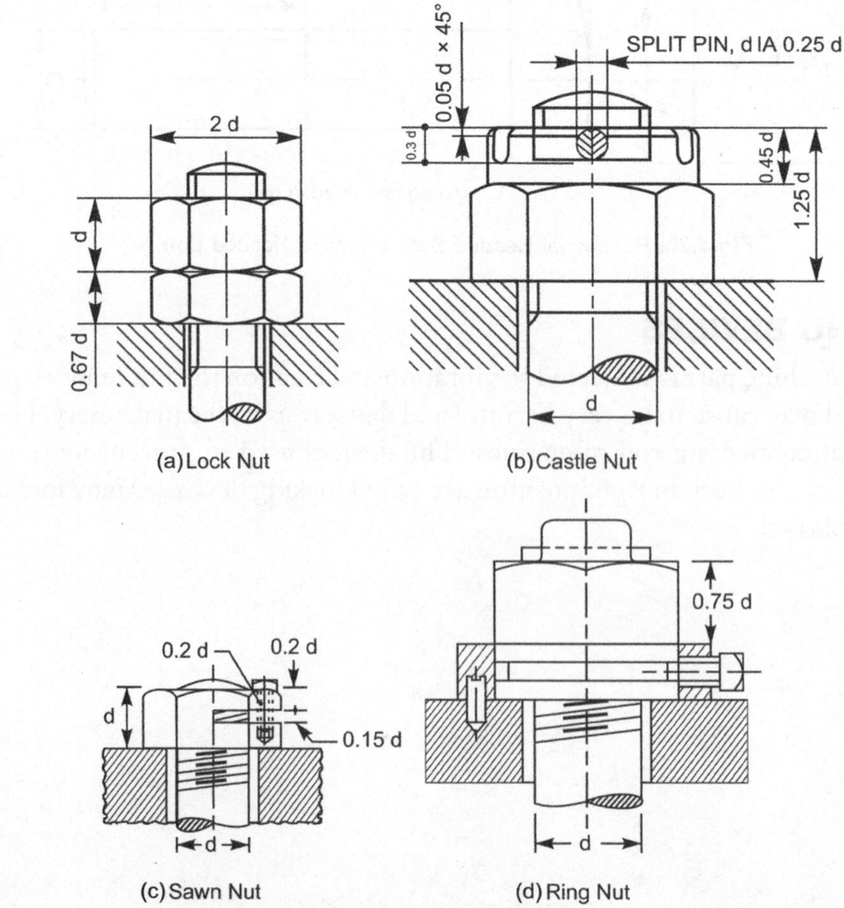

(a) Lock Nut (b) Castle Nut

(c) Sawn Nut (d) Ring Nut

Fig.4.28: Locking devices

4.5.1 Studs

Stud is a cylindrical piece threaded at both ends and plain in the middle. One end of stud is screws tightly in a tapped hole of one machine part. The plain portion passes through the second machine part and the nut is tightened over it.

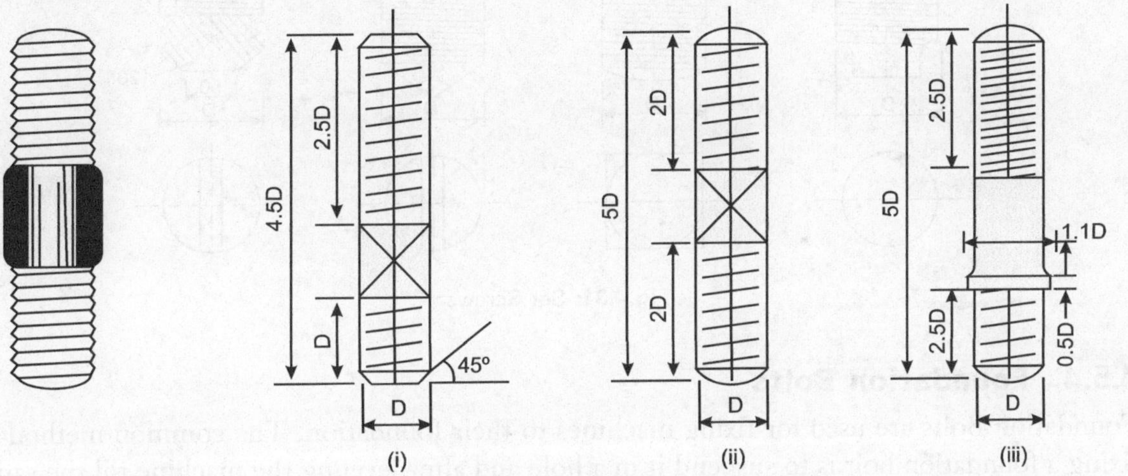

Fig.4.29: Studs

4.5.2 Machine Screws

Machine screws are used in machines for fastening two parts together. One of the parts has a tapped hole and other part has clearance hole.

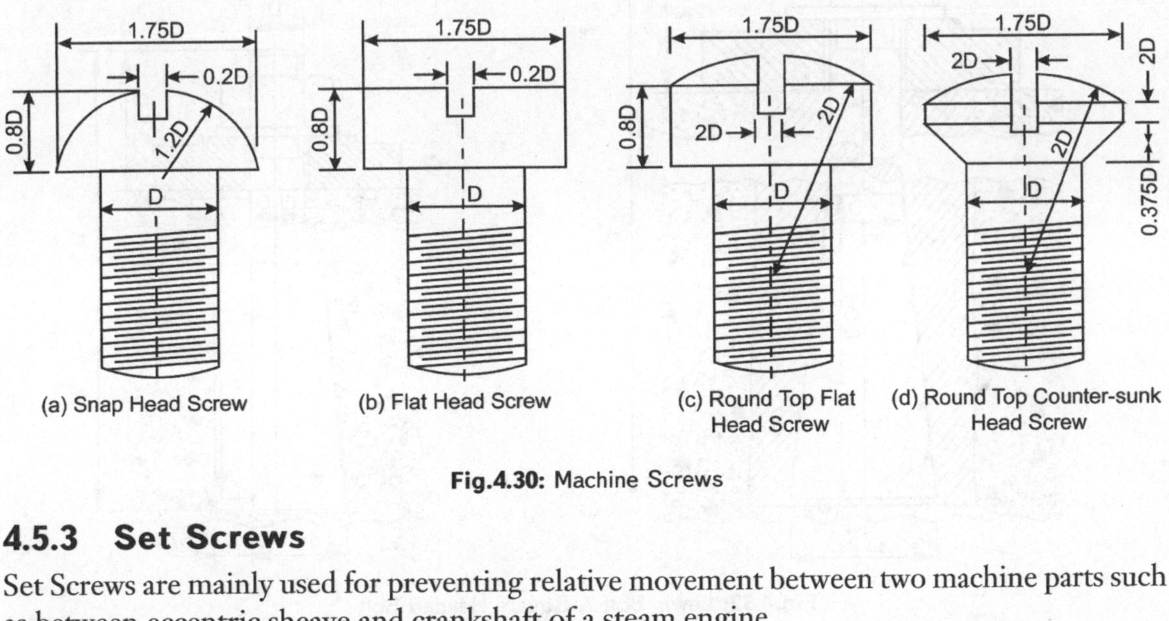

Fig.4.30: Machine Screws

4.5.3 Set Screws

Set Screws are mainly used for preventing relative movement between two machine parts such as between eccentric sheave and crankshaft of a steam engine

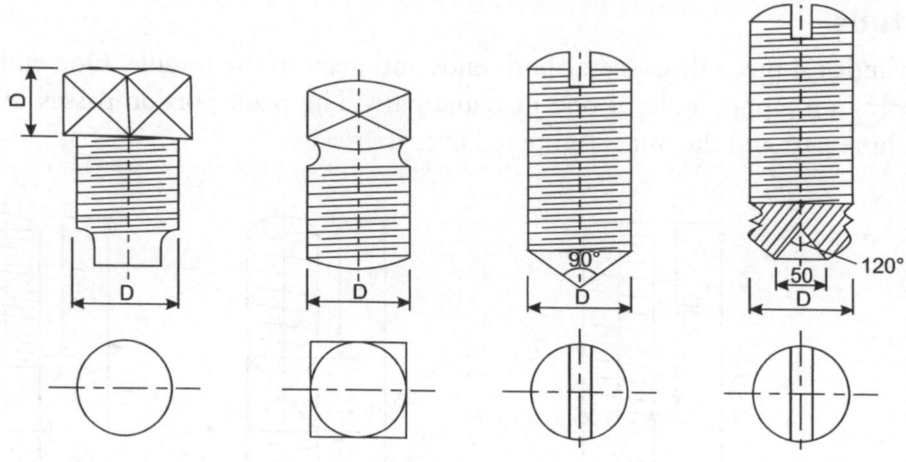

Fig.4.31: Set Screws

4.5.4 Foundation Bolts

Foundation Bolts are used for fixing machines to their foundation. The common method of fixing a foundation bolt is to suspend it in a hole and after leveling the machine fill the same with a fine thin grout consisting of equal of sand and cement.

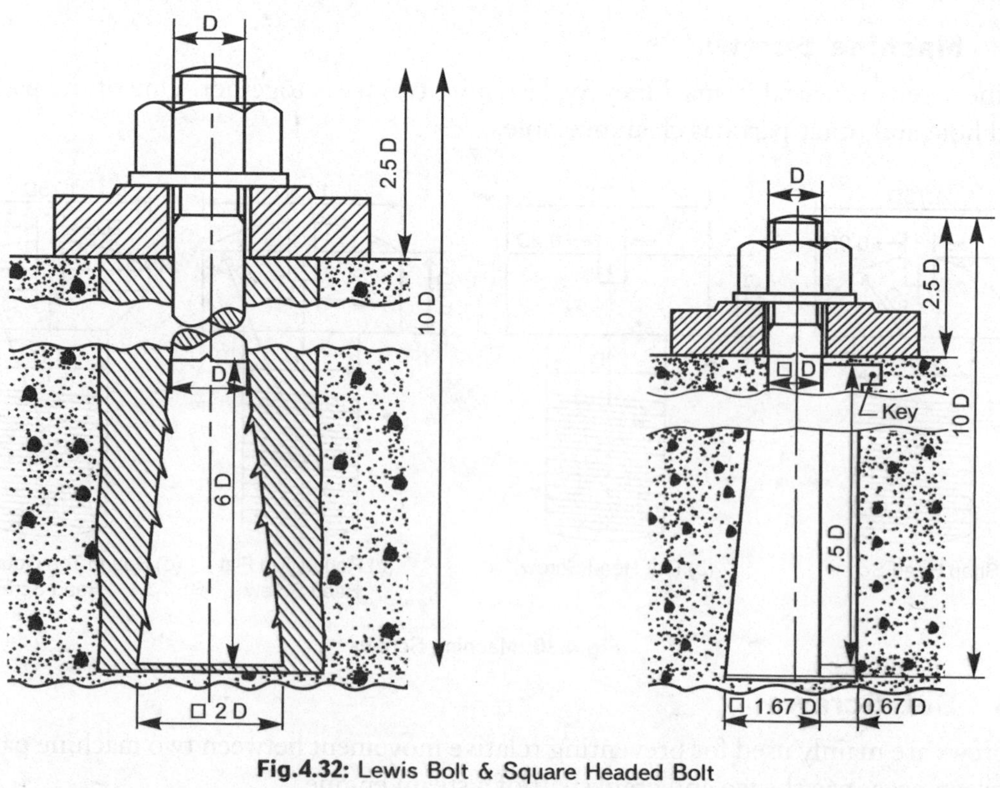

Fig.4.32: Lewis Bolt & Square Headed Bolt

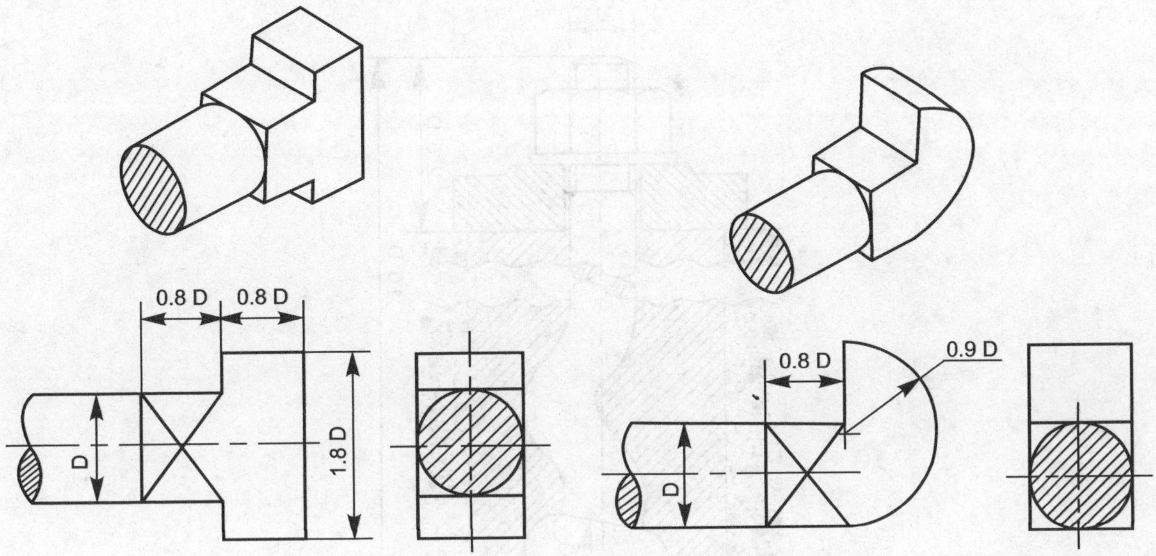

Fig.4.33: T-Headed Bolt & Hook Bolt

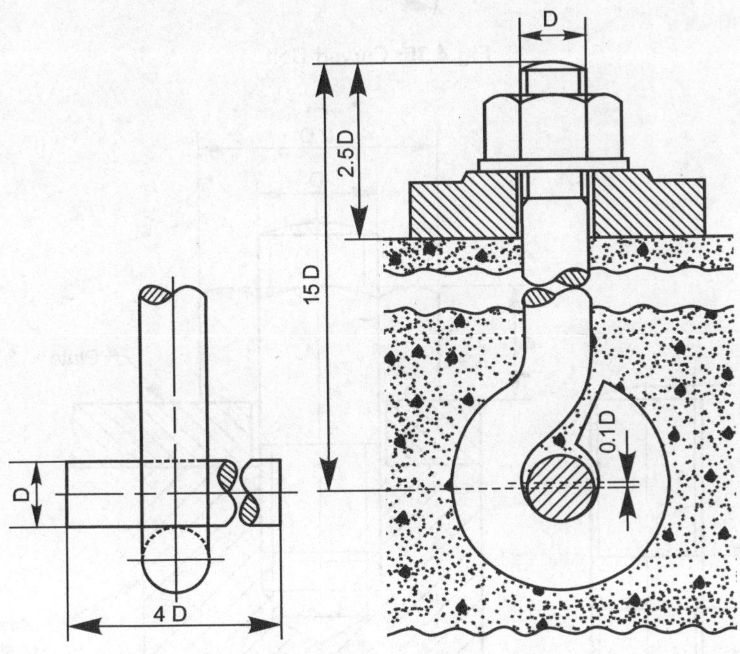

Fig.4.34: Hoop Bolt

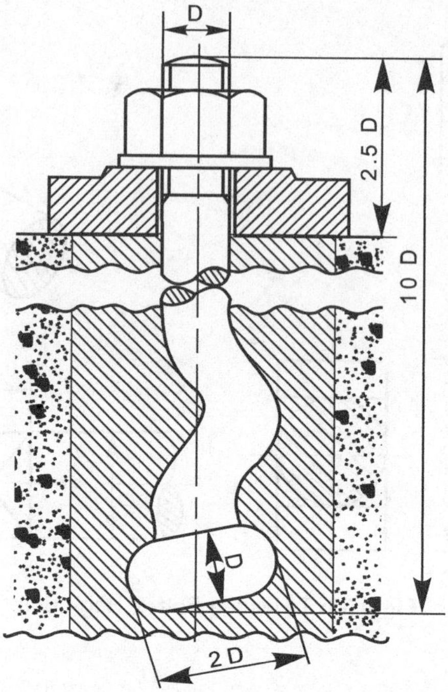

Fig.4.35: Curved Bolt

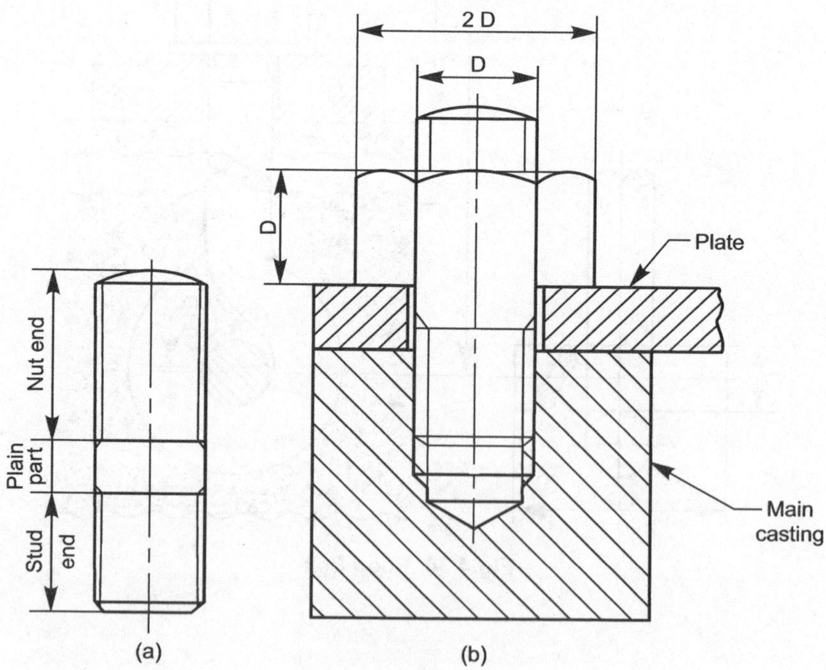

Fig.4.36: Cotter Bolt

Viva Voce Questions

1. What is a fastener and what is meant by fastening?
2. What are the various applications of screwed fasteners?
3. Define the following terms with respect to screw threads:

   (a) Pitch, (b) Pitch diameter (c) Major diameter (d) Minor diameter (e) Lead (f) Crest (g) Root and (h) Thread angle.
4. Distinguish between the following:

   (a) Metric and BSW threads (b) Square and ACME thread (c) Left hand and right hand threads and (d) Pitch and lead of a thread.
5. What is a multi-start thread and how it differs from a single start thread?
6. What are multi-start threads used and why?
7. Where is the pitch and lead in the case of a double start thread?
8. What type of thread is used for the screw jack and lathe lead screw and why?
9. How are the following threads designated as per BIS:

   (a) Metric thread with coarse pitch (b) Metric thread with fine pitch (c) Square thread (d) ACME thread and (e) Worm thread
10. Why hexagonal shape is preferred to square one for nuts?
11. Why are washers used in bolted joints?
12. What is a T-bolt and where is it used?
13. What is an eye-bolt and for what purpose is it used?
14. What is a stud bolt and where is it used?
15. Differentiate between the following:

    (a) Bolt and screw (b) Machine screw and set screw and (c) Cap screw and machine screw.
16. What is a set screw? What is its function?
17. What are locking devices? Where and why are they used?
18. What are foundation bolts and where they are used?

5

BEARINGS & SHAFT COUPLING

BEARINGS

5.1 DEFINITION

It is a device which is used to support the shaft. Normally a shaft is supported by two bearings at ends but if the shaft is long or consists of many mounting (pulleys, wheels, gears, etc.), intermediate support or bearing may be provided to reduce deflection of the shaft. It may also be termed as load bearing support for the shaft.

5.1.1 Types of Bearings:

There are mainly two types of bearings:

1. Sliding Contact Bearing
   (a) Journal Bearing
   (b) Foot-Step Bearing
   (c) Thrust or Collar Bearing
2. Rolling Contact Bearing
   (a) Ball Bearing
   (b) Roller Bearing
   (c) Needle Bearing

5.2 JOURNAL BEARING

These bearings are used for supporting the horizontal shaft. It carry the load perpendicular to the axis of shaft.

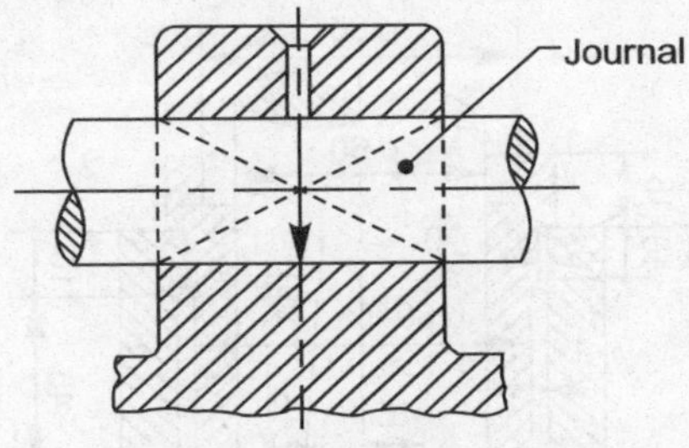

Fig.5.1: Journal Bearing

5.3 FOOT-STEP BEARING

This is known as pivoted bearing. It supports the shaft parallel to its axis. The shaft is kept in vertical position and the end of which rests within bearing.

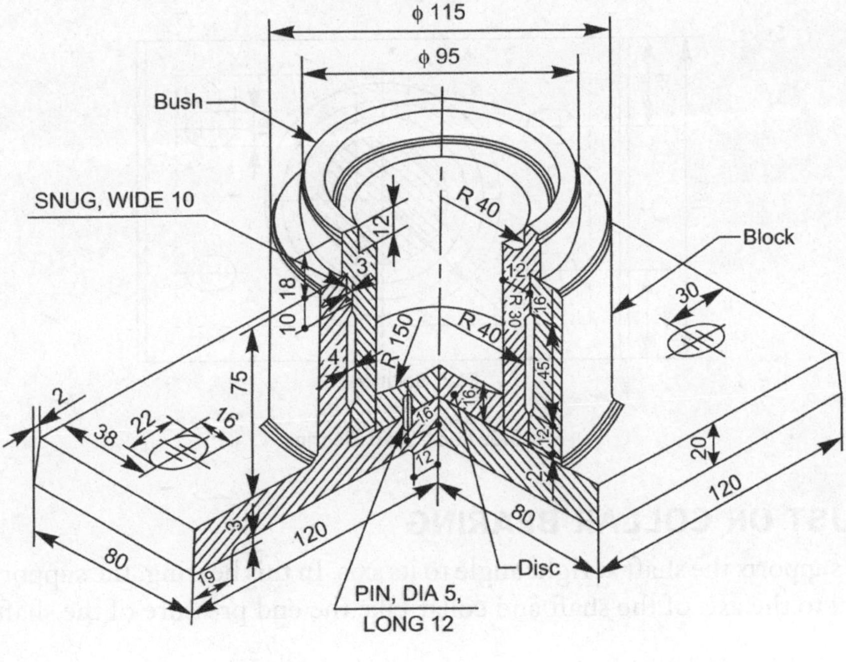

Fig.5.2: Foot step bearing problem

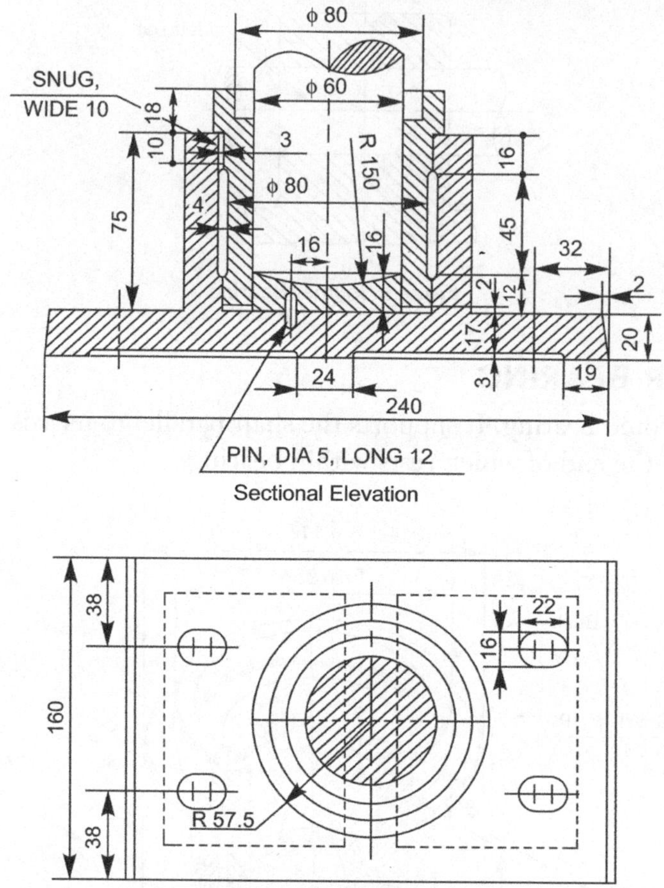

Sectional Elevation

Plan Solution

Fig.5.3: Foot-Step Bearing

5.4 THRUST OR COLLAR BEARING

This bearing supports the shaft at right angle to its axis. In this bearing, the supporting pressure is also parallel to the axis of the shaft and collar take the end pressure of the shaft.

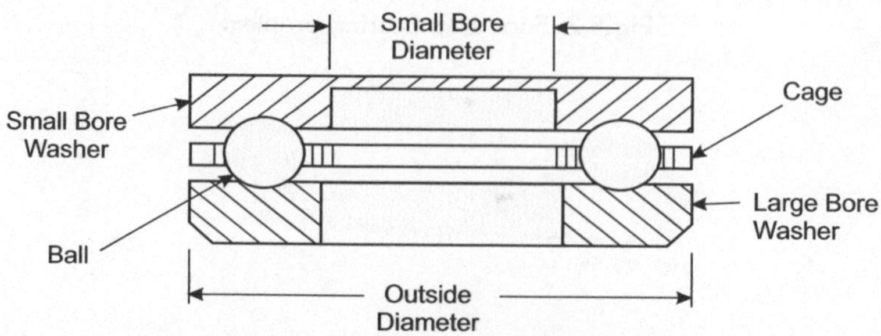

Fig.5.4: Thrust or Collar Bearing

5.5 BALL & ROLLER BEARING

Ball and roller bearing are used as the frictional resistance in these bearings is considerably less than in plain bearings. In ball and roller bearings the rotating pairs are separated by number of balls or rollers. Each ball or roller has rolling contact with the adjacent surfaces of the elements and sliding friction is eliminated and replaced by much lower rolling friction.

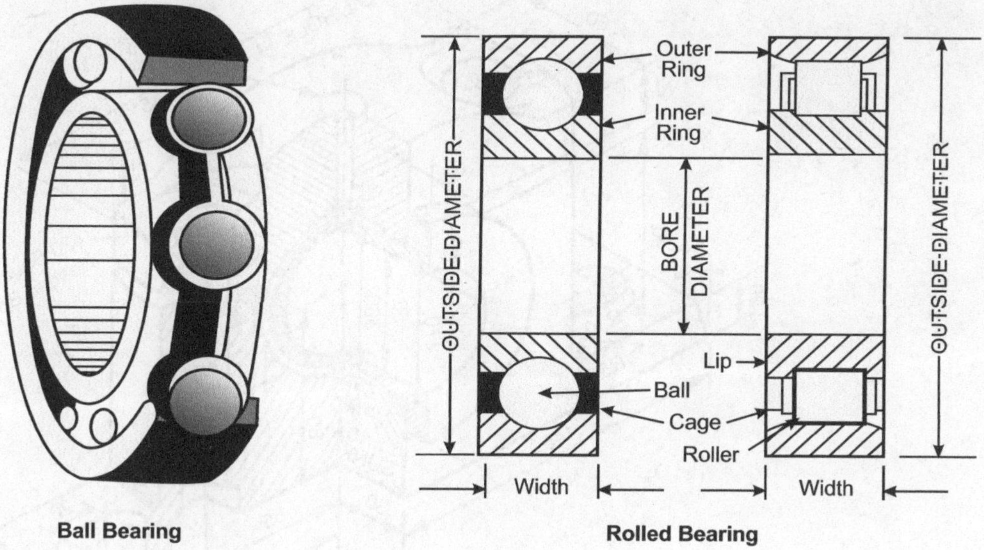

Fig.5.5: Ball & Roller Bearing

5.6 NEEDLE ROLLER BEARING

Needle roller bearings use small diameter of rollers. They are used for radial loads at slow speed and oscillating motion. They have the advantage of light weight and occupy small space. They are used in air-craft industry, live tail stock, centers bench drill spindles etc.

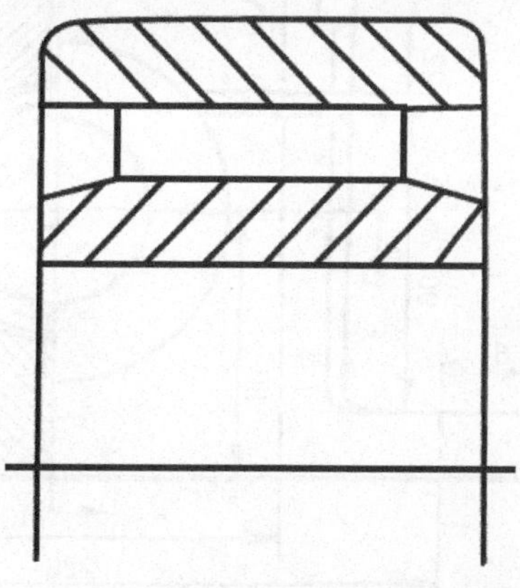

Fig.5.6: Needle Roller Bearing

5.7 PLUMMER BLOCK

This bearing is also known as pedestal bearing. It is a split type of journal bearing and especially used for higher spud and heavy loads. Those bearing consisting of a cast iron block, split type gun metal brasses, a cast iron cap and two mild steel square headed bolt with hexagonal nut.

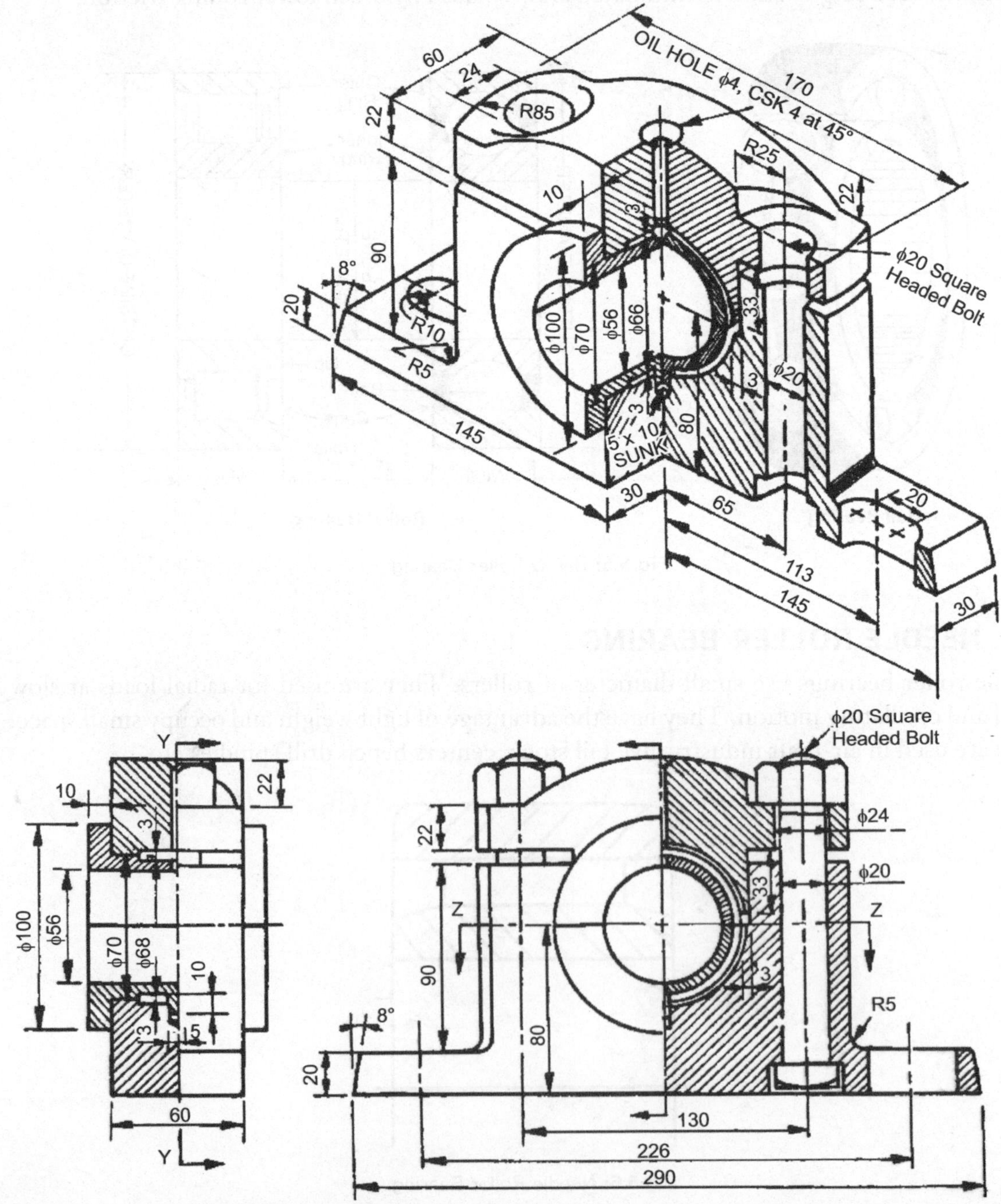

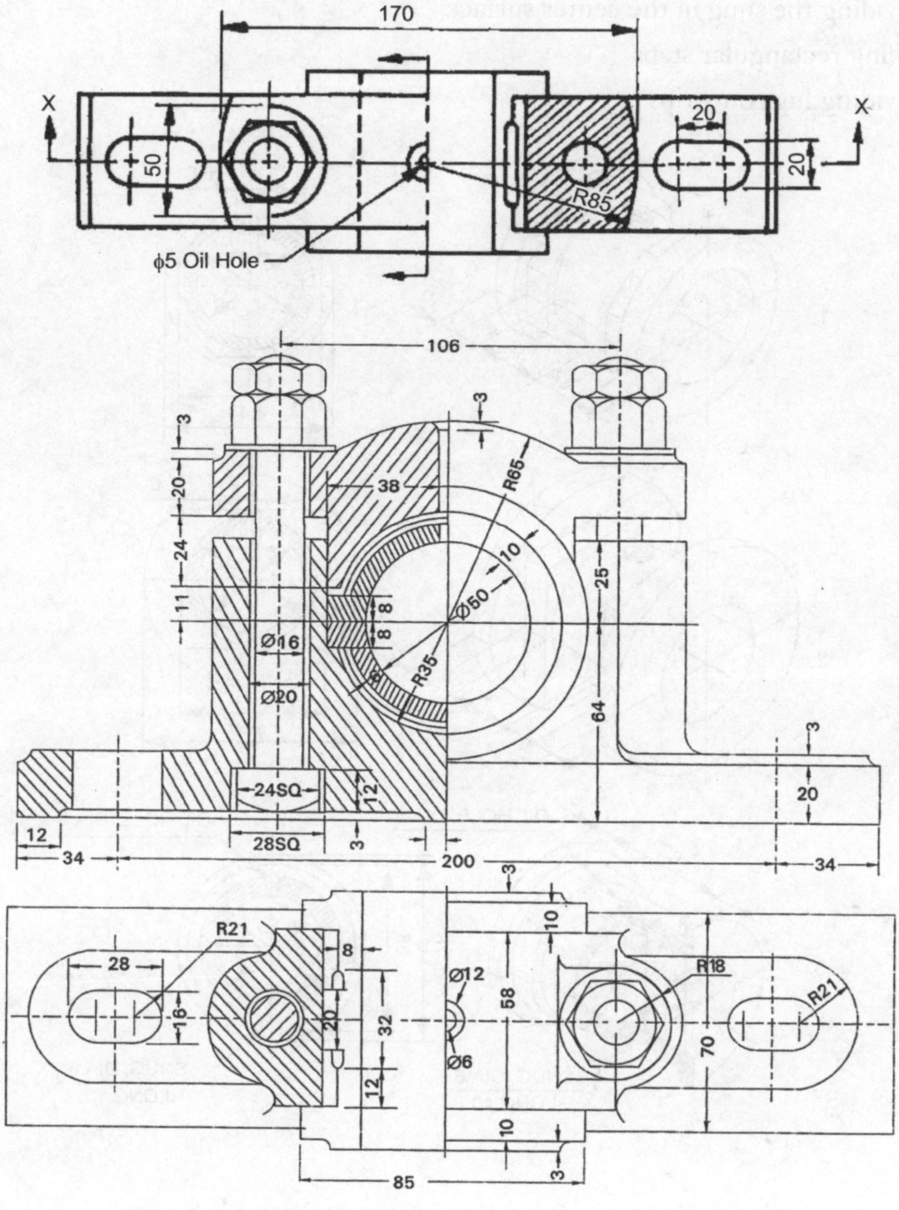

Fig.5.7: Plummer Block

5.8 METHODS OF PREVENTING ROTATION OF BRASSES IN A BEARING

In order to prevent the relative rotation and axial motion of the brasses inside the bearing, in the following methods can be used:

1. By making octagonal steps near the flanges

2. By providing the snug in the center surface
3. By making rectangular steps
4. By providing lugs on strips

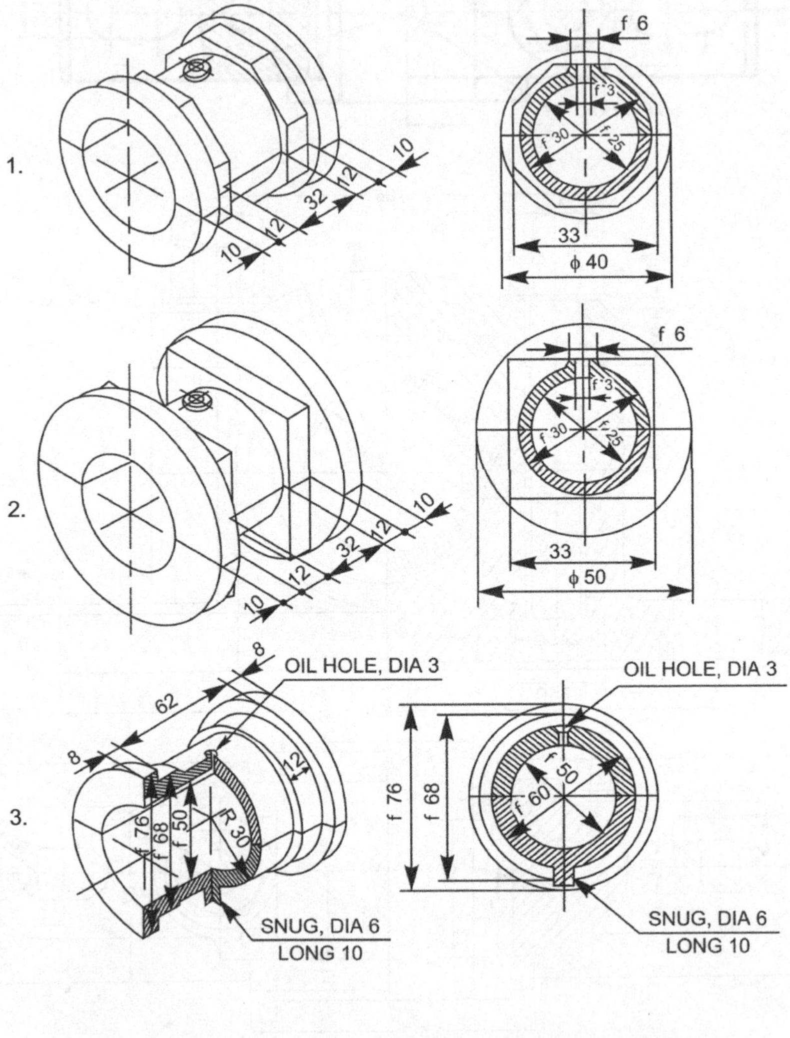

Fig.5.8: Methods of Preventing Rotation of Brasses in Bearings

5.9 SHAFT COUPLING

Shaft coupling is mechanical device used to connect two rotating shafts and absorb misalignment between them. It is used for power and torque transmission between two rotating shafts such as motors, pumps, compressors and generators etc.

Coupling can be classified with respect to the kind of alignment and centre line position of the connecting shafts.

According to above reasons the couplings are mainly two types:

1. Rigid Coupling
   (a) Flange Coupling
   (b) Muff Coupling
   (c) Friction Grip & Compression Coupling
2. Flexible Coupling
   (a) Oldham Coupling
   (b) Universal Joints or Hooks Joints
   (c) Pin type Flexible Couplings

5.9.1 Rigid Coupling or Fast Coupling

These are used when shafts are already positioned in centre line and no central or angular alignment. Their design does not allow any misalignment between shafts and are able to transmit more power than other type of flexible couplings.

Rigid couplings are further subdivided into following groups:

(a) Flange Coupling
(b) Muff Coupling
(c) Friction Grip or Compression Coupling

5.9.2 Flexible Coupling or Non-Rigid Coupling

These are used where rotating shaft are not in centre line positioned and there is misalignment in shafts. Flexible coupling are designed to accommodate misalignment between shafts.

These are further subdivided into following groups:

(a) Oldham Coupling
(b) Universal Joints or Hooks Joints
(c) Pin type Flexible Coupling

5.9.3 Unprotected type Flange Coupling

This is a standard form of coupling and is used extensively. It consists of two similar cast iron flanges to which the shafts are keyed with the help of sunk taper keys.

For sketching of unprotected flange coupling the following properties may be used:

Diameter of Hub	:	1.8D+5 mm
Lengths of Hub	:	1.3D+3 mm
Pitch Circle Diameter	:	2.2D+35 mm
Thickness of Flange	:	0.33D+3 mm
Number of Bolt	:	6 above 55 up to 150 shafts

5.9.4 Protected type Flange Coupling

Each Flange is provided with annular projection for covering bolt heads and nuts. It consists of a turned projection on one flange called spigot, which fits into a recess in other flange.

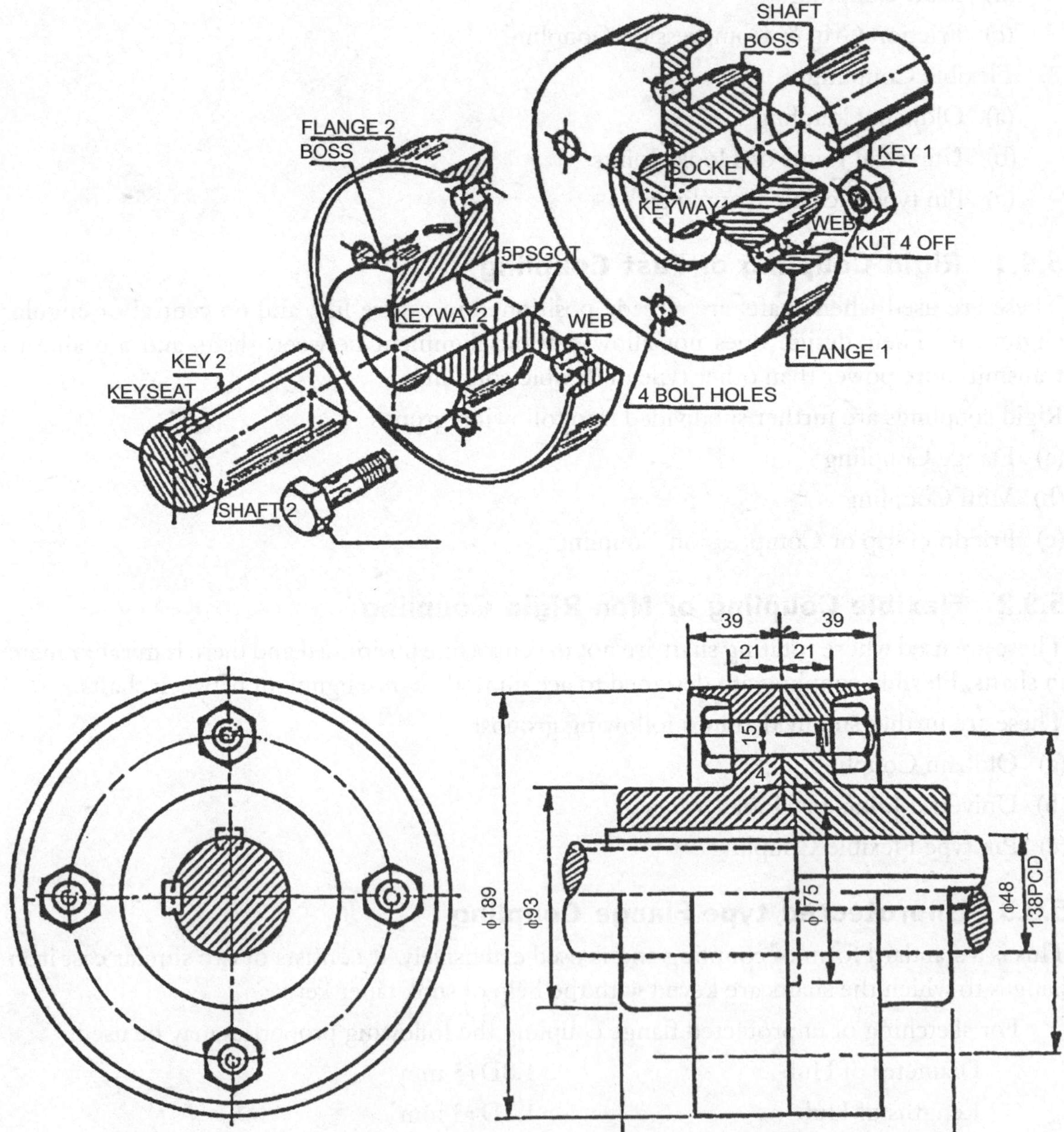

Fig.5.9: Protected type Flange Coupling

For sketching of protected flange coupling, the following proportions may be used:

Diameter of Hub	:	1.8D+5 mm
Length of Hub	:	1.3D+3 mm
Pitch Circle Diameter	:	2.2D+35 mm
Outside Diameter of Flange	:	2.6D+75 mm
Thickness of Flange	:	0.33D+3 mm
Shroud width	:	Thickness of Flange+ Height of nut + 3 mm
Shroud Thickness	:	6 to 10 mm

5.9.5 Muff Coupling

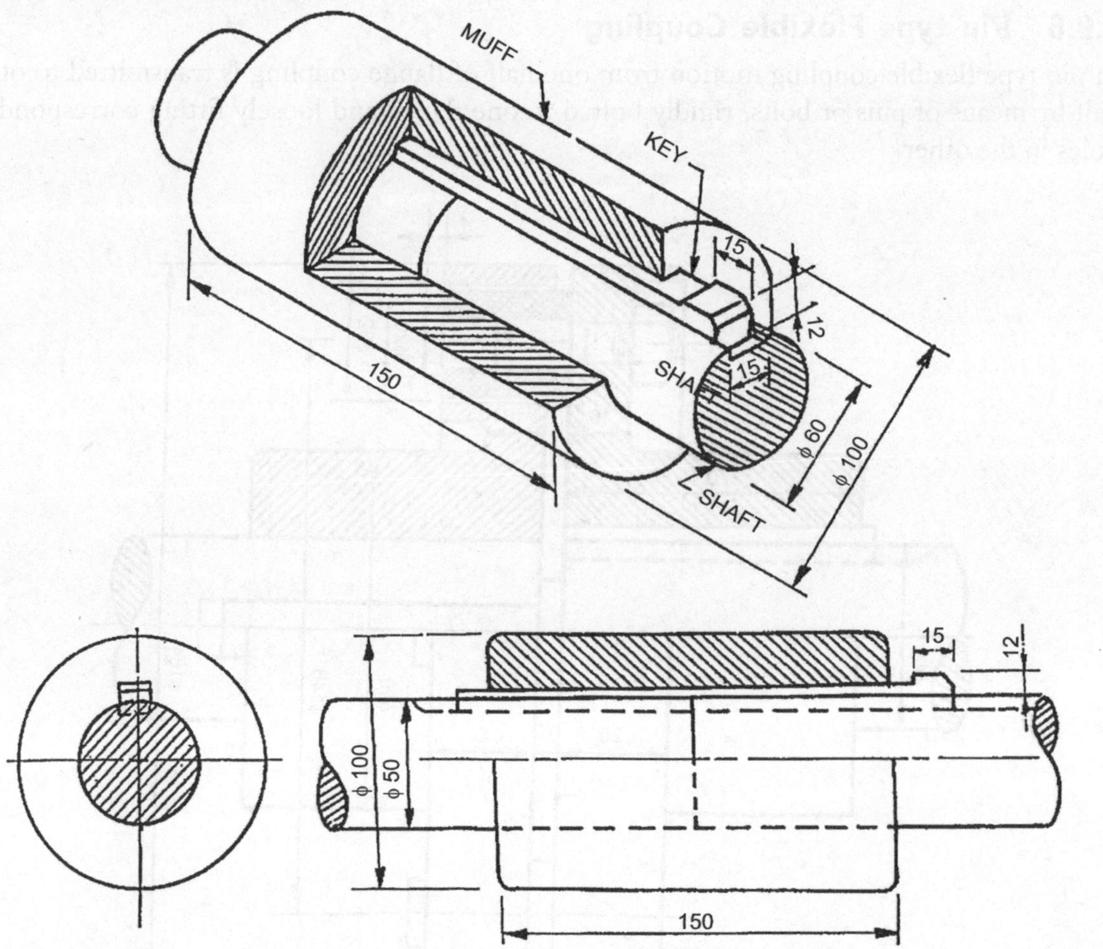

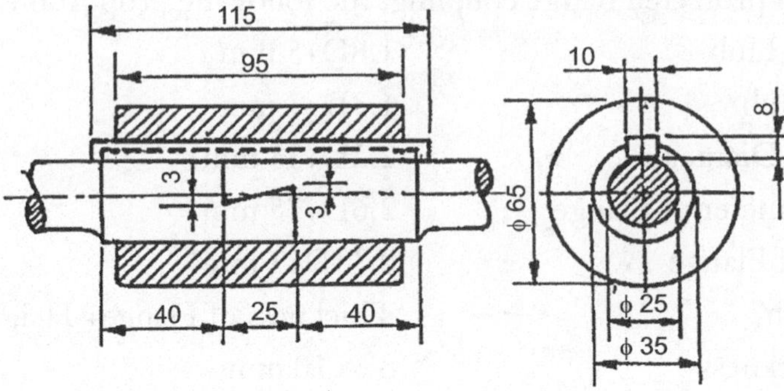

Fig.5.10: Muff Coupling

5.9.6 Pin type Flexible Coupling

In pin type flexible coupling motion from one half of flange coupling is transmitted to other half by means of pins or bolts, rigidly bolted to one flange and loosely fitting corresponding holes in the other.

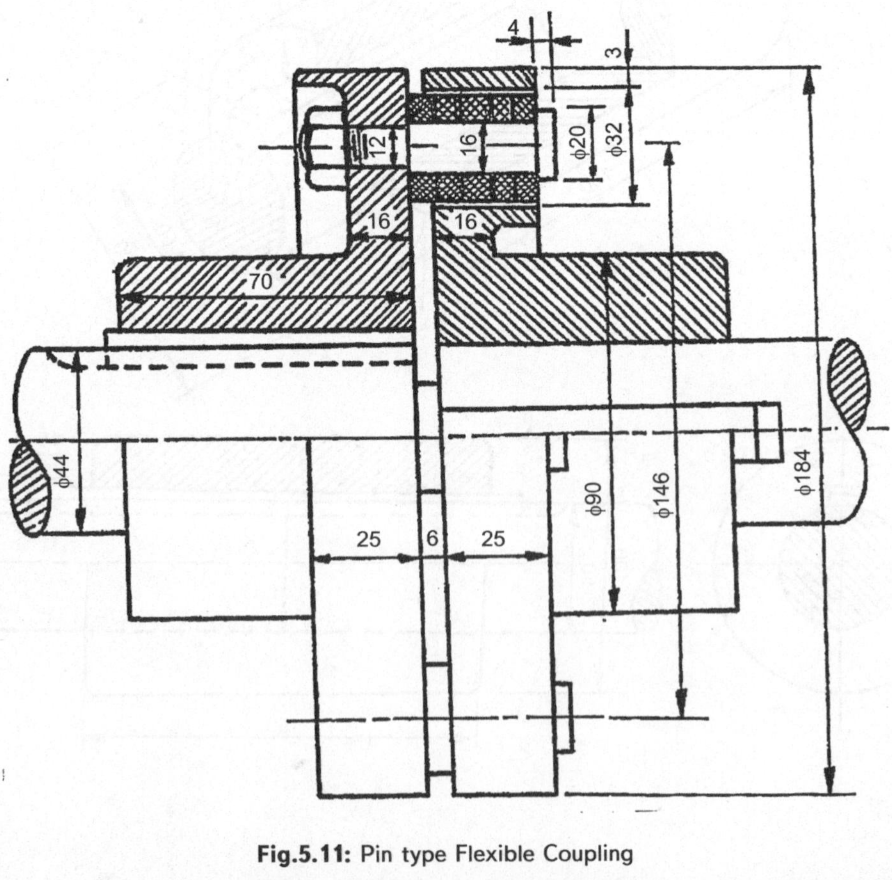

Fig.5.11: Pin type Flexible Coupling

5.9.7 Oldham Coupling

It is used to connect two shafts whose axis are parallel but these shafts are not in line.

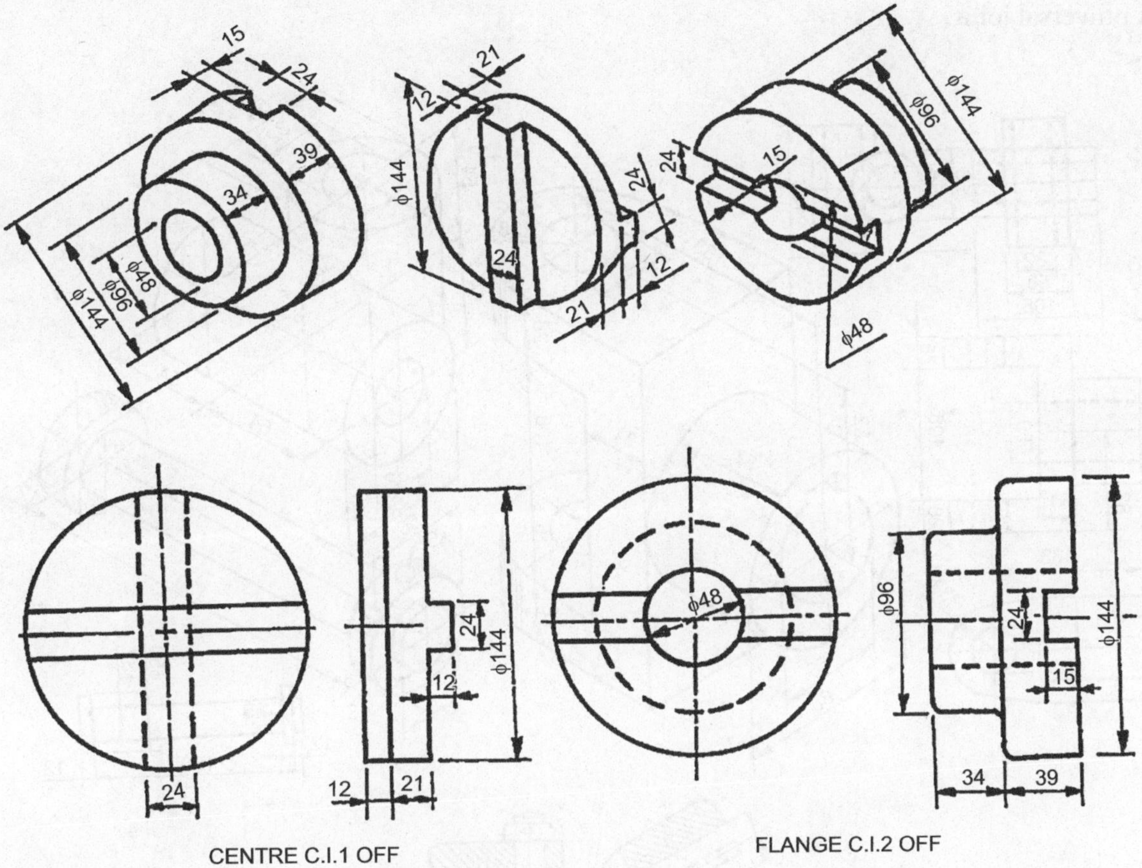

Fig.5.12: Oldham Coupling

5.9.8 Hooks Joints

This is used to connect two intersecting shafts. It is consist of a centre block having two arms at right angles to each other. The forks are pin-jointed to this centre block. This is also known as universal joint.

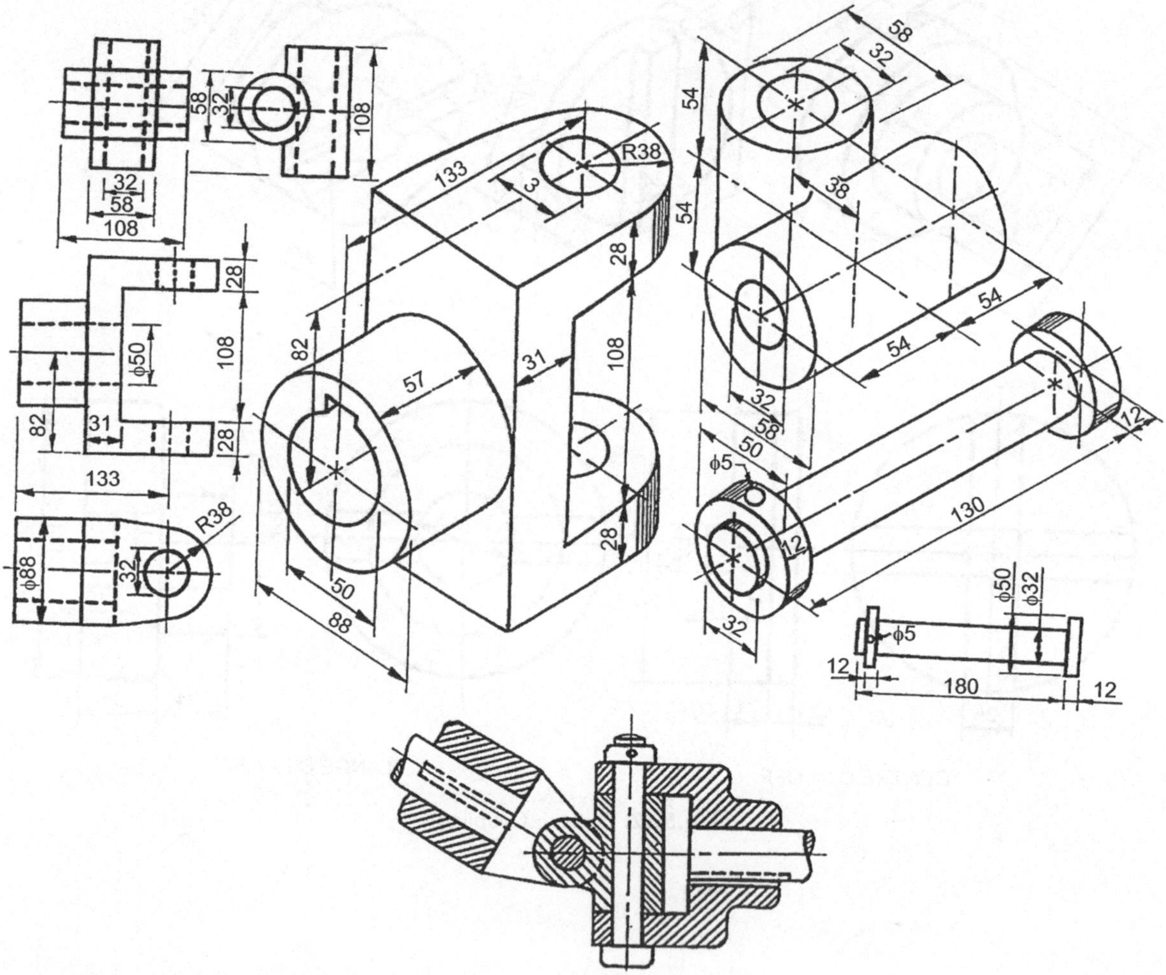

Fig.5.13: Hooks Joint

Viva Voce Questions

1. What is a bearing and what is meant by journal?
2. How are bearings classified?
3. Name the different forms of journal bearings.
4. Under what conditions, a pedastal bearing is preferred?
5. Name the various parts of a plummer block.
6. How the bolts are prevented from rotation in a plummer block?
7. What are the commonly used bearing materials?
8. Why collars are provided at the sides of bearings brasses?
9. What is a snug? What is the function of it in the bearing?
10. Why countersunk hole is provided at the top of the body of the hearing'?
11. Why elongated holes are generally provided in the base of a hearing?
12. Why is the base of the bearing generally kept hollow at the bottom?
13. Why a disc is provided at the shaft end in a pivot hearing?
14. Distinguish between:
    (a) Sliding contact bearings and anti-friction bearings,
    (b) Bracket and hanger bearings,
    (c) Pivot bearing and collar bearing, and
    (d) Journal bearing and thrust bearing.
15. What is a rolling contact bearing?
16. Why are rolling contact bearings called anti-friction bearings?
17. What are the different shapes of the rolling elements used in anti-friction bearings?
18. What is a shaft coupling ?
19. Name different types of shaft couplings.
20. What is the basis, on which shaft couplings are classified?
21. Name three types of rigid shaft couplings. State why they arc called rigid?
22. State where and why split-muff coupling is used in preference to solid muff coupling?
23. What is a flange coupling and why is it so named ?
24. Why are the annular recesses provided at the side of flanges in a protected flange coupling?
25. How flanges are made in a marine coupling?
26. What are the uses of a flexible coupling?
27. What is a universal coupling?

6

ASSEMBLY DRAWING

Assembly drawing demonstrates how number of separate parts drawing, detailed parts, standard components and specifications come together in a unified assembly. Assembly drawings can be used to represent items that consist of more than one components, it shows how the components fit together. Assembly drawing is needed for all products or inventions that have more than one part.

It is a technical drawing that defines the action illustration to show how the different parts fit together in sequential order sets to give instructions on how a product is assembled.

The objective of this chapter is related with the formal ways of presenting a part to be manufactured in detail and the structures that is formed by several parts aligned to each other's by appropriate assembly element such as threaded fasteners, keys, springs etc.

6.1 WORKING DRAWINGS

The drawings that are used to give informations to manufacture or construction of a machine are called working drawing.

It must include all the knowledge for the production of a machine or structure explicitly so that no further information is required to complete the production. Working drawing includes the following:

(i) The graphical representation of the shape of each part, namely shape description.
(ii) The dimensions of each part namely size.
(iii) Explanatory notes on the description drawing, giving the specification of material heat treatment and surface finish.
(iv) Title descriptive on each drawing.
(v) Relationships of each part to others.
(vi) Part list.

6.2 TYPES OF WORKING DRAWING

In general there are two classes of working drawing:

1. Detailed Drawing
2. Assembly Drawing
3. Production Drawing

6.2.1 Detailed Drawing

It is the drawing of a single part that includes a complete and exact description, its form, dimensions and construction.

6.2.2 Assembly Drawing

A complete assembly drawing is presentation of the product or structure put together showing all parts in their operational positions. The separate part come to assembly department after their manufacturing processes are finished and in this department put together according to assembly drawing.

Some small machining operations may be necessary during assembly process such as drilling, reaming or hand finishing.

6.2.3 Production Drawing

Production drawing shows complete information for the production or manufacturing of a machine or structure.

6.3 PROBLEMS OF ASSEMBLY DRAWINGS

6.3.1 Problem 1 (Plummer Block)

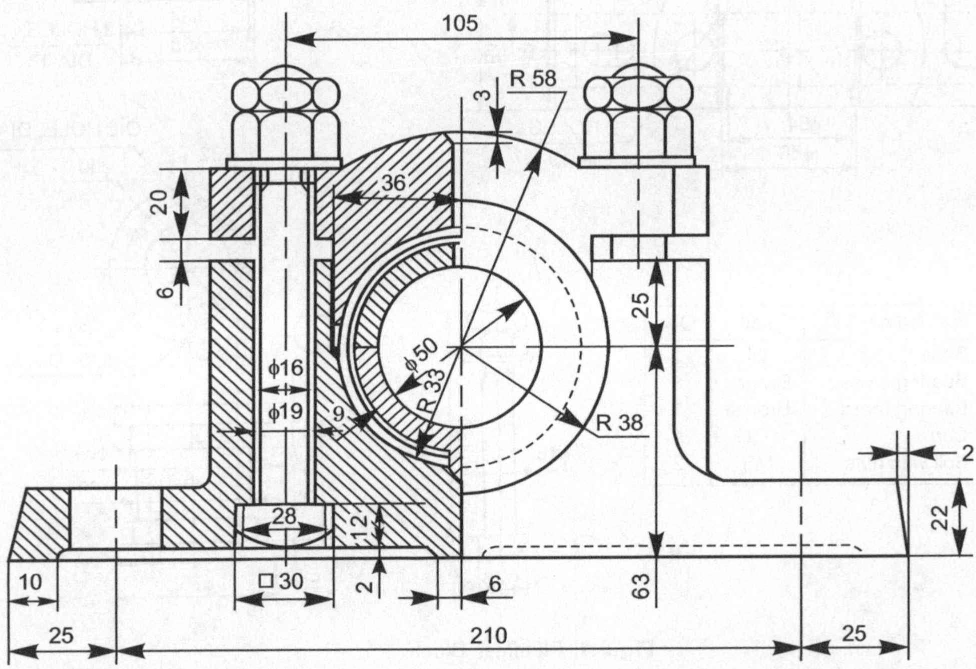

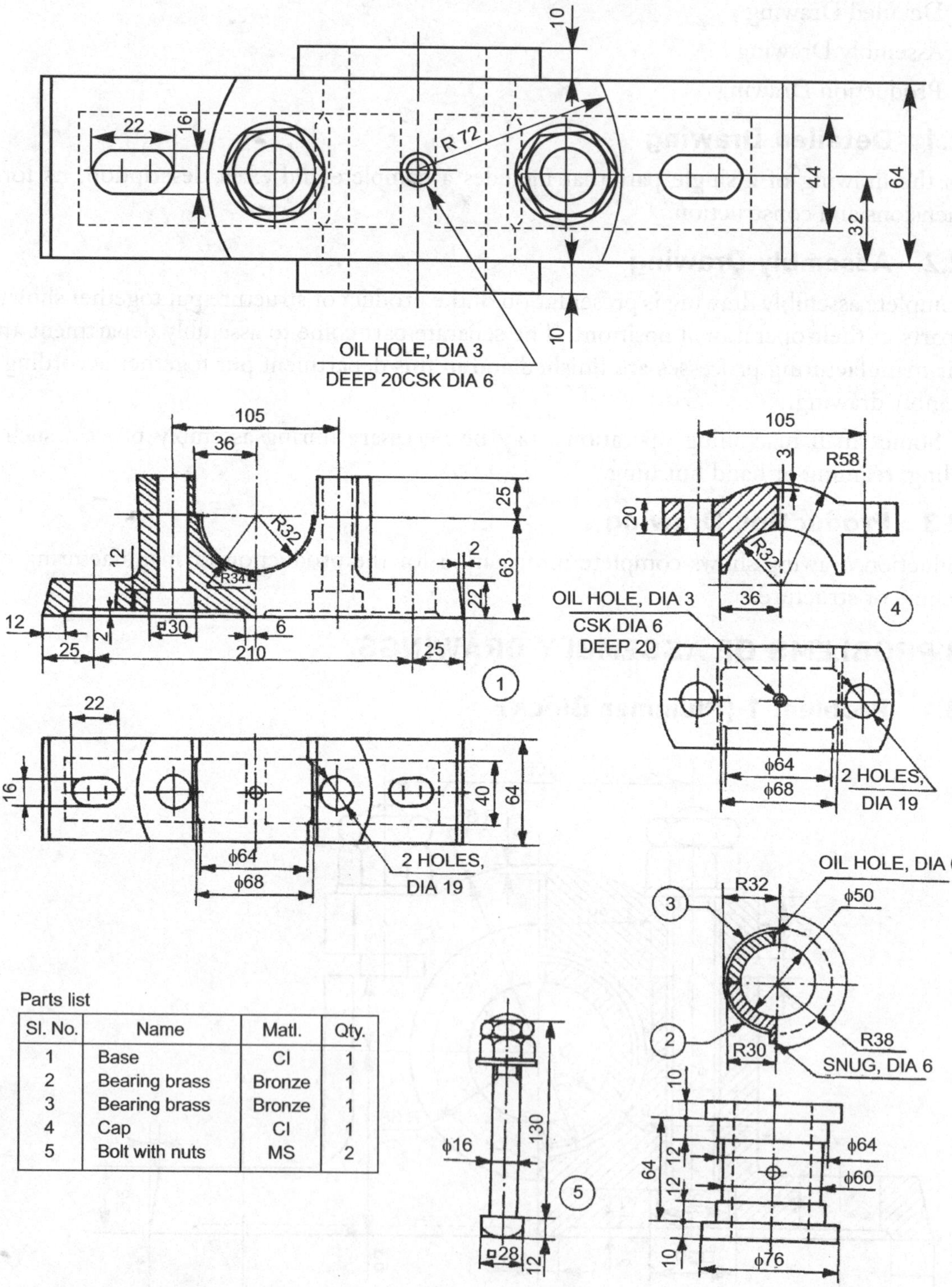

Parts list

Sl. No.	Name	Matl.	Qty.
1	Base	CI	1
2	Bearing brass	Bronze	1
3	Bearing brass	Bronze	1
4	Cap	CI	1
5	Bolt with nuts	MS	2

Fig.6.1: Plummer Block

6.3.2 Problem 2 (Screw Jack)

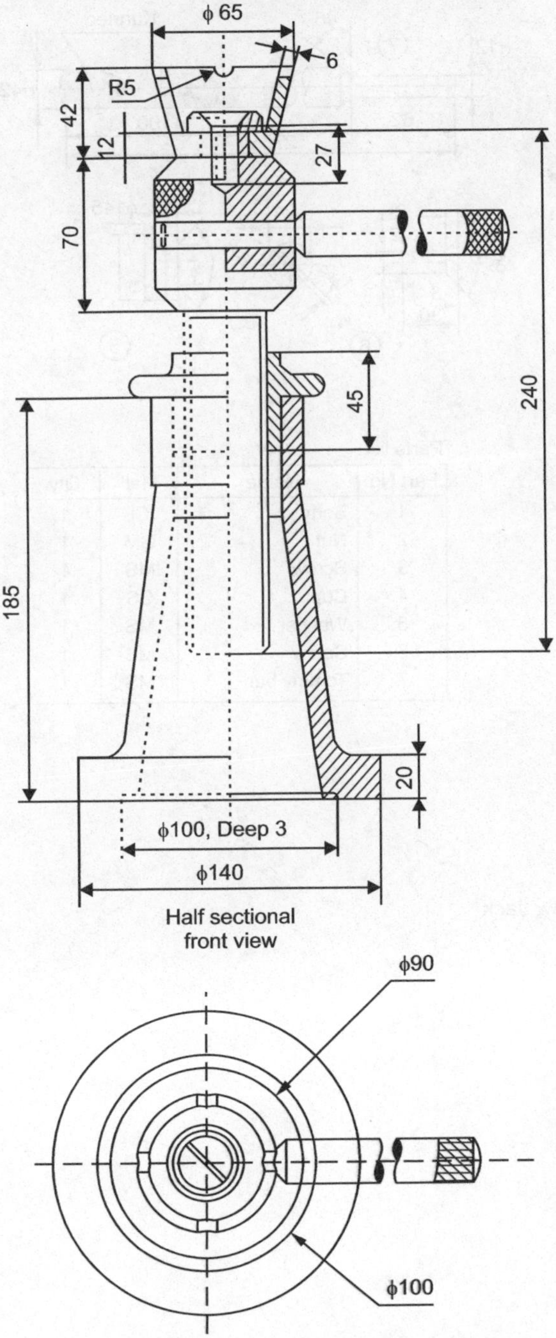

PART NO	NAME	MATERIAL	NO. OFF
01	BODY	CAST IRON	1
02	SCREW SPINDLE	Fe 410 W 1	
03	CUP	CAST STEEL	1
04	NUT	GUN METAL	1
05	WASHER	FE 410 W	1
06	CSK SCREW	Fe 410 W	6
07	TOMMY BAR	Fe410 W	1

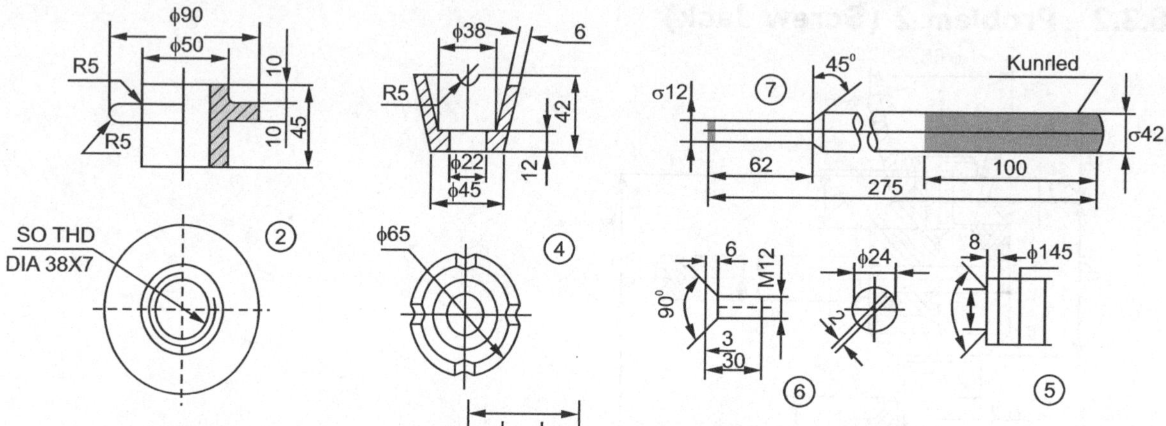

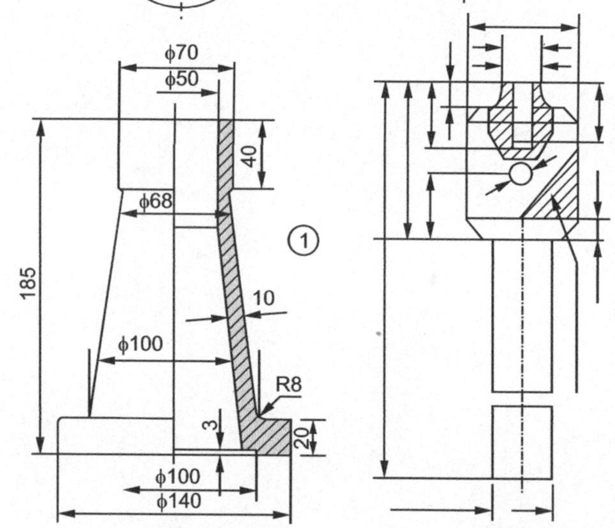

Parts list

Part No.	Name	Matl	Qty
1	Body	CI	1
2	Nut	GM	1
3	Screw	MS	1
4	Cup	CS	1
5	Washer	MS	1
6	Screw	MS	1
7	Tommy bar	MS	1

Fig.6.2: Screw Jack

6.3.3 Problem 3 (Swivel Bearing)

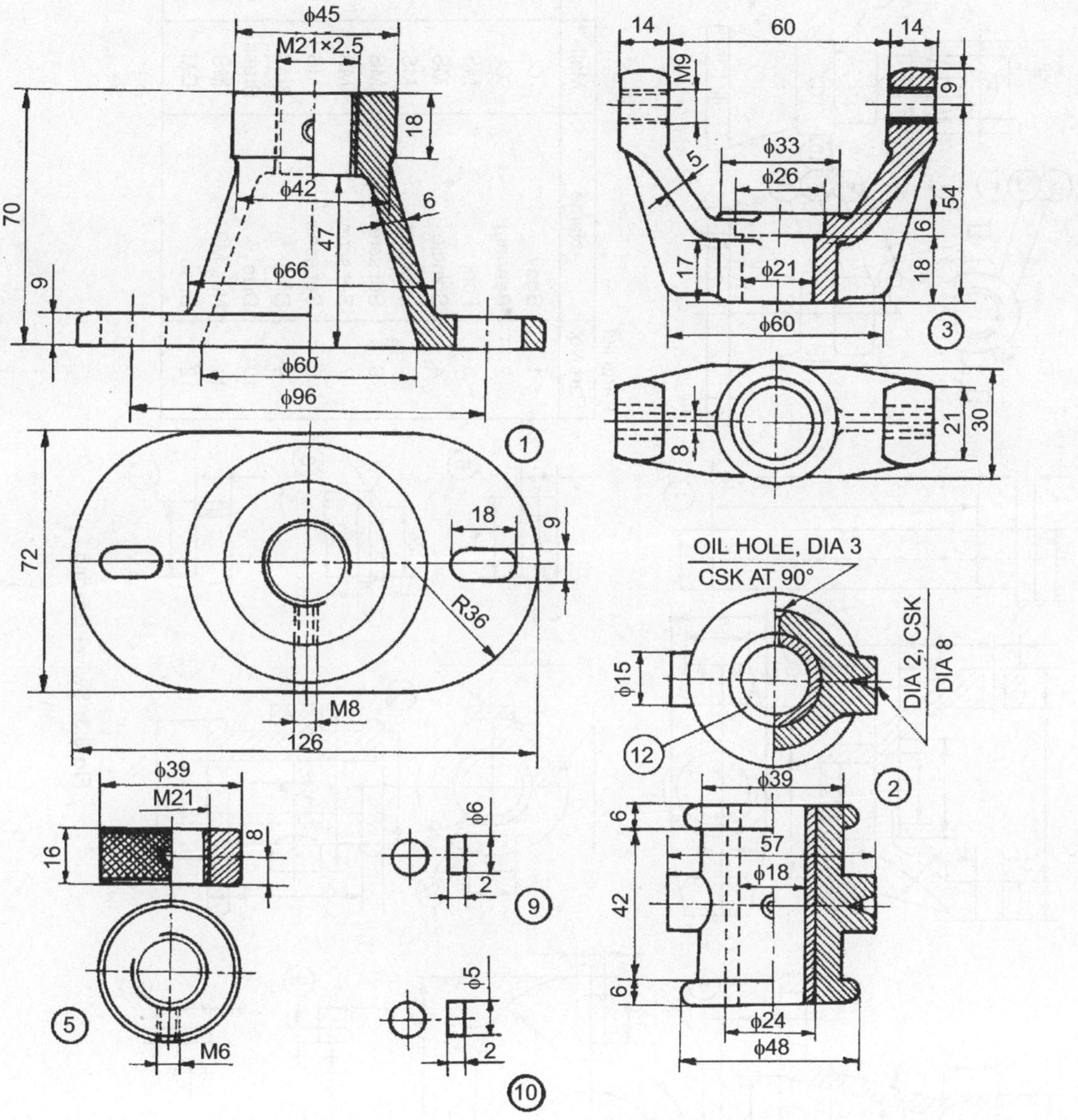

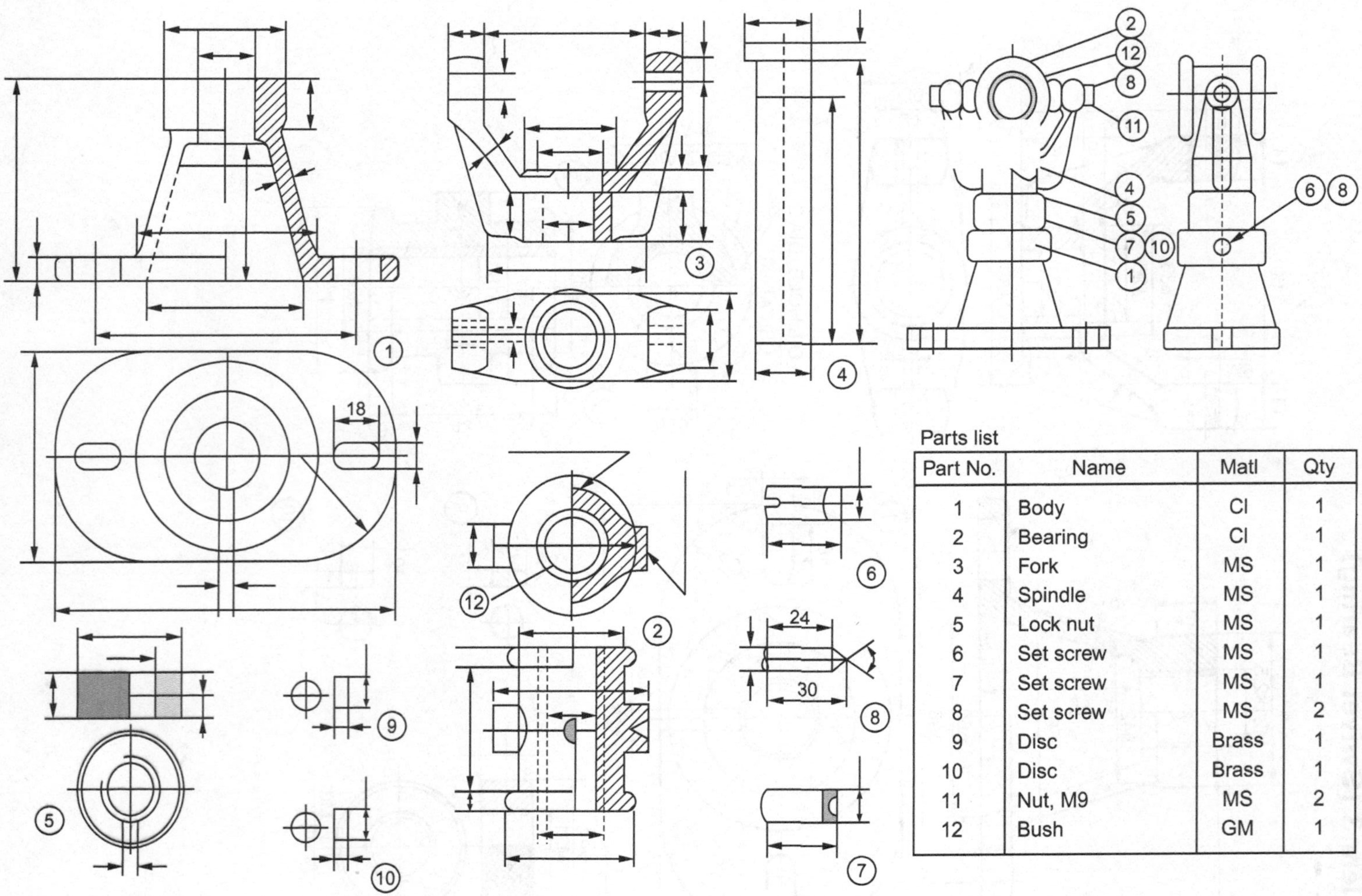

Parts list

Part No.	Name	Matl	Qty
1	Body	CI	1
2	Bearing	CI	1
3	Fork	MS	1
4	Spindle	MS	1
5	Lock nut	MS	1
6	Set screw	MS	1
7	Set screw	MS	1
8	Set screw	MS	2
9	Disc	Brass	1
10	Disc	Brass	1
11	Nut, M9	MS	2
12	Bush	GM	1

Fig.6.3: Swivel Bearing

6.3.4 Problem 4 (Lathe Tail Stock)

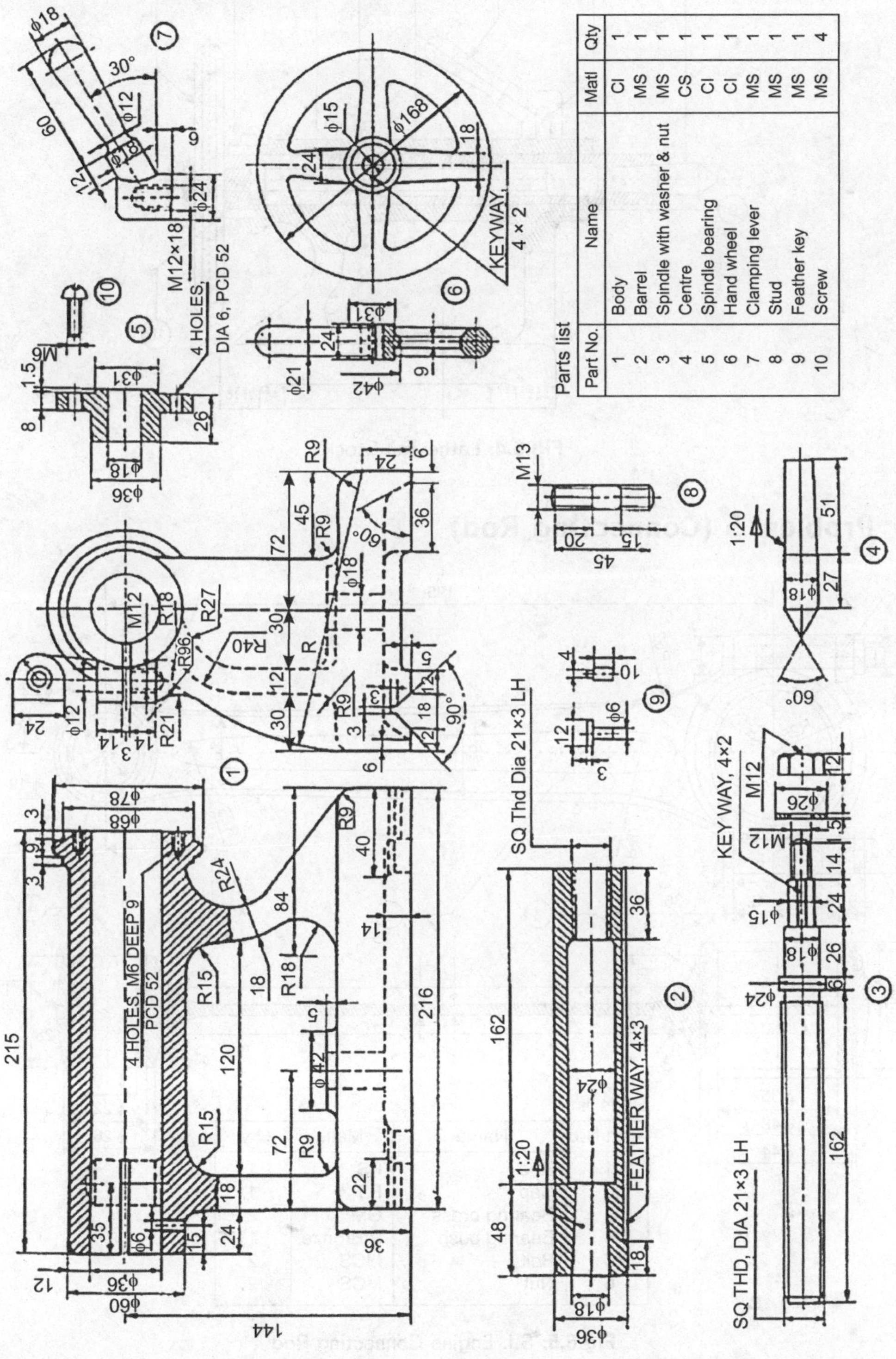

Parts list

Part No.	Name	Matl	Qty
1	Body	CI	1
2	Barrel	MS	1
3	Spindle with washer & nut	MS	1
4	Centre	CS	1
5	Spindle bearing	CI	1
6	Hand wheel	CI	1
7	Clamping lever	MS	1
8	Stud	MS	1
9	Feather key	MS	1
10	Screw	MS	4

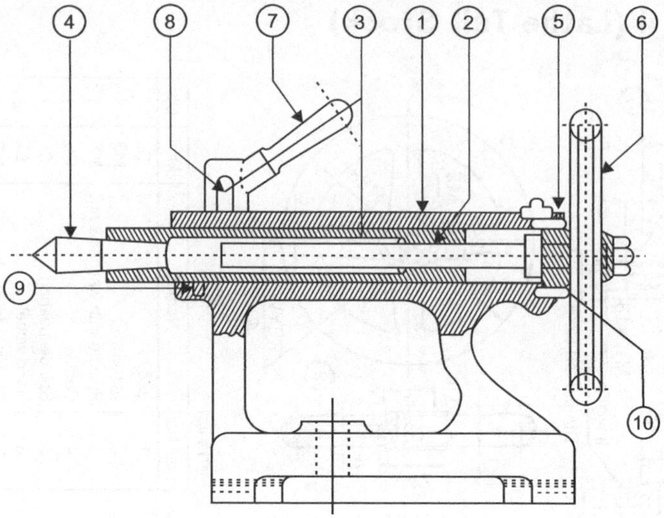

Fig.6.4: Lathe Tail Stock

6.3.5 Problem 5 (Connecting Rod)

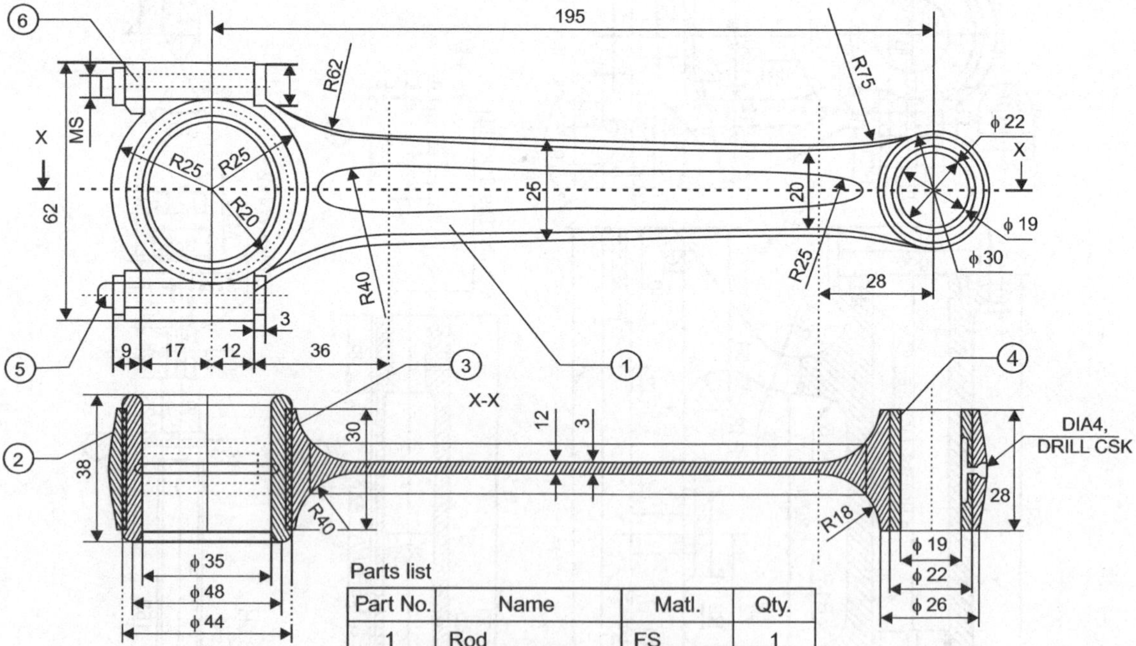

Parts list

Part No.	Name	Matl.	Qty.
1	Rod	FS	1
2	Cap	FS	1
3	Bearing brass	GM	2
4	Bearing bush	P Bronze	1
5	Bolt	MCS	2
6	Nut	MCS	2

Fig.6.5: S.I. Engine Connecting Rod

6.3.6 Problem 6 (Steam Stop Valve)

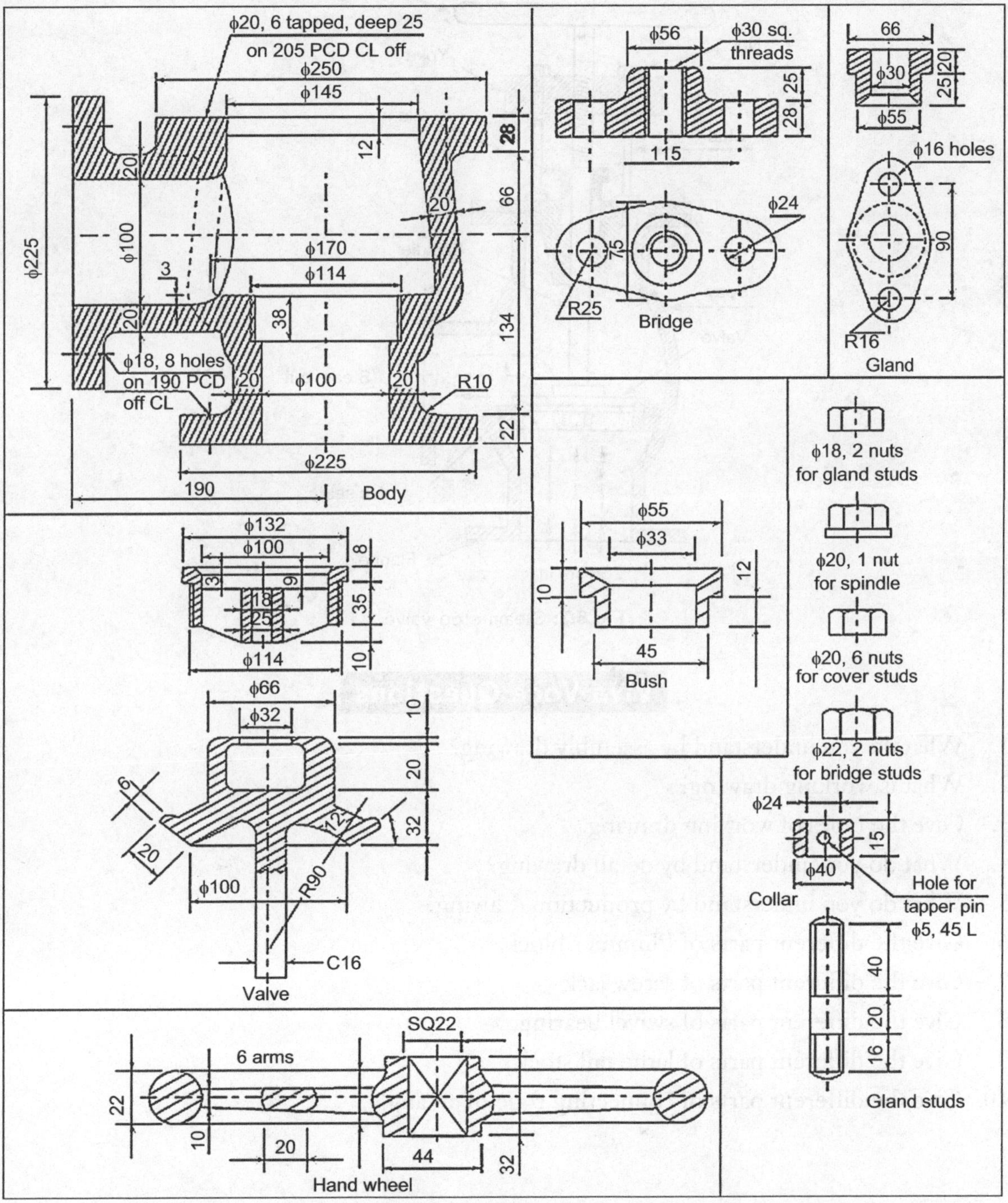

Fig.6.6: Details of components of steam stop valve

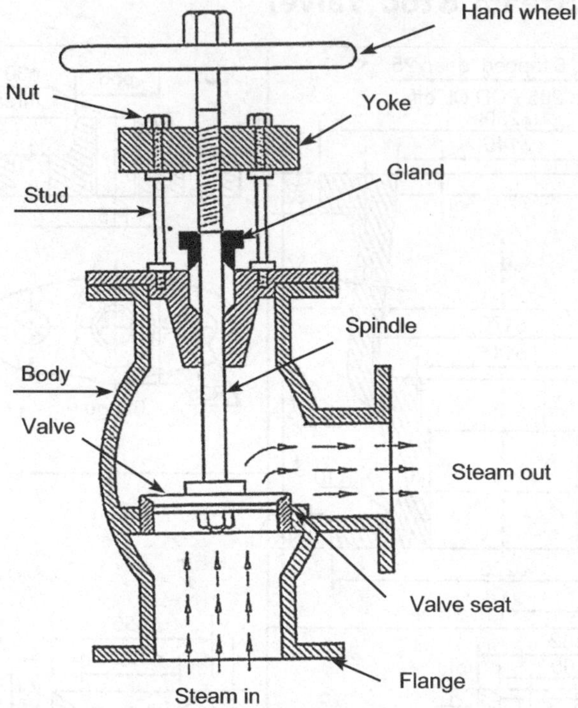

Fig.6.7: Steam stop valve

Viva Voce Questions

1. What do you understand by assembly drawing?
2. What is working drawing?
3. Give the types of working drawing.
4. What do you understand by detail drawing?
5. What do you understand by production drawing?
6. Give the different parts of Plummer block.
7. Give the different parts of screw jack.
8. Give the different parts of swivel bearing.
9. Give the different parts of lathe tail stock.
10. Give the different parts of connecting rode of an angle.

7

POWER TRANSMISSION DRIVES

7.1 INTRODUCTION

In engineering practice and day to day general purpose, the power or rotary motion from one place to another is at a considerable distance which is transmitted by means of following drives:

1. Belt Drive
2. Rope Drive
3. Chain Drive
4. Gear Drive

The amount of power transmitted depends upon the following factors :

(i) The velocity of the belt.

(ii) The tension under which the belt is placed on the pulleys.

(iii) The arc of contact between the belt and the smaller pulley.

(iv) The conditions under which the belt is used.

(v) The shafts should be properly in line to insure uniform tension across the belt section.

(vi) The pulleys should not be too close together, in order that the arc of contact on the smaller pulley may be as large as possible.

(vii) The pulleys should not be so far apart as to cause the belt to weigh heavily on the shafts, thus increasing the friction load on the bearings.

7.2 BELT DRIVE

The belt is used to transmit power from one shaft to another by means of pulleys which rotate at the same speed or at different speeds.

7.2.1 Selection of Belt Drive

Following are the various important factors upon which the selection of a belt drive depends:

(i) Speed of the driving and driven shafts

(ii) Speed reduction ratio
(iii) Power to be transmitted
(iv) Centre distance between the shafts
(v) Positive drive requirements
(vi) Shafts layout
(vii) Space available
(viii) Service conditions

7.2.2 Types of Belts

There are following three types of belts which are generally used:

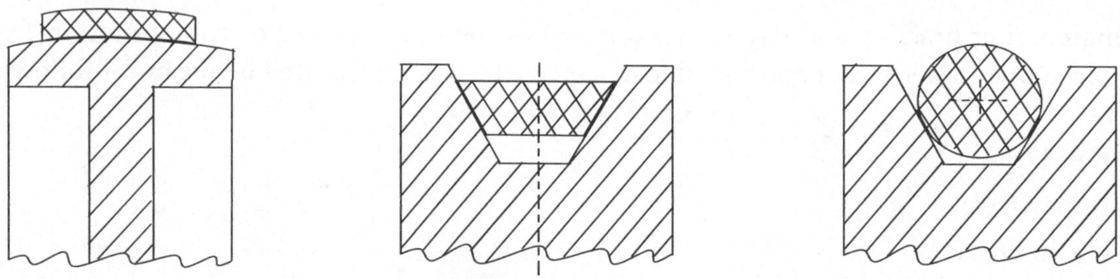

(a) Flat Belt and Pulley (b) V-belt and Pulley (c) Circular Belt or Rope Pulley

Fig.7.1: Types of Belts

1. **Flat Belt:** The flat belt, as shown in Fig. 7.1 (a), is mostly used in the factories and workshops, where a moderate amount of power is to be transmitted, from one pulley to another when the two pulleys are not more than 8 meters apart.
2. **V- Belt:** The V-belt, as shown in Fig. 7.1 (b), is mostly used in the factories and workshops, where a moderate amount of power is to be transmitted, from one pulley to another, when the two pulleys are very near to each other.
3. **Circular Belt or Rope:** The circular belt or rope, as shown in Fig. 7.1 (c), is mostly used in the factories and workshops, where a great amount of power is to be transmitted, from one pulley to another, when the two pulleys are more than 8 meters apart.

7.2.3 Types of Belt Drives

The power, from one pulley to another, may be transmitted by any one of the following three types of belt drives:

1. **Simple Belt Drive or Open Belt Drive:** Open belt drive is shown in Fig. 7.2.

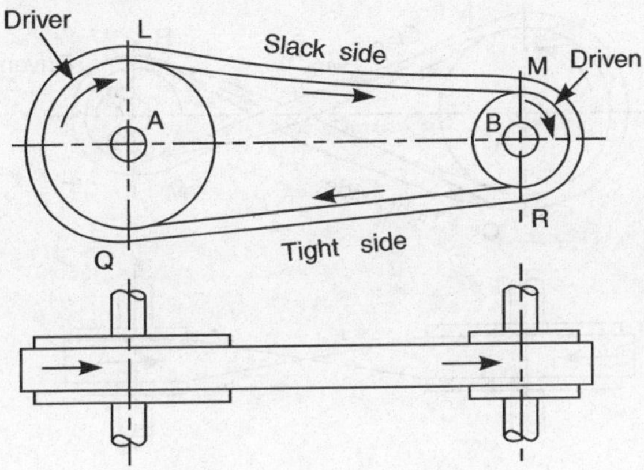

Fig.7.2: Open Belt Drive

2. **Compound Belt Drive:** Compound Belt Drive is shown in Fig. 7.3.

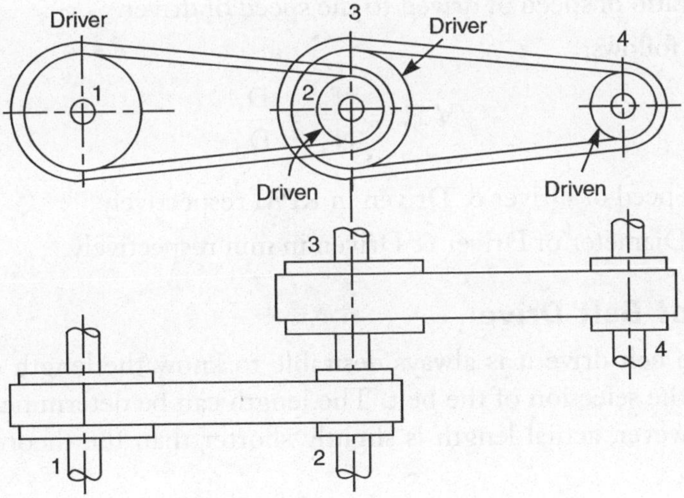

Fig.7.3: Compound Belt Drive

3. **Cross Belt Drive:** Cross belt drive is shown in Fig. 7.4.

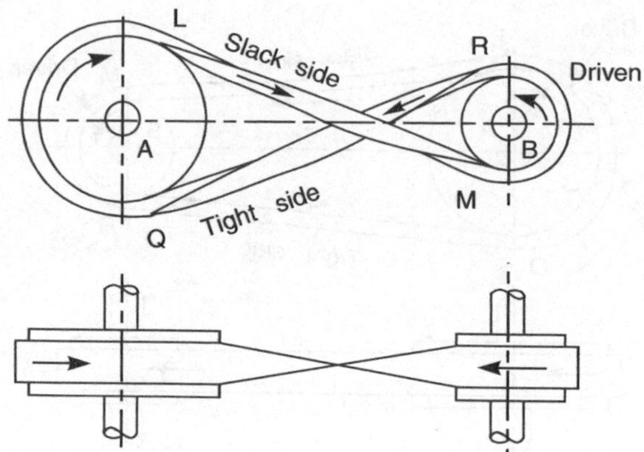

Fig.7.4: Cross Belt Drive

7.2.4 Velocity Ratio of Belt Drive

It is defined as the ratio of speed of driven to the speed of driver.

It can be written as follows:

$$V.R. = \frac{N_2}{N_1} = \frac{D_1}{D_2}$$

Where N_1 & N_2 = Speed of Driver & Driven in RPM respectively

D_1 & D_2 = Diameter of Driver & Driven in mm respectively.

7.2.5 Length of Belt Drive

For any type of the belt drive it is always desirable to know the length of belt required. It will be required in the selection of the belt. The length can be determined by the geometric considerations. However, actual length is slightly shorter than the theoretically determined value

7.2.5.1 Length of Open Belt Drive

Length of open belt drive is given by following relation:

$$L = \pi(R+r) + 2c + \frac{(R-r)^2}{c}$$

Where R and r are the radius of driver and driven pulley respectively and C is centre distance between centre of pulleys.

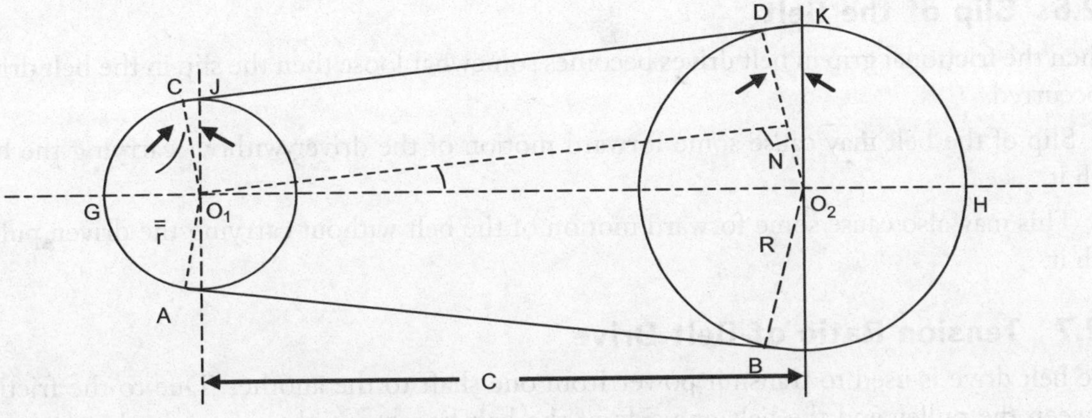

Fig.7.5: Length of Open Belt Drive

7.2.5.2 Length of Cross Belt Drive

Length of cross belt drive is given by following relation:

$$L = \pi(R + r) + 2c + \frac{(R - r)^2}{c}$$

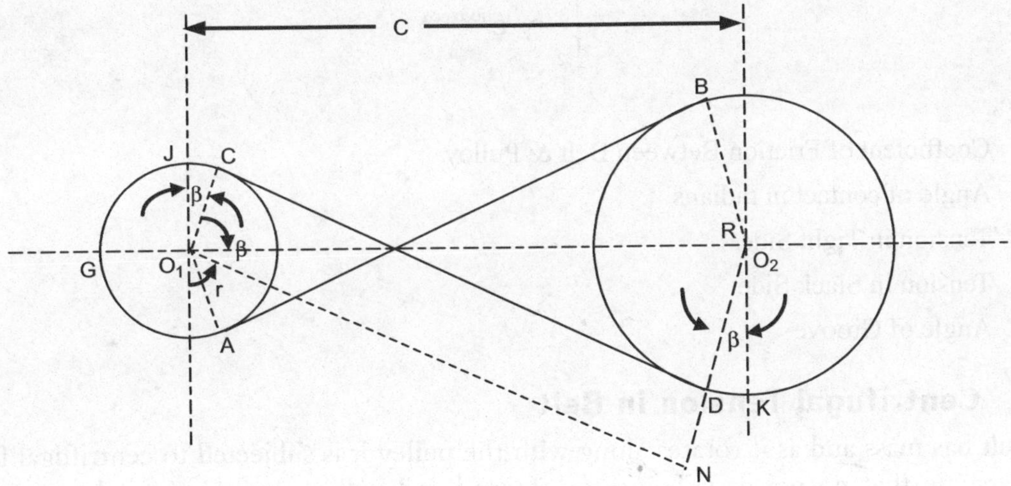

Fig.7.6: Length of Cross Belt Drive

7.2.6 Slip of the Belt

When the frictional grip in belt drives becomes somewhat loose then the slip in the belt drives is occurred.

Slip of the belt may cause some forward motion of the driver without carrying the belt with it.

This may also cause some forward motion of the belt without carrying the driven pulley with it.

7.2.7 Tension Ratio of Belt Drive

The belt drive is used to transmit power from one shaft to the another. Due to the friction between the pulley and the belt one side of the belt becomes tight side and other becomes slack side.

- Tension Ratio for flat belt is given by:

$$\frac{T_1}{T_2} = e^{\mu\theta}$$

- Tension Ratio for V-belt is given by:

$$\frac{T_1}{T_2} = e^{\mu\theta\operatorname{cosec}\alpha}$$

Where,

μ = Coefficient of Friction Between Belt & Pulley

θ = Angle of contact in radians

T_1 = Tension in Tight Side

T_2 = Tension in Slack Side

α = Angle of Groove

7.2.8 Centrifugal Tension in Belt

The belt has mass and as it rotates along with the pulley it is subjected to centrifugal forces. If we assume that no power is being transmitted and pulleys are rotating, the centrifugal force will tend to pull the belt as shown in Fig. 7.7 and, thereby, a tension in the belt called centrifugal tension will be introduced.

Centrifugal tension in belt is given by:

$$T_c = mV^2$$

Where m = Mass per unit length of belt & V = Velocity of Belt

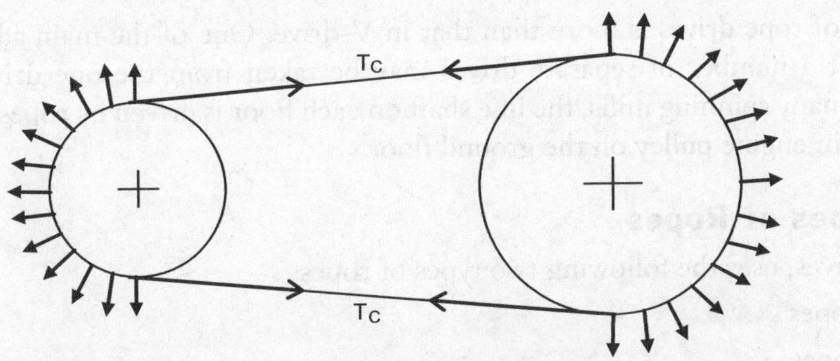

Fig.7.7: Centrifugal Tension in Belt

7.2.9 Power Transmitted by Belt Drive

The power transmitted by the belt depends on the tension on the two sides and the belt speed.

Let T_1 be the tension on the tight side in 'N' (Newton)

T_2 be the tension on the slack side in 'N', and

V be the velocity of the belt in m/sec.

Then power transmitted by the belt is given by:

$$P = (T_1 - T_2)V \text{ Watt}$$

Condition for Maximum Power Transmitted by belt is given by:

$$T_c = \frac{T_t}{3}$$

$$V = \sqrt{\frac{T_t}{3m}}$$

Where,

T_c = Centrifugal Tension in Belt in N

T_t = Total Tension in Belt in N

V = Belt Velocity in m/s

m = Mass per unit length of Belt

7.3 ROPE DRIVE

The rope drives are widely used where a large amount of power is to be transmitted, from one pulley to another, over a considerable distance. It may be noted that the use of flat belts is limited for the transmission of moderate power from one pulley to another when the two pulleys are not more than 8 meters apart. If large amounts of power are to be transmitted by the flat belt, then it would result in excessive belt cross-section. It may be noted that frictional grip in case of rope drives is more than that in V-drive. One of the main advantage of rope drives is that a number of separate drives may be taken from the one driving pulley. For example, in many spinning mills, the line shaft on each floor is driven by ropes passing directly from the main engine pulley on the ground floor.

7.3.1 Types of Ropes

The rope drives, uses the following two types of ropes:

1. Fiber Ropes
2. Wire Ropes

The fiber ropes operate successfully when the pulleys are about 60 meters apart, while the wire ropes are used when the pulleys are up to 150 meters apart.

1. **Fiber Ropes:** The ropes for transmitting power are usually made from fibrous materials such as hemp, manila and cotton. Since the hemp and manila fibers are rough, therefore the ropes made from these fibers are not very flexible and possesses poor mechanical properties. The hemp ropes have less strength as compared to manila ropes. When the hemp and manila ropes are bent over the sheave (or pulley), there is some sliding of fibers, causing the rope to wear and chafe internally. In order to minimize this defect, the rope fiber are lubricated with a tar, tallow or graphite. The lubrication also makes the rope moisture proof. The hemp ropes are suitable only for hand operated hoisting machinery and as the ropes for lifting tackle, hooks etc.

   The cotton ropes are very soft and smooth. The lubrication of cotton ropes is not necessary. But if it is done, it reduces the external wear between the rope and the grooves of its sheaves. It may be noted that manila ropes are more durable and stronger than cotton ropes. The cotton ropes are costlier than manila ropes.
2. **Wire Ropes:** When a large amount of power is to be transmitted over long distances from one pulley to another (pulleys are of 150 meters apart), then wire ropes are used. The wire ropes are widely used in elevators, mine hoists, cranes, conveyors, hauling devices and suspension bridges. The wire ropes run on grooved pulleys but they rest on the bottom of the grooves and are not wedged between the sides of the grooves.

7.4 CHAIN DRIVE

In belt and rope drive, slip is major problem. Therefore to avoid slipping chain drive is used to transmit power from one place to another.

The chains are made up of rigid links which are hinged together in order to provide the necessary flexibility for warping around the driving and driven wheels. The wheels have projecting teeth and fit into the corresponding recesses, in the links of the chain as shown in Fig. 7.8. The wheels and the chain are thus constrained to move together without slipping and ensures perfect velocity ratio. The toothed wheels are known as **sprocket wheels** or simply **sprockets.**

The chains are mostly used to transmit motion and power from one shaft to another, when the distance between the centers of the shafts is short such as in bicycles, motor cycles, agricultural machinery, road rollers, etc.

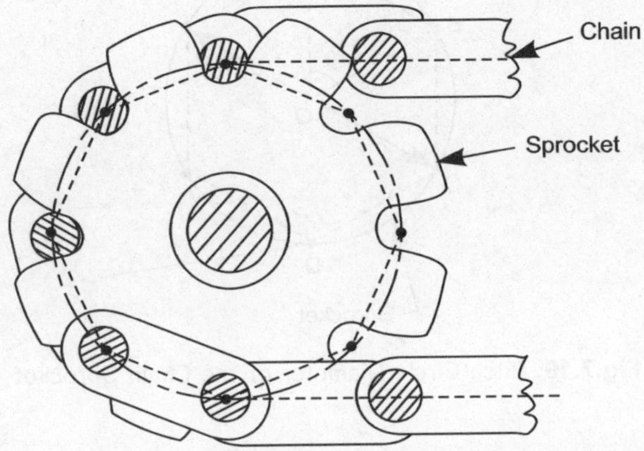

Fig.7.8: Chain Drive

7.4.1 Terminology of Chain Drive

The following terms are used in chain drive:

1. **Pitch of the Chain :** It is the distance between the hinge centre of a link and the corresponding hinge centre of the adjacent link as shown in Fig. 7.9. It is usually denoted by p.

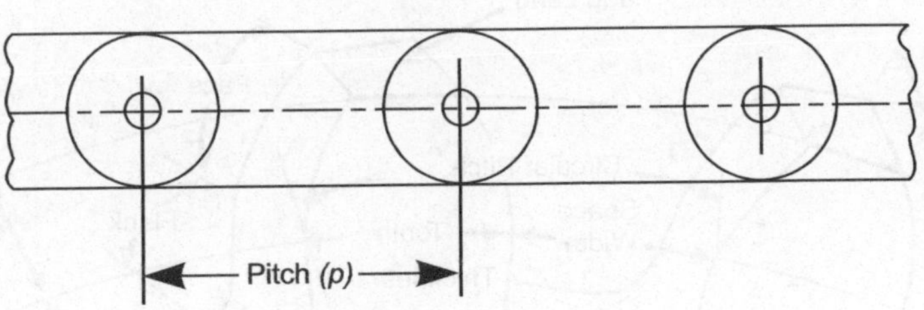

Fig.7.9: Pitch of the Chain

2. **Pitch Circle Diameter of the Chain Sprocket:** It is the diameter of the circle on which the hinge centres of the chain lie, when the chain is wrapped round a sprocket as shown in Fig. 7.10.

   The points A, B, C, and D are the hinge centres of the chain and the circle drawn through these centres is called pitch circle and its diameter (d) is known as pitch circle diameter.

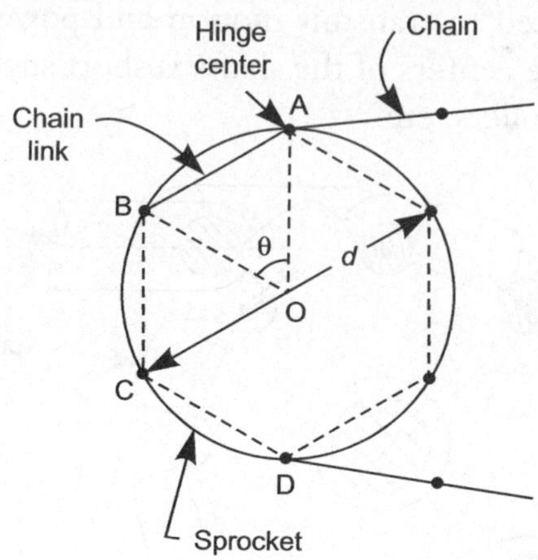

Fig.7.10: Pitch Circle Diameter of the Chain Sprocket

7.4 GEAR DRIVE

Gears are also used for power transmission. This is accomplished by the successive engagement of teeth. The two gears transmit motion by the direct contact like chain drive. Gears also provide positive drive.

7.4.1 Gear Terminology

There are some important terms for gear which are shown in Fig. 7.11.

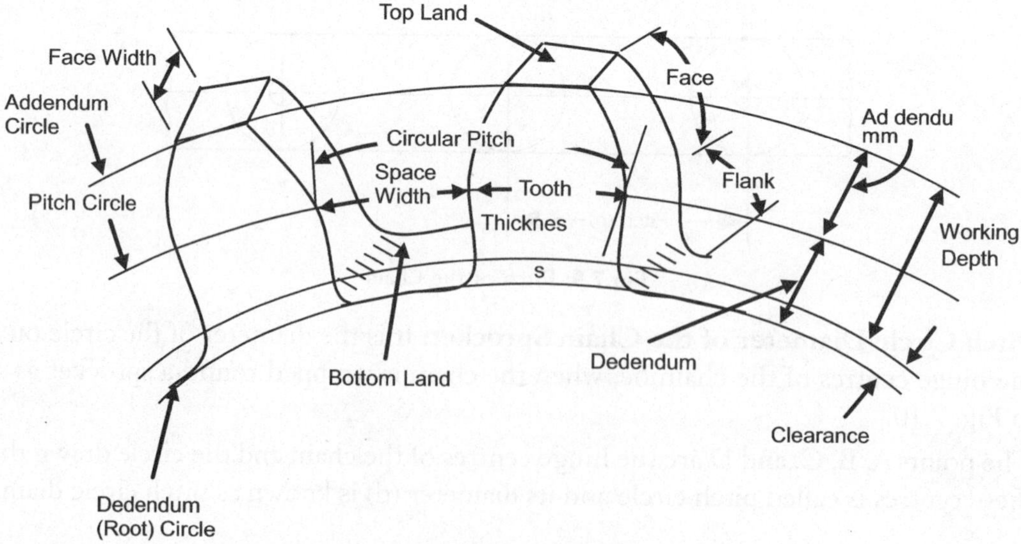

Fig.7.11: Gear Terminology

1. Pitch Circle or Pitch Curve

It is the theoretical curve along which the gear rolls without slipping on the corresponding pitch curve of other gear for transmitting equivalent motion.

2. Pitch Point

It is the point of contact of two pitch circles.

3. Pinion

It is the smaller of the two mating gears. It is usually the driving gear.

4. Rack

It is type of the gear which has infinite pitch circle diameter.

5. Circular Pitch

It is the distance along the pitch circle circumference between the corresponding points on the consecutive teeth.

If d is diameter of the pitch circle and 'T' be number of teeth, the circular pitch (P_c) is given by:

$$P_c = \frac{\pi d}{T}$$

6. Diamental Pitch

It is defined as the number of teeth per unit pitch circle diameter. Therefore, diamental pitch (P_d) can be expressed as

$$P_d = \frac{T}{d}$$

7. Module

It is the ratio of the pitch circle diameter to the number of teeth. Therefore, the module (m) can be expressed as

$$m = \frac{d}{T}$$

8. Addendum Circle & Addendum

It is the circle passing through the tips of gear teeth and addendum is the radial distance between pitch circle and the addendum circle.

9. Dedendum Circle & Dedendum

It is the circle passing through the roots of the teeth and the dedendum is the radial distance between root circle and pitch circle.

10. Full Depth of Teeth & Working Depth

Full depth is sum of addendum and dedendum and working depth is sum of addendums of the two gears which are in mesh.

11. Tooth Thickness & Space Width

Tooth thickness is the thickness of tooth measured along the pitch circle and space width is the space between two consecutive teeth measured along the pitch circle. They are equal to each other and measure half of circular pitch.

12. Top Land &d Bottom Land

Top land is the top surface of the tooth and the bottom land is the bottom surface between the adjacent fillets.

13. Face & Flank

Tooth surface between the pitch surface and the top land is called face whereas flank is tooth surface between pitch surface and the bottom land.

14. Pressure Line & Pressure Angle

The driving tooth exerts a force on the driven tooth along the common normal. This line is called pressure line. The angle between the pressure line and the common tangent to the pitch circles is known as pressure angle.

15. Path of Contact

The path of contact is the locus of a point of contact of two mating teeth from the beginning of engagement to the end of engagement.

16. Arc of Approach & Arc of Recess

Arc of approach is the locus of a point on the pitch circle from the beginning of engagement to the pitch point. The arc of recess is the locus of a point from pitch point up to the end of engagement of two mating gears.

17. Arc of Contact

It is the locus of a point on the pitch circle from the beginning of engagement to the end of engagement of two mating gears.

Arc of Contact = Arc of Approach + Arc of Recess

18. Angle of Action

It is the angle turned by a gear from beginning of engagement to the end of engagement of a pair of teeth.

Angle of action = Angle turned during arc of approach + Angle turned during arc of recess

7.4.2 Gears Classification

There are different types of arrangement of shafts which are used in practice. According to the relative positions of shaft axes, different types of gears are used.

1. **Parallel Shafts:** In this arrangement, the shaft axes lie in parallel planes and remain parallel to one another. The following type of gears are used on these shafts:

   (i) Spur Gear: These gears have straight teeth with their alignment parallel to the axes. These gears are shown in Fig. 7.12 (a & b). The contact between the two meshing teeth is along a line whose length is equal to entire length of teeth. It may be observed that in external meshing, the two shafts rotate opposite to each other whereas in internal meshing the shafts rotate in the same sense.

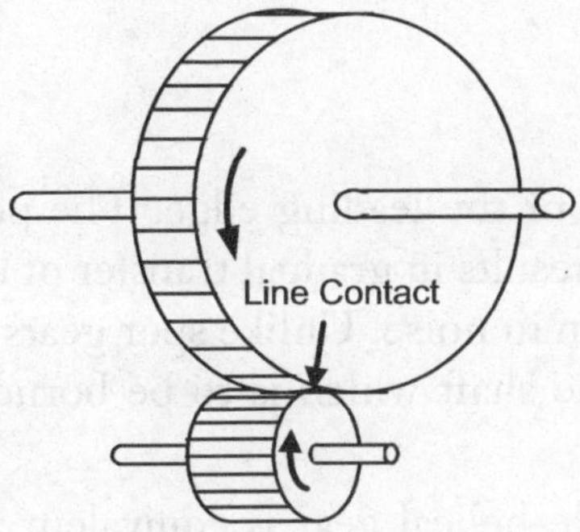

(a) External Meshing

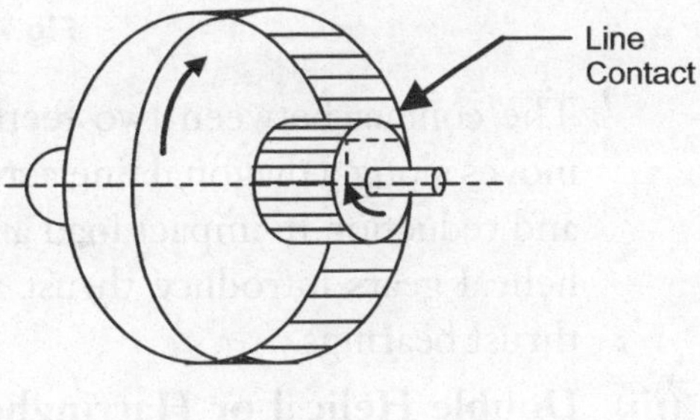

(b) Internal Meshing

Fig.7.12: Spur Gears

If the gears mesh externally and diameter of one gear becomes infinite, the arrangement becomes 'Spur Rack and Pinion'. This is shown in Fig. 7.13. It converts rotary motion into translatory motion, or vice-versa.

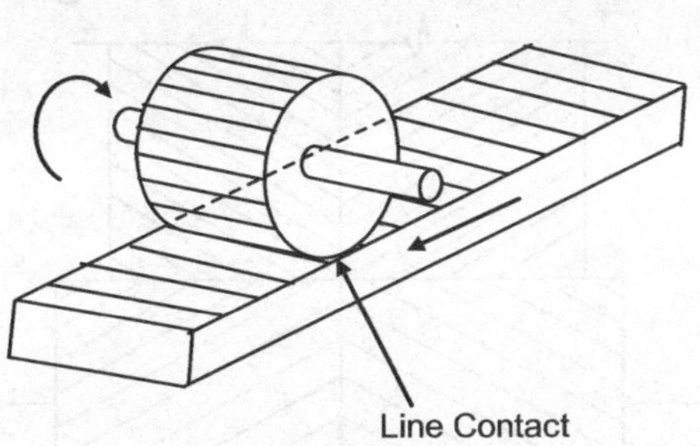

Fig.7.13: Spur Rack & Pinion

   (ii) Helical Gears: In helical gears, the teeth make an angle with the axes of the gears which is called helix angle. The two meshing gears have same helix angle but its layout is in opposite sense as shown in Fig. 7.14.

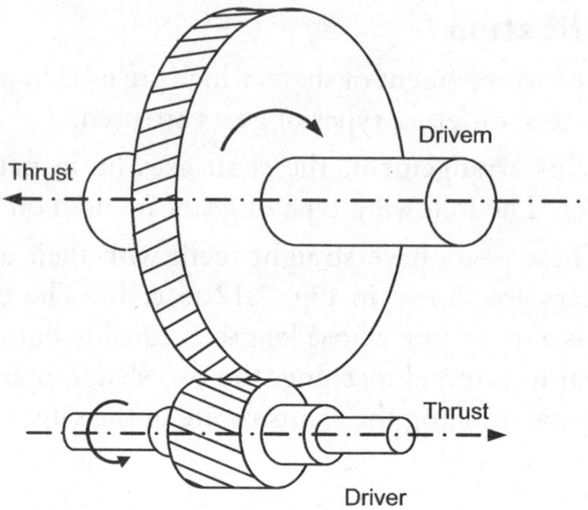

Fig.7.14: Helical Gear

The contact between two teeth occurs at a point of the leading edge. The point moves along a diagonal line across the teeth. This results in gradual transfer of load and reduction in impact load and thereby reduction in noise. Unlike spur gears the helical gears introduce thrust along the axis of the shaft which is to be borne by thrust bearings.

(iii) **Double Helical or Harringbone Gear:** A double-helical gear is equivalent to a pair of helical gears having equal helix angle secured together, one having a right-hand helix and the other a left-hand helix. The teeth of two rows are separated by a groove which is required for tool run out. The axial thrust which occurs in case of single-helical gears is eliminated in double helical gears. If the left and right inclinations of a double helical gear meet at a common apex and groove is eliminated in it, the gear is known as herringbone gear as shown in Fig. 7.15.

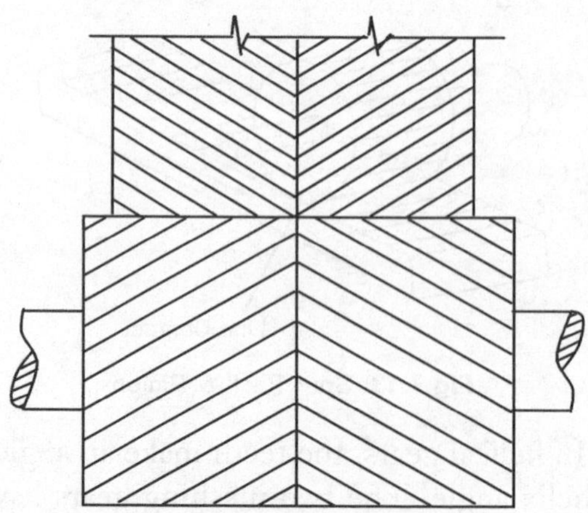

Fig.7.15: Double Helical Gear

2. **Intersecting Shaft:** The motion between two intersecting shafts is equivalent to rolling of two conical frustums from kinematical point of view.

   (i) **Straight Bevel Gear:** These gears have straight teeth which are radial to the point of intersection of the shaft axes. Their teeth vary in cross section throughout their length. Generally, they are used to connect shafts at right angles. These gears are shown in Fig. 7.16. The teeth make line contact like spur gears. As a special case, gears of the same size and connecting two shafts at right angle to each other are known as mitre gears.

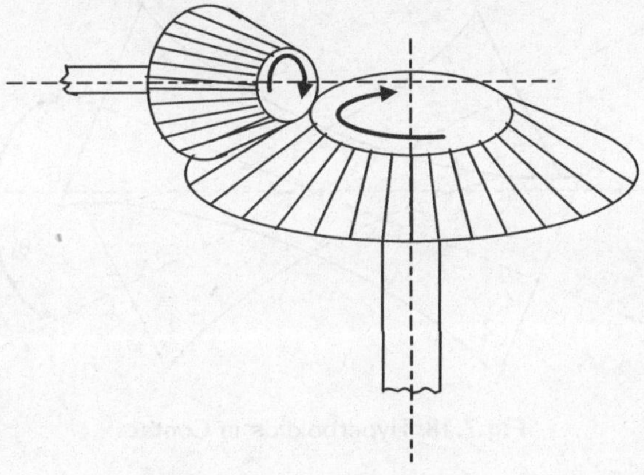

Fig.7.16: Straight Bevel Gear

   (ii) **Spiral Gear:** When the teeth of a bevel gear are inclined at an angle to the face of the bevel, these gears are known as spiral bevel gears or helical bevel gears. A gear of this type is shown in Fig. 7.17. They run quitter in action and have point contact. If spiral bevel gear has curved teeth but with zero degree spiral angle, it is known as zero bevel gear.

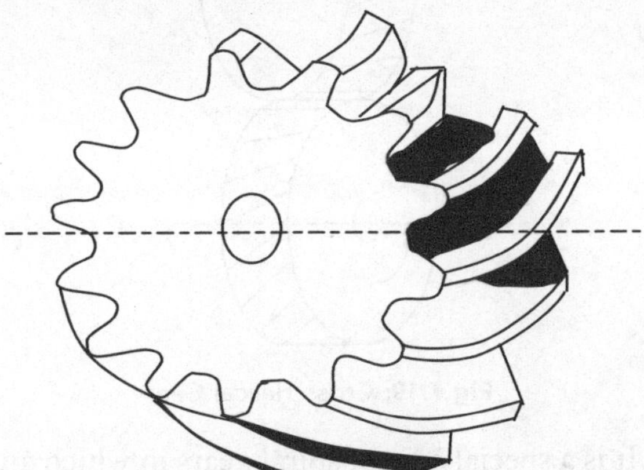

Fig.7.17: Spiral Gear

3. **Skew Shafts:** These shafts are non-parallel and non-intersecting. The motion of the two mating gears is equivalent to motion of two hyperboloids in contact as shown in Fig. 7.18. The angle between the two shafts is equal to the sum of the angles of the two hyperboloids. That is

$$\phi = \theta_1 + \theta_2$$

The minimum perpendicular distance between the two shafts is equal to the sum of the throat radii.

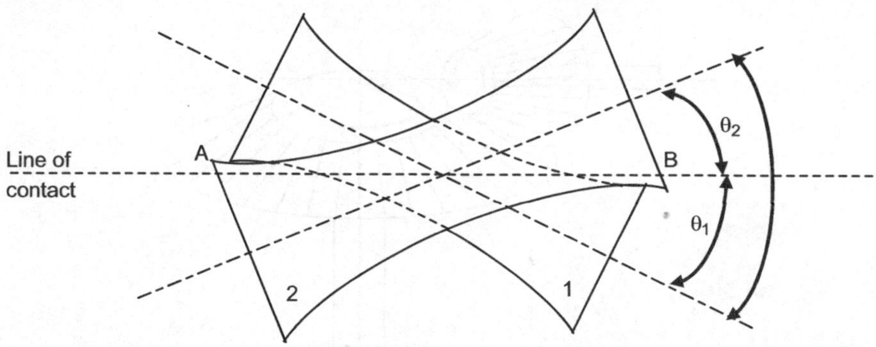

Fig.7.18: Hyperboloids in Contact

(i) **Cross-Helical Gear:** They can be used for any two shafts at any angle as shown in Fig. 7.19 by a suitable choice of helix angle. These gears are used to drive feed mechanisms on machine tool.

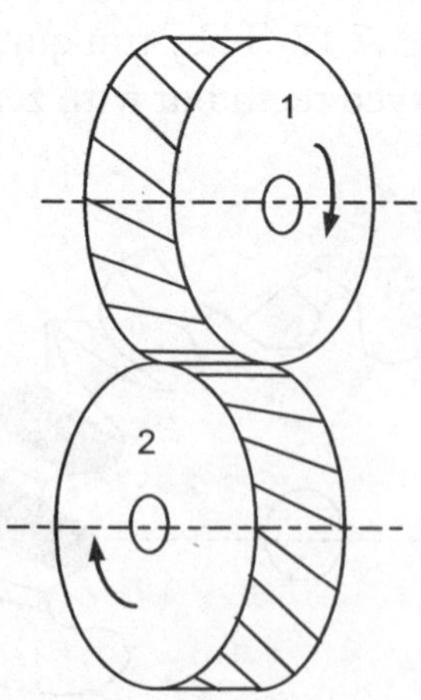

Fig.7.19: Cross Helical Gear

(ii) **Worm Gear:** It is a special case of spiral gears in which angle between the two axes is generally right angle. The smaller of the two gears is called worm which has large spiral angle. These are shown in Fig. 7.20.

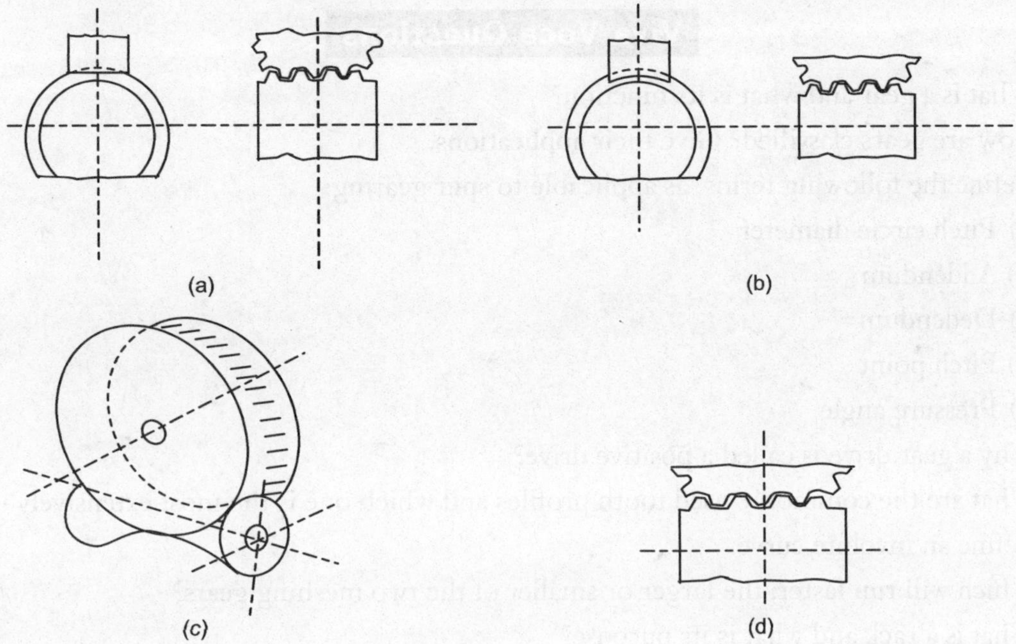

Fig.7.20: Worm Gear

(iii) Hypoid Gear: These gears are of hyperboloids though look like spiral bevel gears. The hypoid pinion is larger and stronger than a spiral bevel pinion. They have quit and smooth action and have larger number of teeth is contact as compared to straight bevel gears. These gears are used in final drive of vehicles. They are shown in Fig. 7.21.

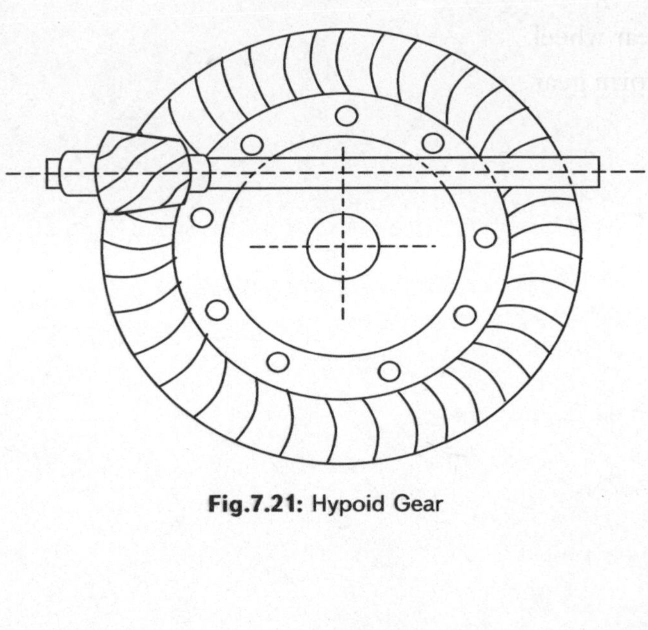

Fig.7.21: Hypoid Gear

Viva Voce Questions

1. What is a gear and what is its function?
2. How are gears classified? Give their applications.
3. Define the following terms, as applicable to spur gearing:
   (a) Pitch circle diameter
   (b) Addendum
   (c) Dedendum
   (d) Pitch point
   (e) Pressure angle
4. Why a gear drive is called a positive drive?
5. What are the commonly used tooth profiles and which one is the most extensively used?
6. Define an involute curve.
7. Which will run faster; the larger or smaller of the two meshing gears?
8. What is a rack and what is its purpose?
9. What is the difference between a rack and a pinion?
10. Distinguish between:
    (a) Spur and helical gear
    (b) Single helical gear and double helical gear
    (c) Spur and bevel gear
    (d) Gear and gearing
    (e) Pinion and gear wheel
    (f) Worm and worm gear

8

BASICS DRAWING SOFTWARES

8.1 AUTO-CAD

8.1.1 Introduction

Computer aided drawing is the main basic tool of the drawing. Learning to use a CAD system is similar to learning a new language. It is necessary to begin with the basic alphabet and learn how to use it correctly and effectively through practice. It will require learning some new concepts and skills as well as learning a different vocabulary. Nowadays, the majority of the Mechanical CAD systems are capable of creating three-dimensional solid models. All CAD systems create designs using basic geometric entities and many of the constructions used in technical designs are based upon two-dimensional planar geometry. In order to become effective and efficient in using a CAD system, we must learn to create geometric entities quickly and accurately. In examining the different types of planar geometric entities, the importance of lines and circles becomes obvious. Triangles and polygons are planar figures bounded by straight lines. Ellipses and splines can be constructed by connecting arcs with different radii. As one gains some experience in creating lines and circles, similar procedures can be applied to create other geometric entities. In this chapter, the different ways of creating lines and circles in AutoCAD are explained.

8.1.2 Starting the Auto-CAD

1. Select the AutoCAD option on the Program menu or select the AutoCAD icon on the Desktop. Click Start Drawing to start a new drawing.

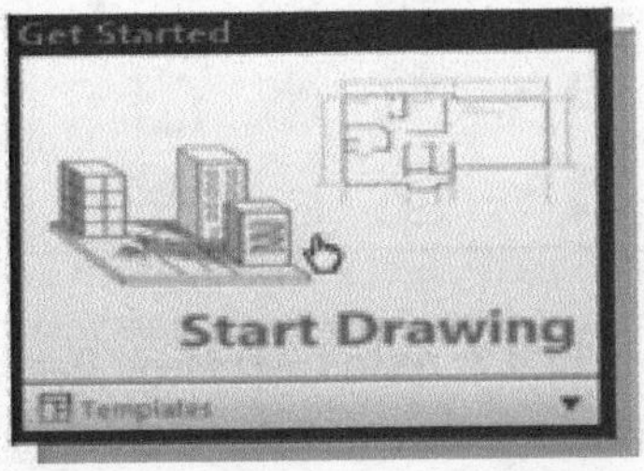

Fig.8.1: Startup of Auto-CAD

- Once the program is loaded into memory, the AutoCAD main drawing screen will appear on the screen.
- Note that AutoCAD automatically assigns generic names, Drawing X, as new drawings are created. In our example, AutoCAD opened the graphics window using the default system units and assigned the drawing name Drawing1.

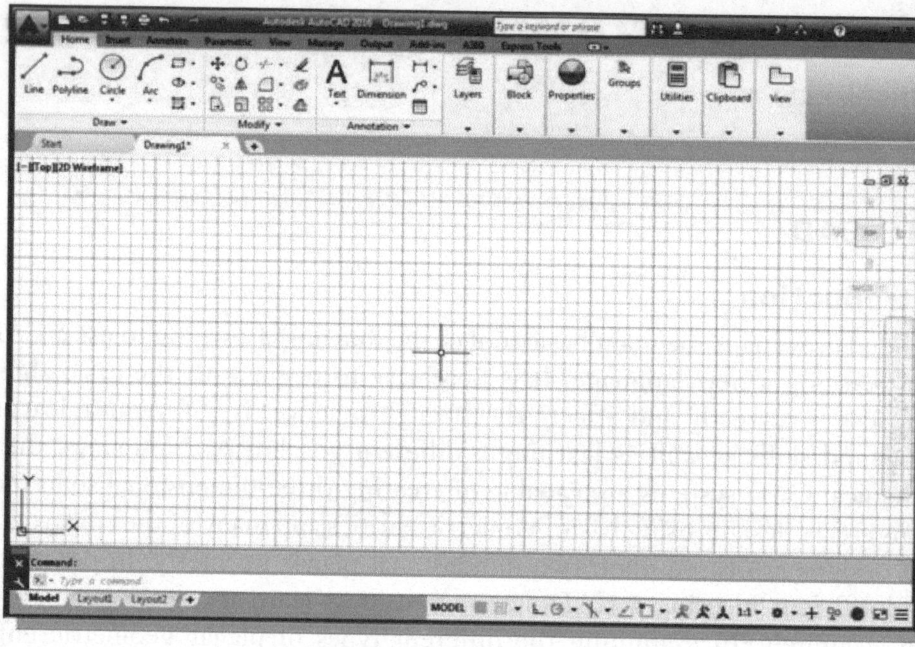

Fig.8.2: Auto-CAD Window

2. If necessary, click on the down-arrow in the Quick Access bar and select Show Menu Bar to display the AutoCAD Menu Bar. The Menu Bar provides access to all AutoCAD commands.

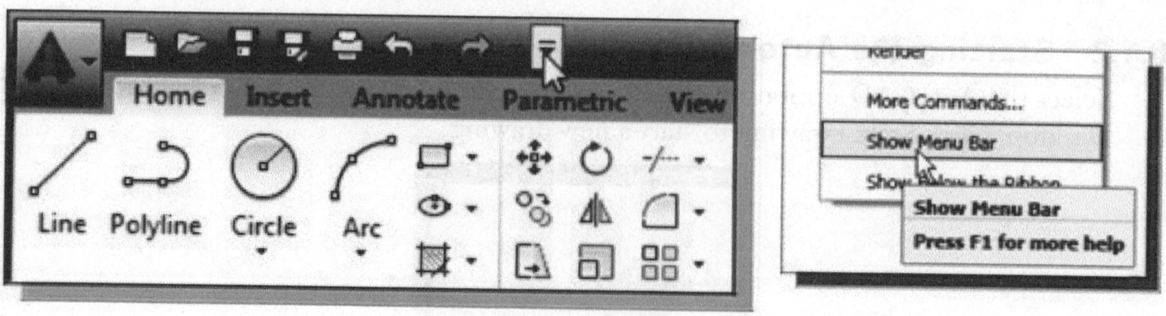

Fig.8.3: Auto-CAD Menu Bar

3. To switch on the AutoCAD Coordinates Display, use the Customization option at the bottom right corner.

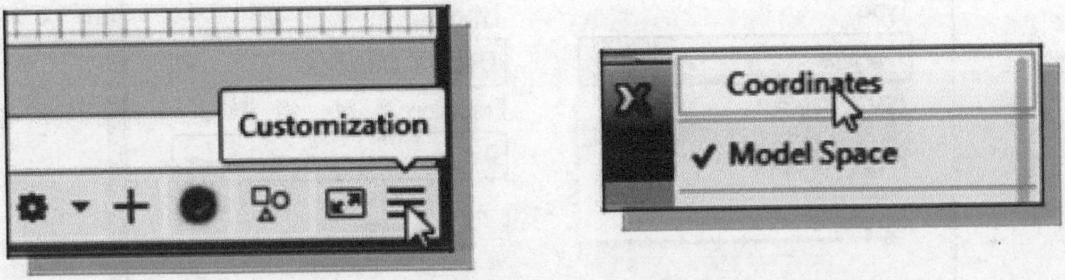

Fig.8.4: Auto-CAD Coordinates Display

8.1.3 Drawing Units Setup

Every object constructed in a CAD system is measured in units. It starting determine the system of units within the CAD system before creating the first geometric entities.

1. In the Menu Bar select: [Format] ◇ [Units]

   The AutoCAD Menu Bar contains multiple pull-down menus where all of the AutoCAD commands can be accessed. Click on the Length Type option to display the different types of length units available. Confirm the Length Type is set to Decimal.

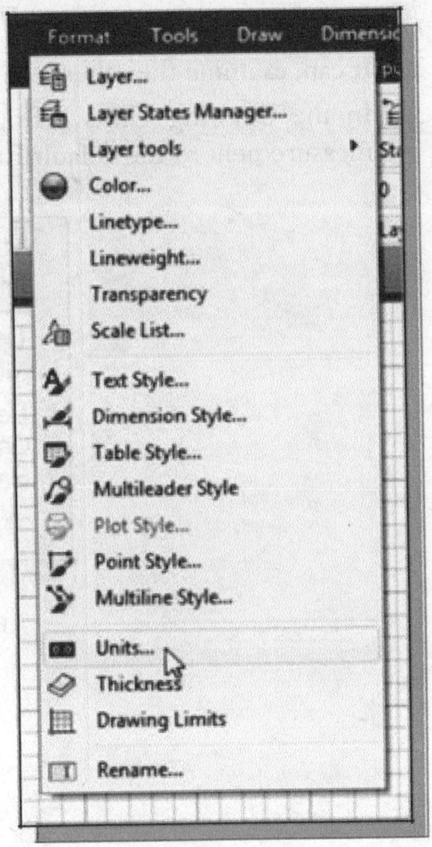

Fig.8.5: Drawing Units Setup

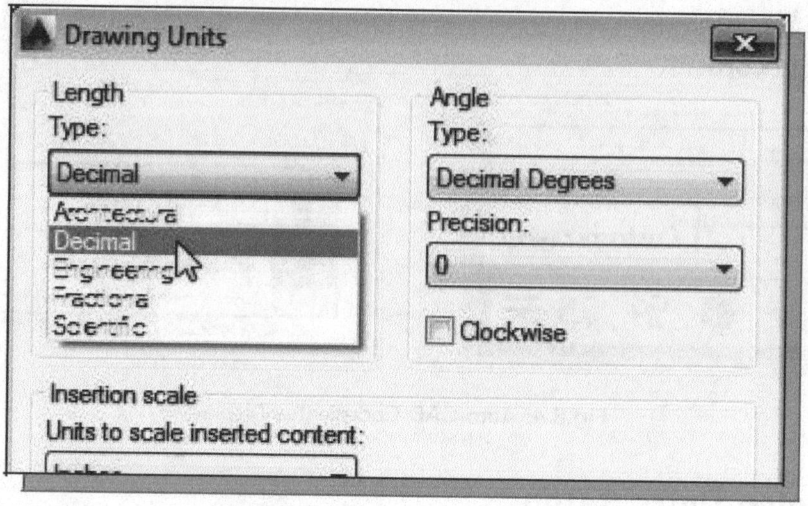

Fig.8.6: Drawing Unit to Decimal

2. It can, examine the other settings that are available.
3. In the Drawing Units dialog box, set the Length Type to Decimal. It will set the measurement to the default English units, inches.

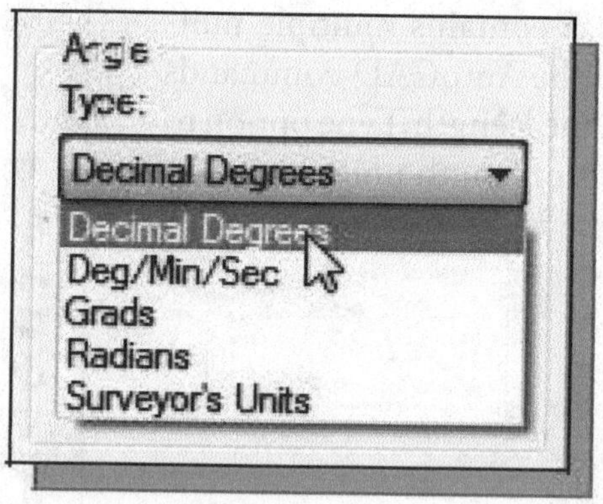

Fig.8.7: Drawing Units Setup

4. Set the Precision to two digits after the decimal point.

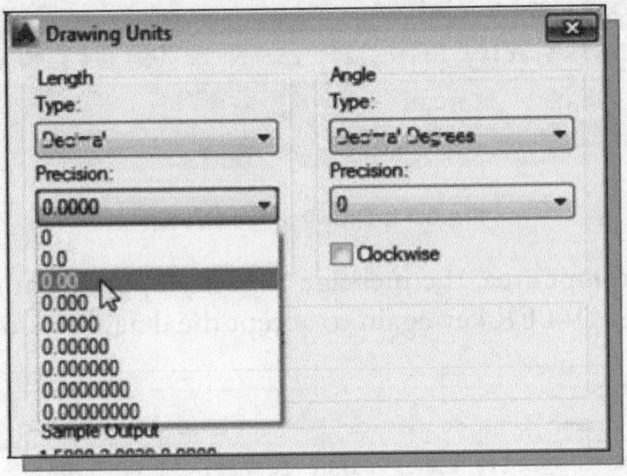

Fig.8.8: Drawing Units Setup

5. Pick OK to exit the Drawing Units dialog box.

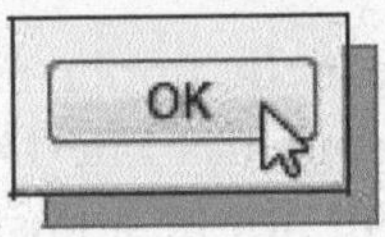

Fig.8.9: Drawing Units Setup

8.1.4 Drawing Area Setup

In next step, set up the Drawing Limits by entering a command in the command prompt area. Setting the Drawing Limits controls the extents of the display of the grid. It also serves as a visual reference that marks the working area. It can also be used to prevent construction outside the grid limits and as a plot option that defines an area to be plotted/printed.

1. In the Menu Bar select: [Format] □ [Drawing Limits]
2. In the command prompt area, the message "Reset Model Space Limits: Specify lower left corner or [On/Off] <0.00,0.00>:" is displayed. Press the ENTER key once to accept the default coordinates <0.00,0.00>.

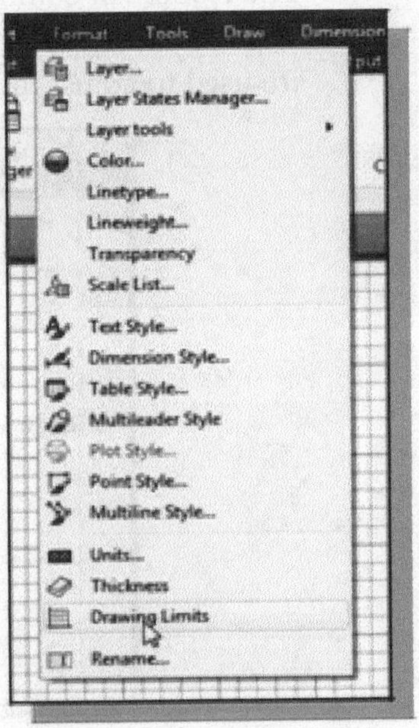

Fig.8.10: Drawing Area Setup

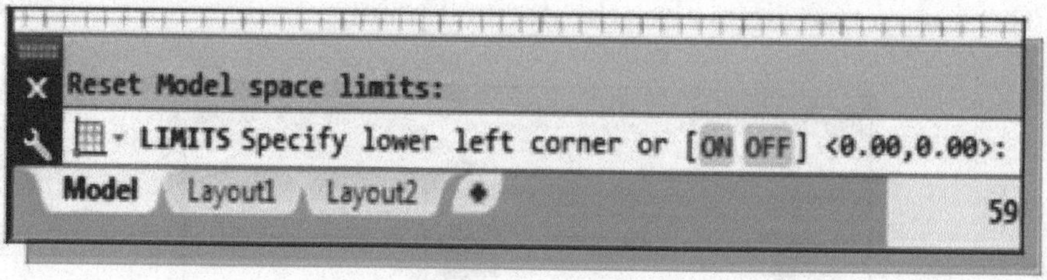

Fig.8.11: Drawing Area Setup

3. In the command prompt area, the message "Specify upper right corner<12.00,9.00>:" is displayed. Press the ENTER key again to accept the default coordinates <12.00,9.00>.

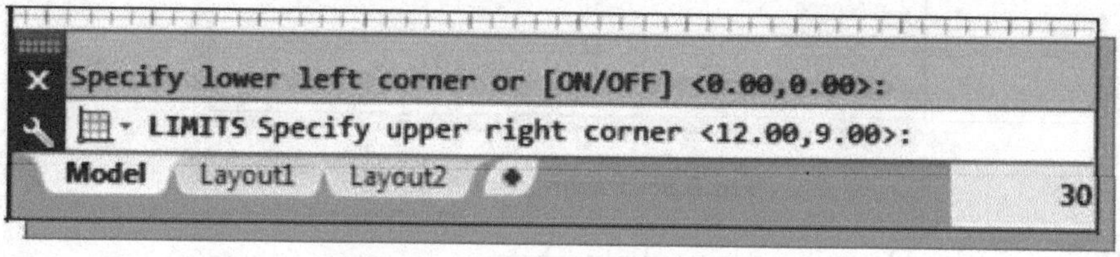

Fig.8.12: Drawing Area Setup

4. It can, move the graphics cursor near the upper-right corner inside the drawing area and note that the drawing area is unchanged. (The Drawing Limits command is used to set the drawing area, but the display will not be adjusted until a display command is used.)
5. Inside the Menu Bar area select: [View] □ [Zoom] □ [All]
   - The Zoom All command will adjust the display so that all objects in the drawing are displayed to be as large as possible. If no objects are constructed, the Drawing Limits are used to adjust the current viewport.

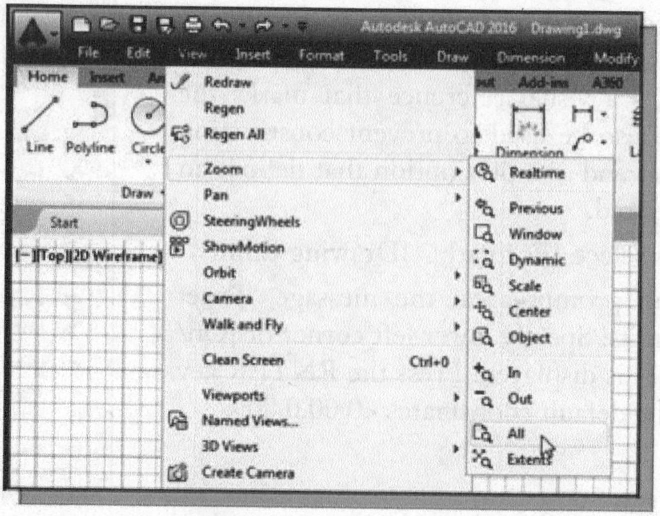

Fig.8.13: Drawing Area Setup

6. Move the graphics cursor near the upper-right corner inside the drawing area and note that the display area is updated.
7. Click the function key [F7] once to turn off the display of the Grid lines.

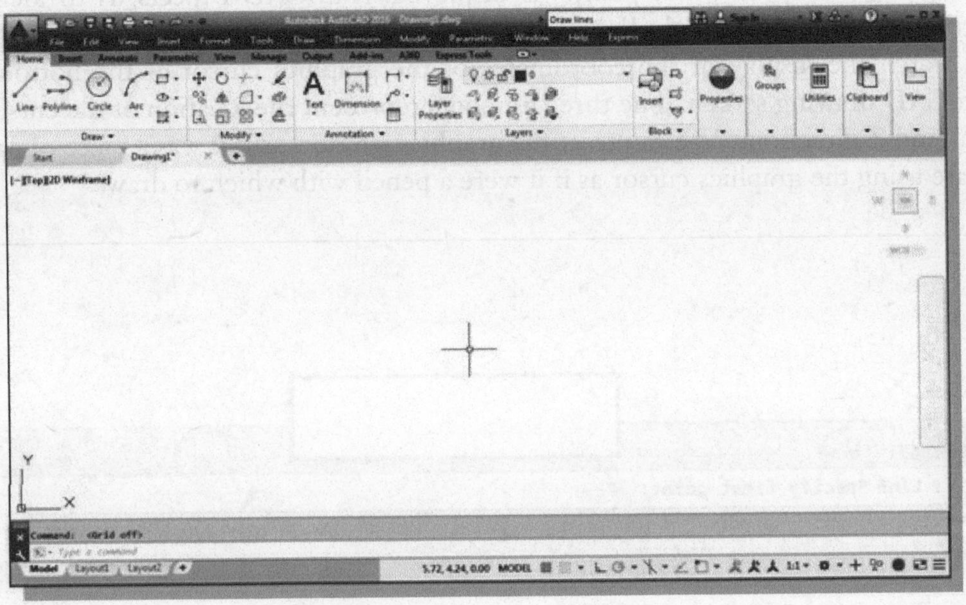

Fig.8.14: Drawing Area Setup

- Note that function key [F7] is a quick key, which can be used to quickly toggle on/off the grid display.

8.1.5 Drawing Lines with the LINE Command

1. Move the graphics cursor to the first icon in the Draw panel. It is the Line icon. Note that a brief description of the Line command appears next to the cursor.

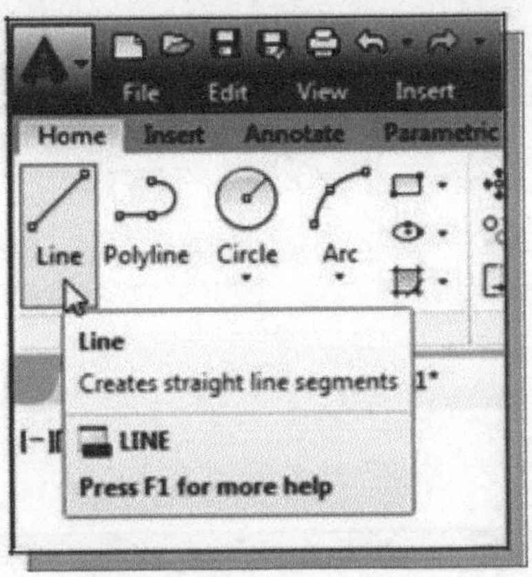

Fig.8.15: Drawing Line

2. Select the icon by clicking once with the left-mouse-button, which will activate the Line command.
3. In the command prompt area, near the bottom of the AutoCAD drawing screen, the message "_line Specify first point:" is displayed. AutoCAD expects us to identify the starting location of a straight line. Move the graphics cursor inside the graphics window and watch the display of the coordinates of the graphics cursor at the bottom of the AutoCAD drawing screen. The three numbers represent the location of the cursor in the X, Y, and Z directions. We can treat the graphics window as if it was a piece of paper and we are using the graphics cursor as if it were a pencil with which to draw.

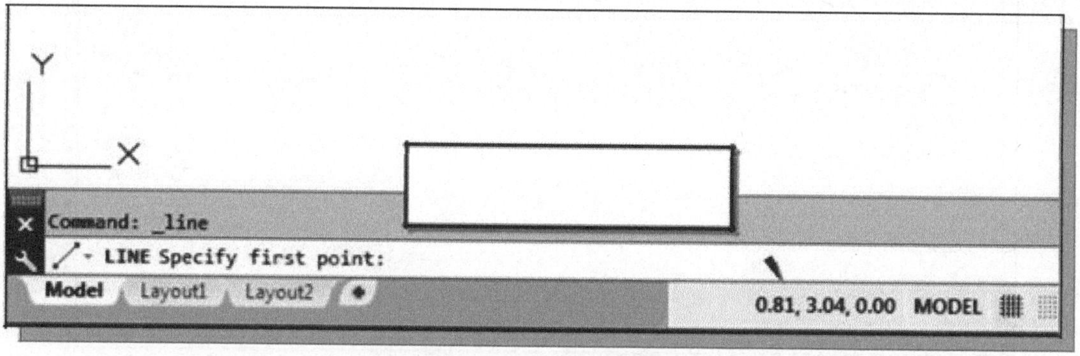

Fig.8.16: Line Drawing Window

4. A location about one-third from the bottom of the graphics window is started. Left-click once to position the starting point of our first line. This will be point 1 of our sketch. Next, move the cursor upward and toward the right side of point1. Notice the rubber-band line that follows the graphics cursor in the graphics window. Left-click again (point 2) and hence the first line of the sketch is created.

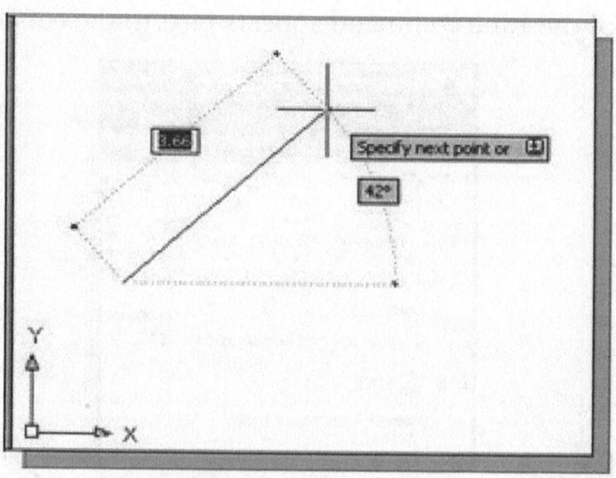

Fig.8.17: Drawing Line

5. Move the cursor to the left of point 2 and create a horizontal line about the same length as the first line on the screen.
6. Repeat the above steps and complete the freehand sketch by adding three more lines (from point 3 to point 4, point 4 to point 5, and then connect to point 5 back to point 1).

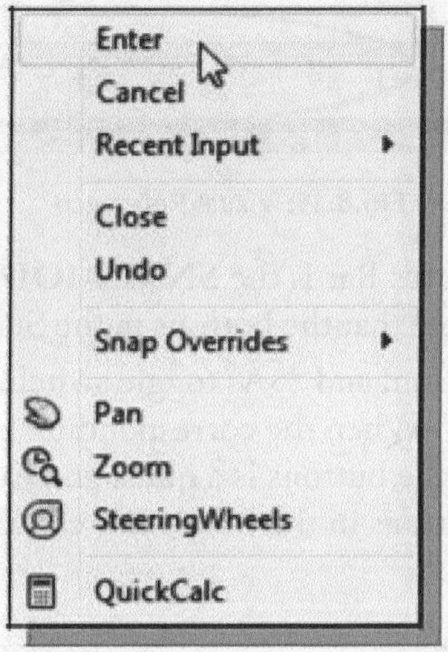

Fig.8.18: Drawing Line using LINE Command

7. Notice that the Line command remains activated even after we connected the last segment of the line to the starting point (point 1) of the sketch. Inside the graphics window, click once with the right-mouse-button and a popup menu appears on the screen.
8. Select Enter with the left-mouse-button to end the Line command. (This is equivalent to clicking the [ENTER] key on the keyboard.)
9. Move the cursor near point 2 and point 3, and estimate the length of the horizontal line by watching the displayed coordinates for each point.

8.1.6 Visual Reference

The method which is used to create the freehand sketch is known as the interactive method , where it use the cursor to specify locations on the screen. However, it is rather difficult to try to create a line of a specific length by watching the displayed coordinates. It would be helpful to know what one inch or one meter looks like on the screen while we are creating entities. **AutoCAD** provides us with many tools to aid the construction of our designs. For example, the **GRID** and **SNAP MODE** options can be used to get a visual reference as to the size of objects and learn to restrict the movement of the cursor to a set increment on the screen.

The **GRID** and **SNAP MODE** options can be turned **ON** or **OFF** through the Status Bar. The Status Bar area is located at the bottom left of the **AutoCAD** drawing screen, next to the cursor coordinates.

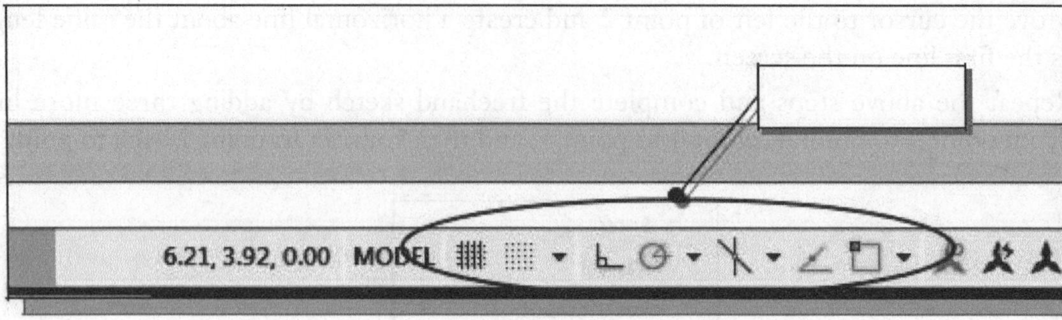

Fig.8.19: Visual Reference

The second button in the Status Bar is the **SNAP MODE** option and the third button is the **GRID DISPLAY** option. Note that the buttons in the Status Bar area serve two functions:

1. The status of the specific option, and 2. As toggle switches, that can be used to turn these special options ON and OFF. When the corresponding button is highlighted, the specific option is turned ON. Using the buttons is a quick and easy way to make changes to these drawing aid options. The buttons in the Status Bar can also be switched on and off in the middle of another command.

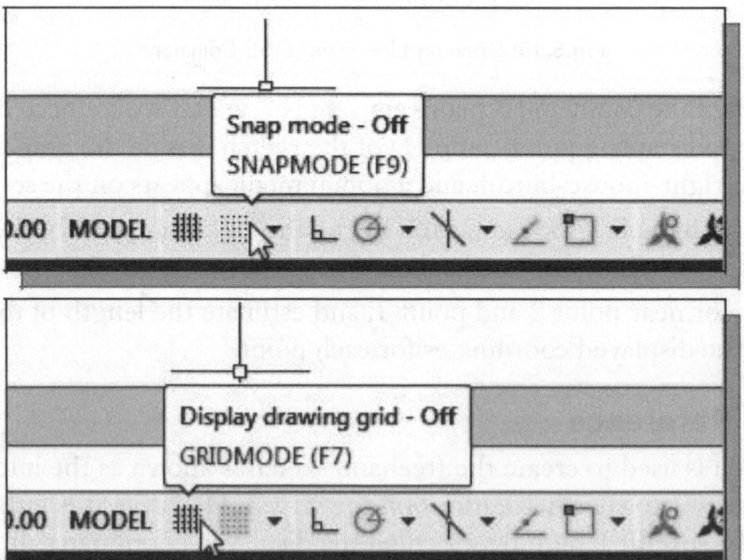

Fig.8.20: Visual Reference

GRID ON

1. Left-click the **GRID** button in the Status Bar to turn **ON** the **GRID DISPLAY** option. (Notice in the command prompt area, the message "<Grid on>" is also displayed.)

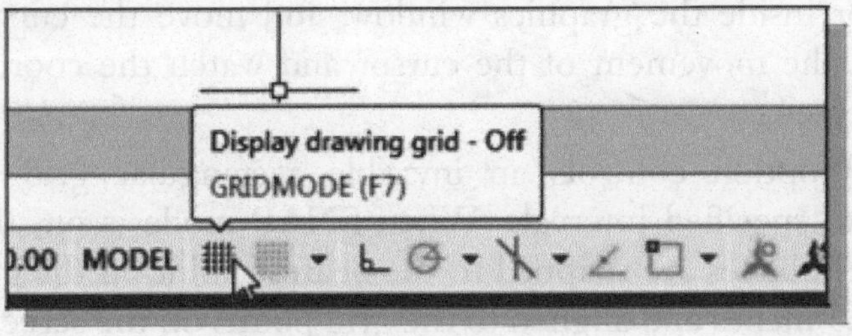

Fig.8.21: Grid ON

2. Move the cursor inside the graphics window, and estimate the distance in between the grid lines by watching the coordinates displayed at the bottom of the screen.

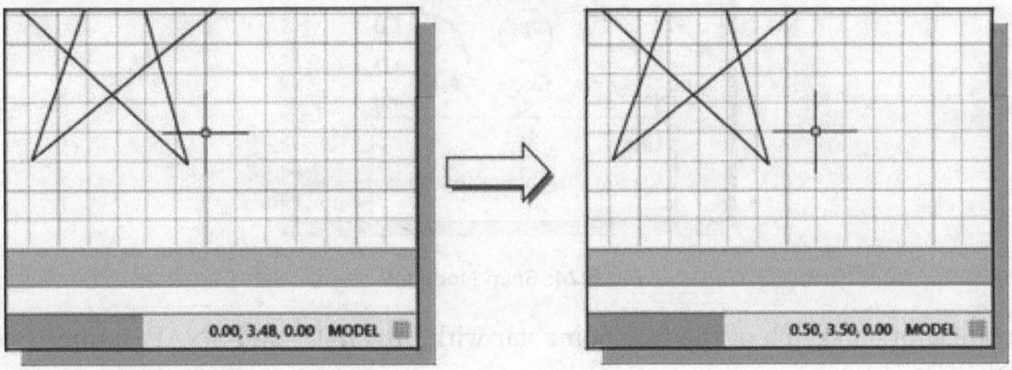

Fig.8.22: Grid ON

3. The **GRID** option creates a pattern of lines that extends over an area on the screen. Using the grid is similar to placing a sheet of grid paper under a drawing. The grid helps you align objects and visualize the distance between them. The grid is not displayed in the plotted drawing. The default grid spacing, which means the distance in between two lines on the screen, is 0.5 inches.

SNAP MODE ON

1. Left-click the **SNAP MODE** button in the Status Bar to turn **ON** the **SNAP** option.

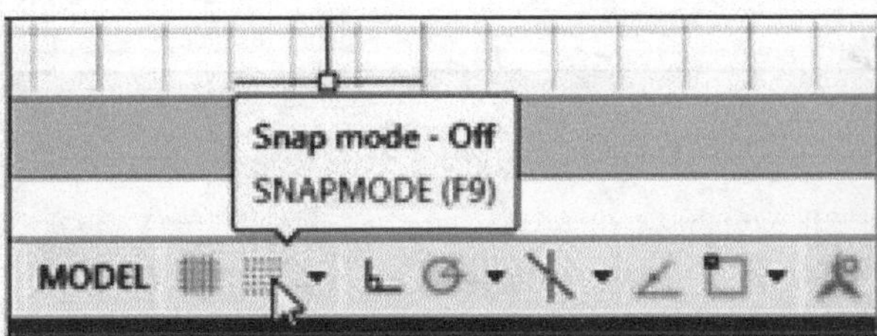

Fig.8.23: Snap Mode ON

2. Move the cursor inside the graphics window, and move the cursor diagonally on the screen. Observe the movement of the cursor and watch the coordinates display at the bottom of the screen.
   - The **SNAP** option controls an invisible rectangular grid that restricts cursor movement to specified intervals. When **SNAP** mode is on, the screen cursor and all input coordinates are snapped to the nearest point on the grid. The default snap interval is 0.5 inches and aligned to the grid points on the screen.
3. Click on the Line icon in the Draw toolbar. In the command prompt area, the message "_line Specify first point:" is displayed.

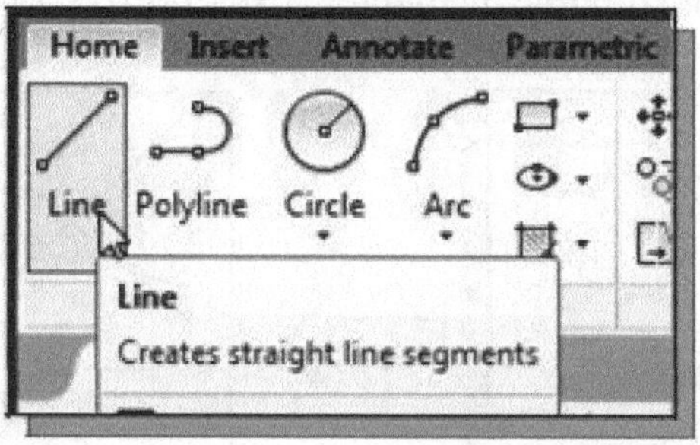

Fig.8.24: Snap Mode ON

4. Create another sketch of the five-point star with the GRID and SNAP options switched ON.

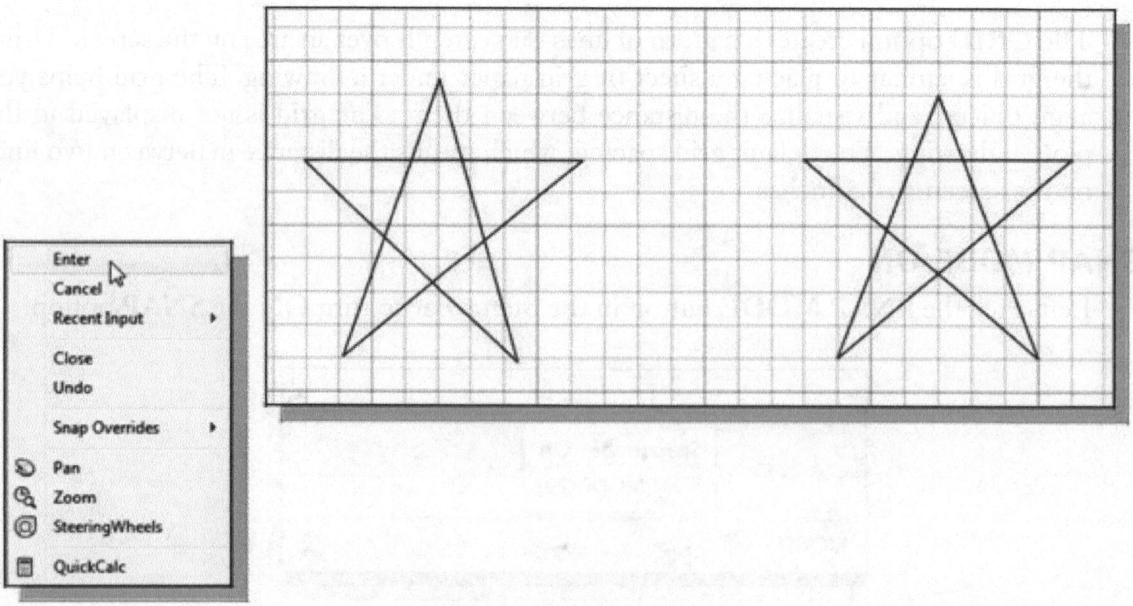

Fig.8.25: Snap Mode ON

5. Use the right-mouse-button and select Enter in the popup menu to end the Line command if you have not done so.

Using the ERASE Command

One of the advantages of using a **CAD** system is the ability to remove entities without leaving any marks. Erase two of the lines can be done very easily by using Erase command.

1. Pick Erase in the Modify toolbar. (The icon is a picture of an eraser at the end of a pencil.) The message "Select objects" is displayed in the command prompt area and **AutoCAD** awaits us to select the objects to erase.

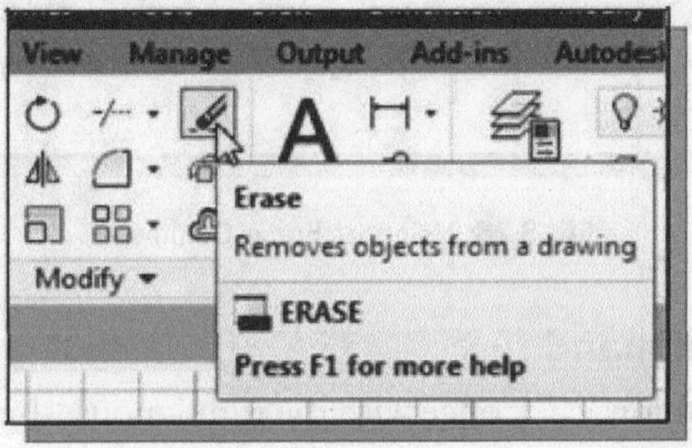

Fig.8.26: Erase Command

2. Left-click the **SNAP MODE** button on the Status Bar to turn **OFF** the **SNAPMODE** option so that we can more easily move the cursor on top of objects. We can toggle the Status Bar options **ON** or **OFF** in the middle of another command.

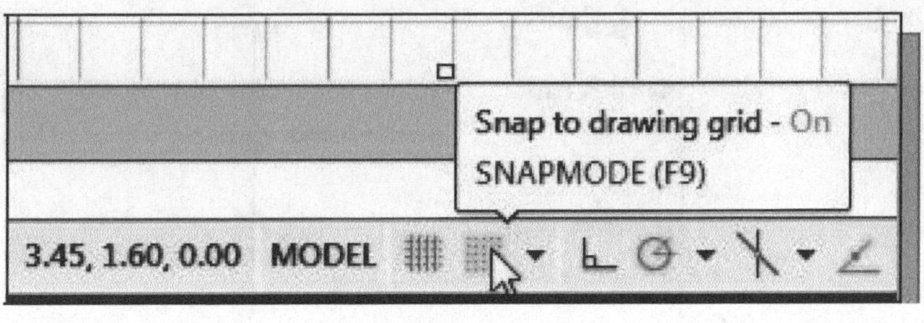

Fig.8.27: Snap mode off

3. Select any two lines on the screen; the selected lines are highlighted as shown in the figure below.
    - To deselect an object from the selection set, hold down the [SHIFT] key and select the object again.
4. Right click right-mouse-click once to accept the selections. The selected two lines are erased.

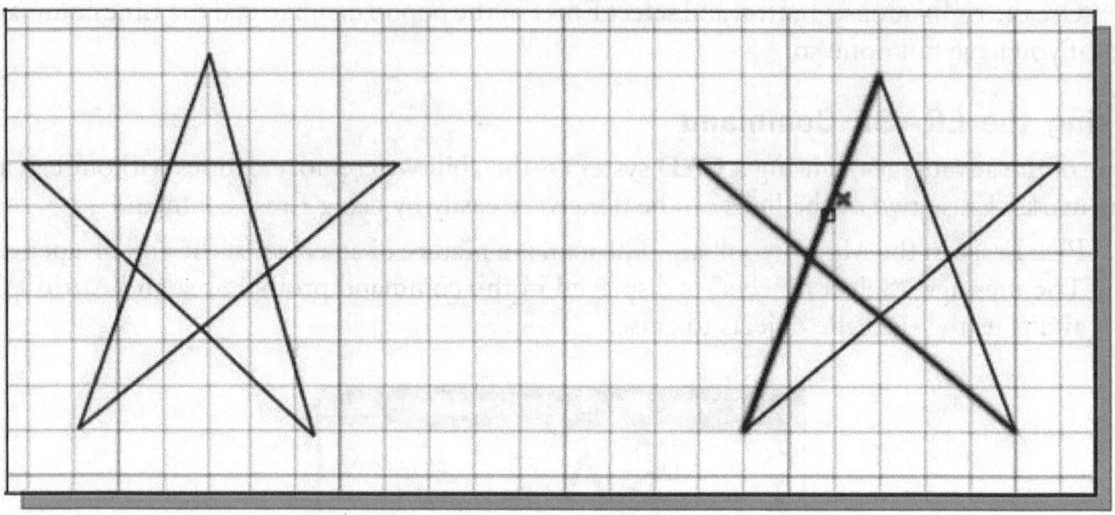

Fig.8.28: Using of Erase Command

Repeat the Last Command

1. Inside the graphics window, click once with the right-mouse-button to bring up the popup option menu.

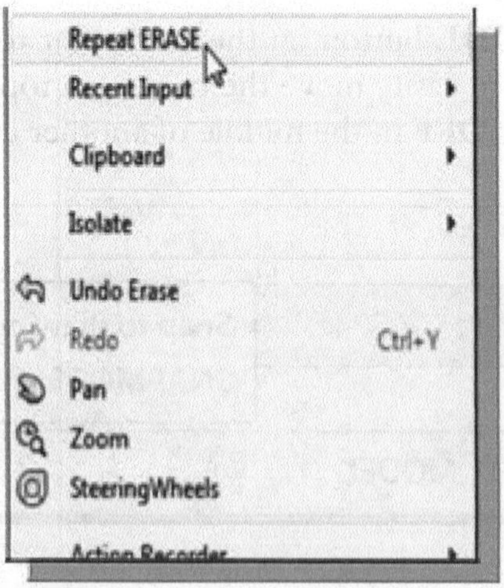

Fig.8.29: Repeat the Cast Command

2. Pick Repeat Erase, with the left-mouse-button, in the popup menu to repeat the last command. Notice the other options available in the popup menu and use them as required.
3. Move the cursor to a location that is above and toward the left side of the entities on the screen. Left-mouse-click once to start a corner of a rubber-band window.

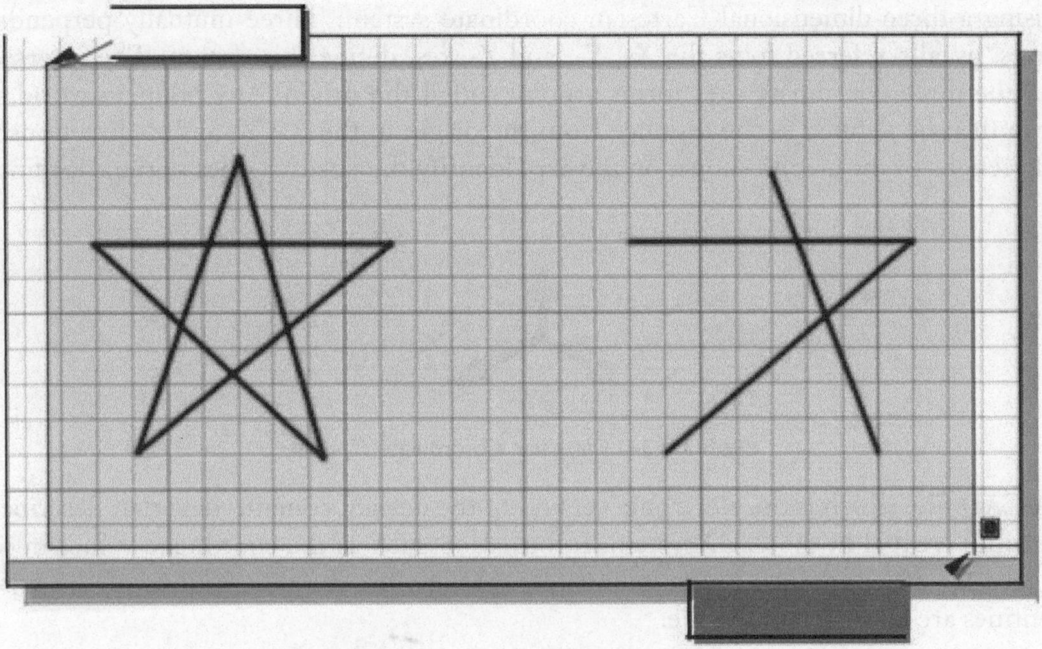

Fig.8.30: Example of use Cast Command

4. Move the cursor toward the right and below the entities, and then left-mouse-click to enclose all the entities inside the selection window. Notice all entities that are inside the window are selected. (Note the enclosed window selection direction is from top left to bottom right.)
5. Inside the graphics window, right-mouse-click once to proceed with erasing the selected entities.
   - On your own, create a free-hand sketch of your choices using the Line command. Experiment with using the different commands have been discussed so far. Reset the status buttons so that only the GRID DISPLAY option is turned ON as shown.

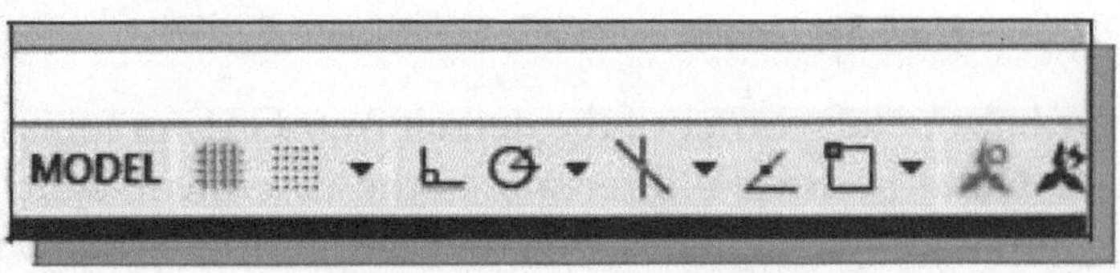

Fig.8.31: Reset of Status Button

The CAD Database and the User Coordinate System

➢ Designs and drawings created in a CAD system are usually defined and stored using sets of points in space, termed as world space. In most CAD systems, the world space is defined using a three-dimensional Cartesian coordinate system. Three mutually perpendicular axes, usually referred to as the X-, Y-, and Z-axes, define this system. The intersection of the three coordinate axes forms a point called the origin. Any point in world space can then be defined as the distance from the origin in the X-, Y- and Z-directions. The directions of the arrows shown on the axes identify the positive sides of the coordinates.

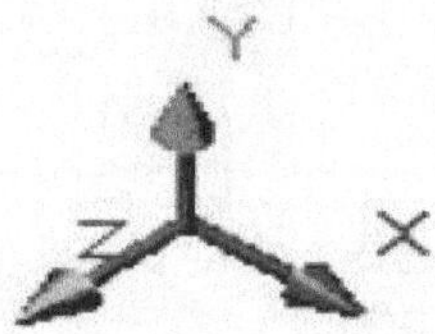

Fig.8.32: 3-D Cartesian Co-ordinate System

➢ A CAD file, which is the electronic version of the design, contains data that describes the entities created in the CAD system. Information such as the coordinate values in world space for all endpoints, center points, etc. along with the descriptions of the types of entities are all stored in the file.

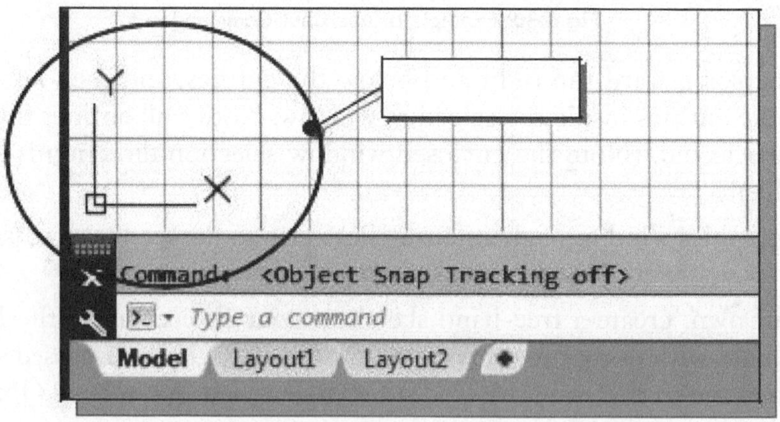

Fig.8.33: Default AutoCAD Co-ordinate System

➢ The icon near the bottom left corner of the default AutoCAD graphics window shows the positive X-direction and positive Y-direction of the coordinate system that is active. In AutoCAD, the coordinate system that is used to create entities is called the user coordinate system (UCS). By default, the user coordinate system is aligned to the world coordinate system (WCS). The world coordinate system is a coordinate system used by AutoCAD as the basis for defining all objects and other coordinate systems defined by the users. The origin of the world coordinate system is taken as a fixed point being used as a reference for all measurements. The default orientation of the Z-axis can be considered as positive values in front of the monitor and negative values inside the monitor.

Changing to the 2D UCS Icon Display

➢ In AutoCAD, the UCS icon is displayed in various ways to help us visualize the orientation of the drawing plane.

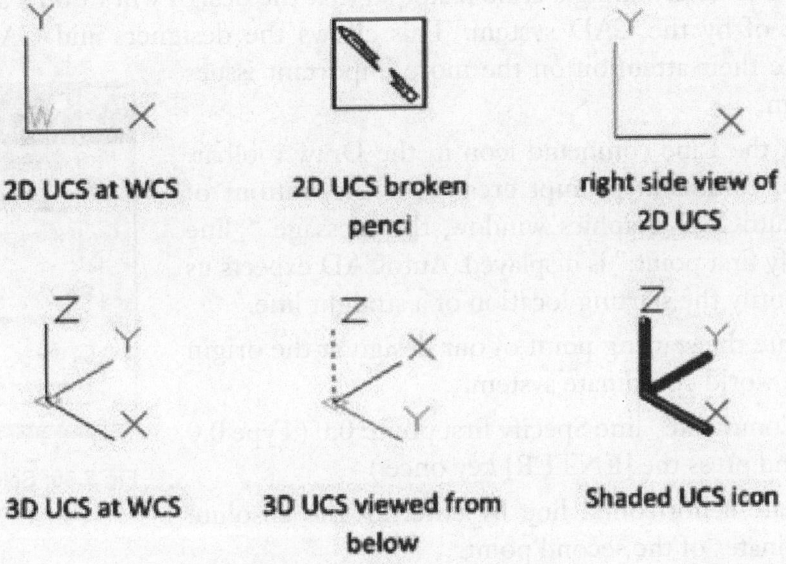

Fig.8.34: 2D UCS Icon Display

The Guide Plate: It create a mechanical design using the different coordinate entry methods.

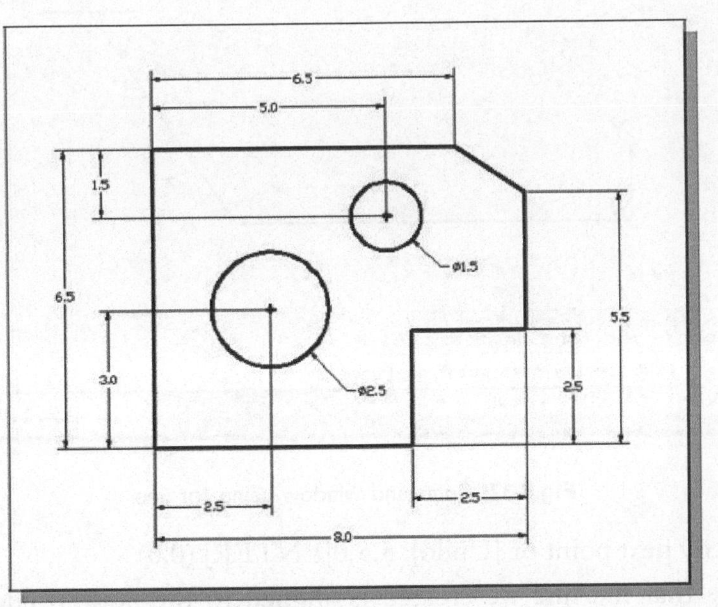

Fig.8.35: Guide Plate

➢ The rule for creating CAD designs and drawings is that they should be created at full size using real-world units. The CAD database contains all the definitions of the geometric entities and the design is considered as a virtual, full-sized object. Only when a printer or plotter transfers the CAD design to paper is the design scaled to fit on a sheet. The tedious task of determining a scale factor so that the design will fit on a sheet of paper is taken care of by the CAD system. This allows the designers and CAD operators to concentrate their attention on the more important issues – the design.

1. Select the Line command icon in the Draw toolbar. In the command prompt area, near the bottom of the AutoCAD graphics window, the message "_line Specify first point:" is displayed. AutoCAD expects us to identify the starting location of a straight line.
2. It locate the starting point of our design at the origin of the world coordinate system.
   - Command: _line Specify first point: 0,0 (Type 0,0 and press the [ENTER] key once.)
3. It create a horizontal line by entering the absolute coordinates of the second point.

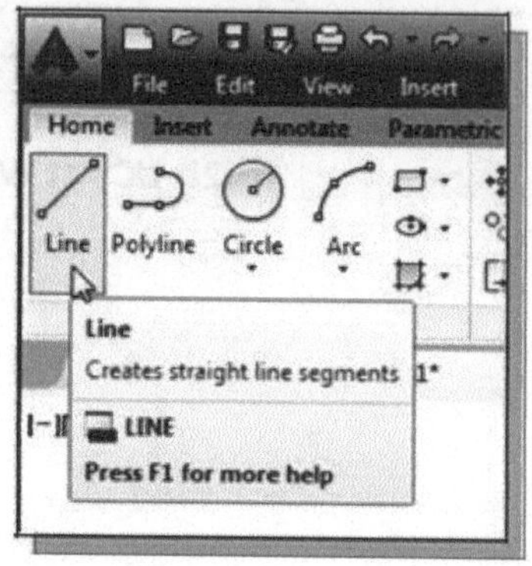

Fig.8.36: Select Line Command from toolbar

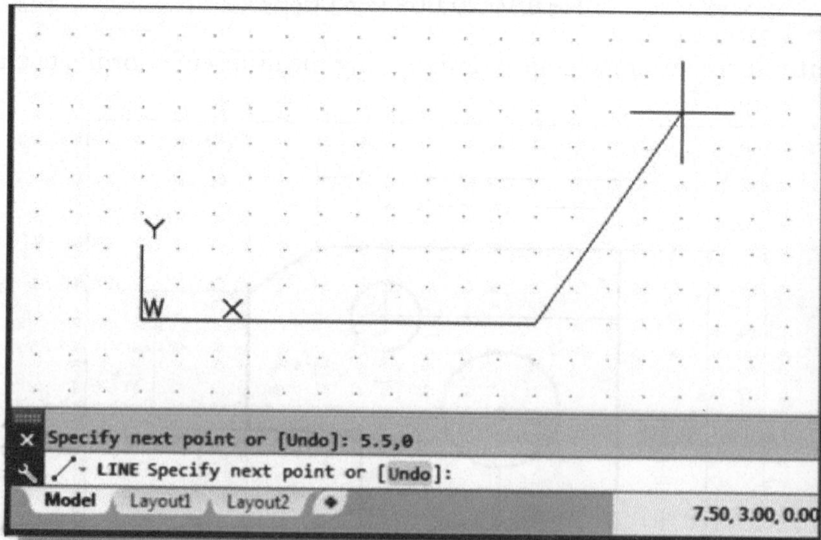

Fig.8.37: Command window using for line

- Specify next point or [Undo]: 5.5,0[ENTER] (0,0)
- Note that the line we created is aligned to the bottom edge of the drawing window. Let us adjust the view of the line by using the Pan Real time command.

4. In the Menu Bar area select: [View]□[Pan]□[Real time]

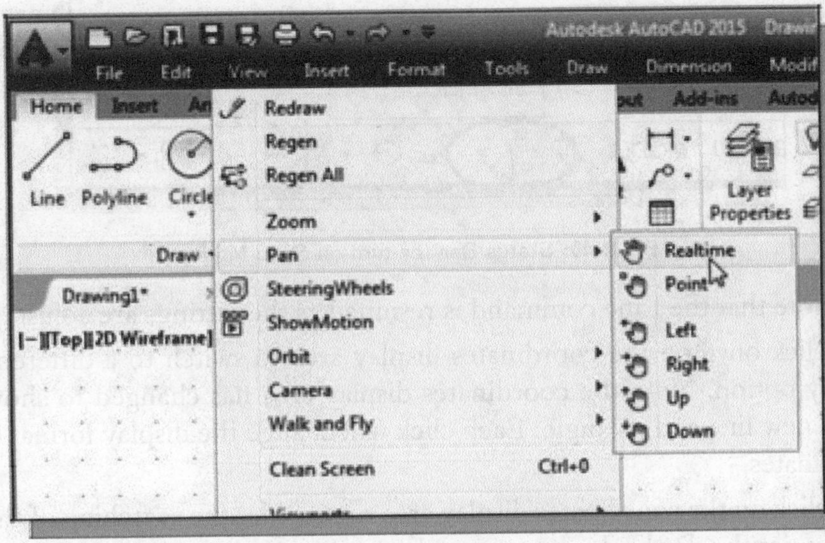

Fig.8.38: Menu Bar

- The available Pan commands enable us to move the view to a different position. The Pan-Real time function acts as if we are using a video camera.

5. Move the cursor, which appears as a hand inside the graphics window, near the center of the drawing window, then push down the left-mouse-button and drag the display toward the right and top side until we can see the sketched line.
6. Press the [Esc] key to exit the Pan-Real-time command. Notice that AutoCAD goes back to the Line command.
7. This will create a vertical line by using the relative rectangular coordinates entry method, relative to the last point we specified:

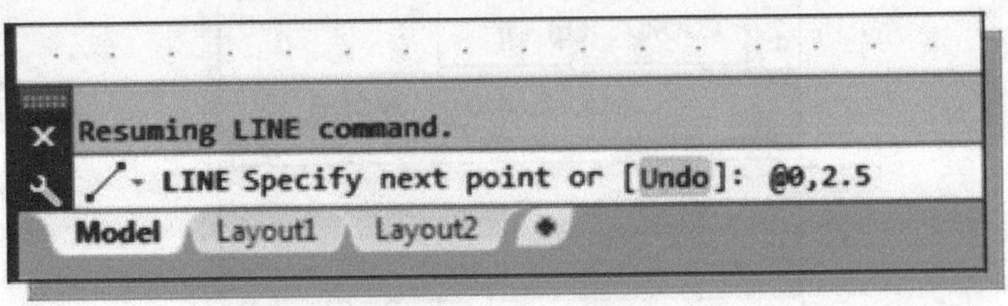

Fig.8.39: Resuming Line Command

- Specify next point or [Close/Undo]: @0,2.5[ENTER]

8. It can mix any of the entry methods in positioning the locations of the endpoints. Move the cursor to the Status Bar area, and turn ON the SNAP MODE option.

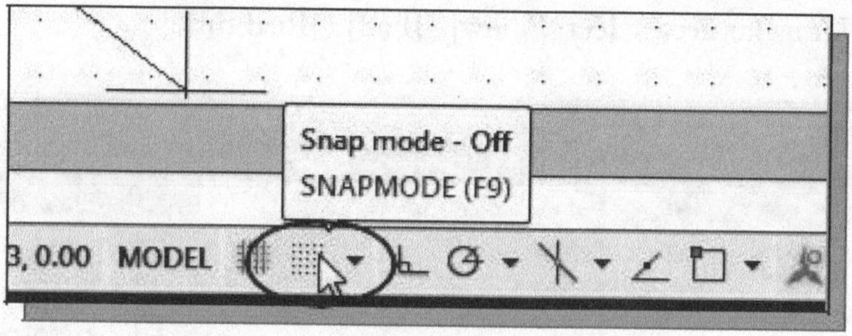

Fig.8.40: Status Bar for turn on Snap Mode

- Note that the Line command is resumed as the settings are adjusted.

9. Left-click once on the coordinates display area to switch to a different coordinate display option. Note the coordinates display area has changed to show the length of the new line and its angle. Each click will change the display format of the cursor coordinates.
10. Left-click on the coordinates display area to provides the switching of the coordinate display; set the display back to using the world coordinate system.
11. Create the next line by picking the location, world coordinates (8,2.5), on the screen.

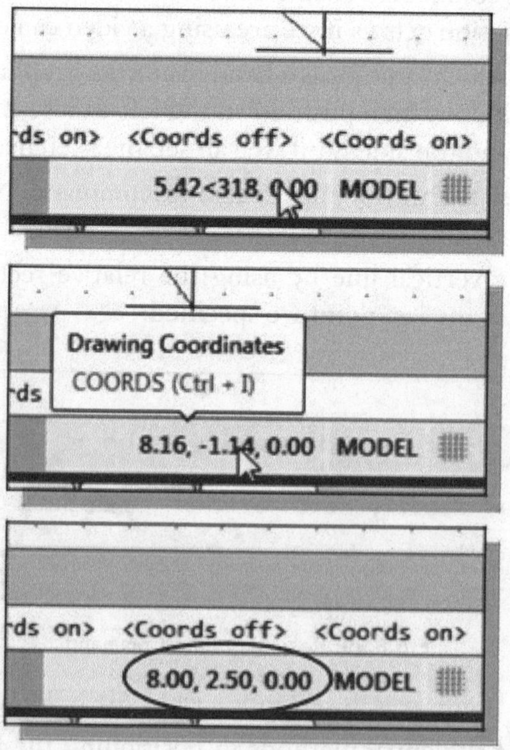

Fig.8.41: Create line location on world coordinates system

12. It will next use the relative polar coordinates entry method, relative to the last point specified:

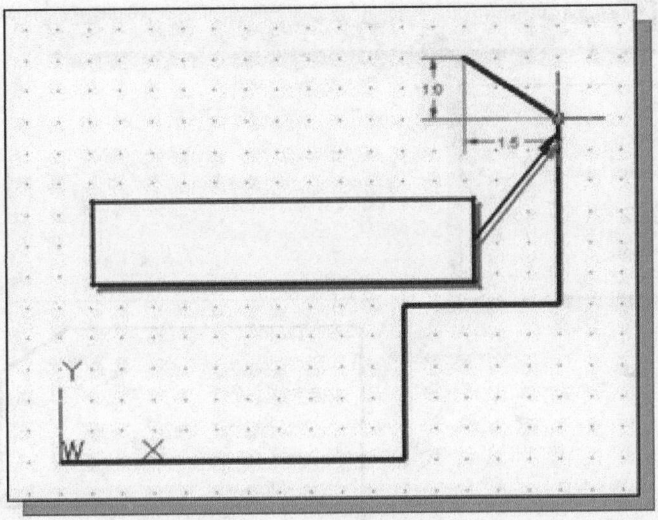

Fig.8.42: Polar Coordinates Method

- Specify next point or [Close/Undo]: @3<90[ENTER] (Distance is 3 inches with an angle of 90 degrees.)

13. Using the relative rectangular coordinates entry method to create the next line, it can imagine a reference coordinate system aligned at the previous point. Coordinates are measured along the two reference axes.

- Specify next point or [Close/Undo]: @-1.5,1[ENTER] (-1.5 and 1 inches are measured relative to the reference point.)

14. Move the cursor directly to the left of the last point and use the direct distance entry technique by entering 6.5[ENTER].
15. For the last segment of the sketch, it can use the Close option to connect back to the starting point. Inside the graphics window, right-mouse-click and a popup menu appears on the screen.
16. Select Close with the left-mouse-button to connect back to the starting point and end the Line command.

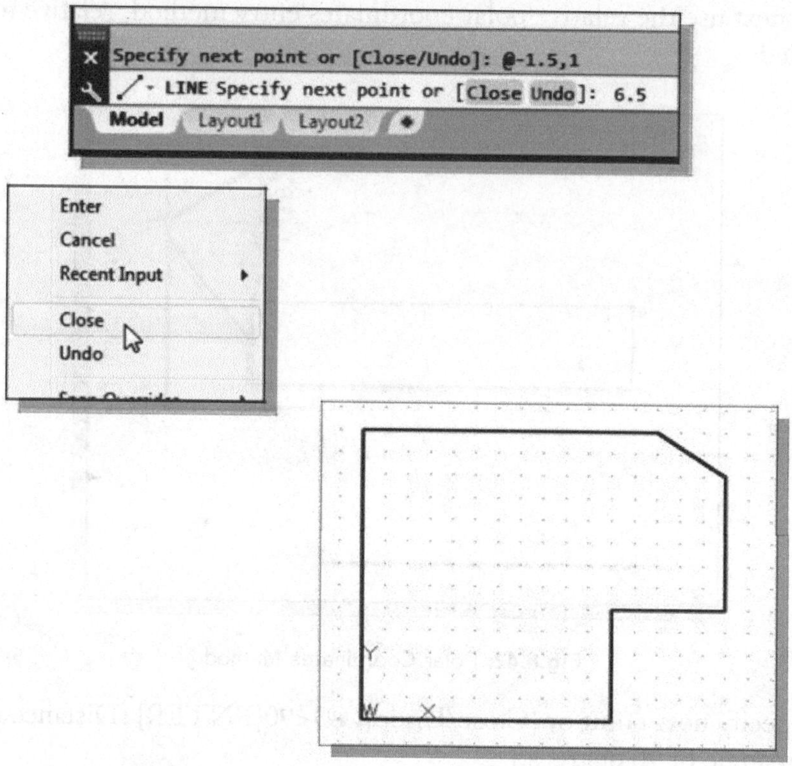

Fig.8.43: Close of LIne Command

Creating Circle

The toolbars in AutoCAD are designed to allow the CAD operator to quickly activate the desired commands.

1. In the Draw toolbar, click on the little triangle below the circle icon. Note that the little triangle indicates additional options are available.

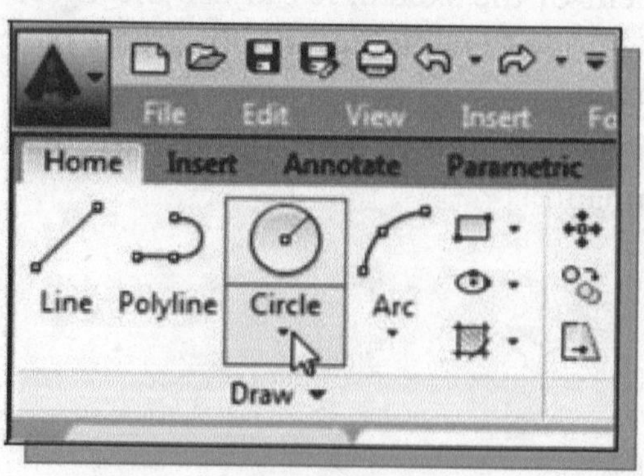

Fig.8.44: Circle Command from Toolbar

2. In the option list, select: [Center, Diameter]

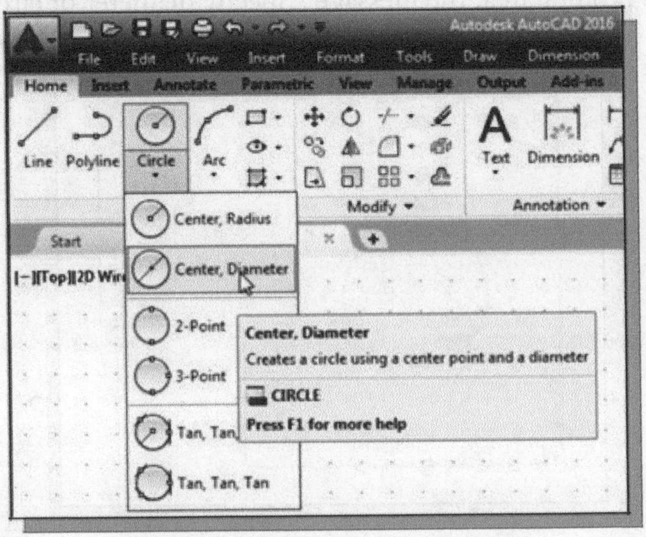

Fig.8.45: Selection of Circle Command

3. Check the different options available under the circle submenu:

   Center, Radius: Draws a circle based on a center point and a radius.

   Center, Diameter: Draws a circle based on a center point and a diameter.

   2 Points: Draws a circle based on two endpoints of the diameter.

   3 Points: Draws a circle based on three points on the circumference.

   TTR–Tangent, Tangent, Radius: Draws a circle with a specified radius tangent to two objects.

TTT–Tangent, Tangent, Tangent: Draws a circle tangent to three objects.

4. In the command prompt area, the message "Specify center point for circle or[3P/2P/Ttr (tan tan radius)]:" is displayed. AutoCAD expects us to identify the location of a point or enter an option. Any of the four coordinate entry methods can be to identify the desired location. This Enter the world coordinates(2.5,3) as the center point for the first circle.

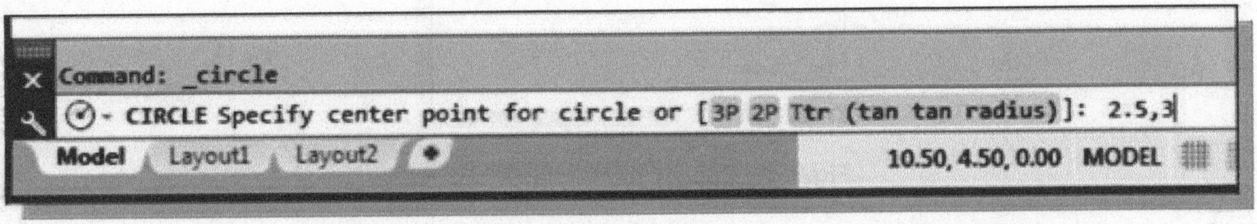

Fig.8.46: Using of Command Window for Circle Command

5. Specify center point for circle or [3P/2P/Ttr (tan tan radius)]: 2.5,3[ENTER]
6. In the command prompt area, the message "Specify diameter of circle:" is displayed.

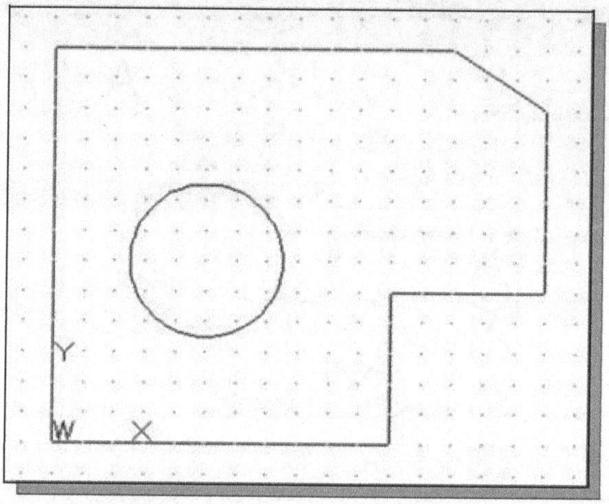

Fig.8.47: Display the specify diameter of circle

7. Specify diameter of circle: 2.5[ENTER]
8. Inside the graphics window, right-mouse-click to bring up the popup option menu.
9. Pick Repeat CIRCLE with the left-mouse-button in the popup menu to repeat the last command.
10. Using the relative rectangular coordinates entry method, relative to the center-point coordinates of the first circle, we specify the location as (2.5,2).
11. Specify center point for circle or [3P/2P/Ttr (tan tan radius)]: @2.5,2[ENTER]

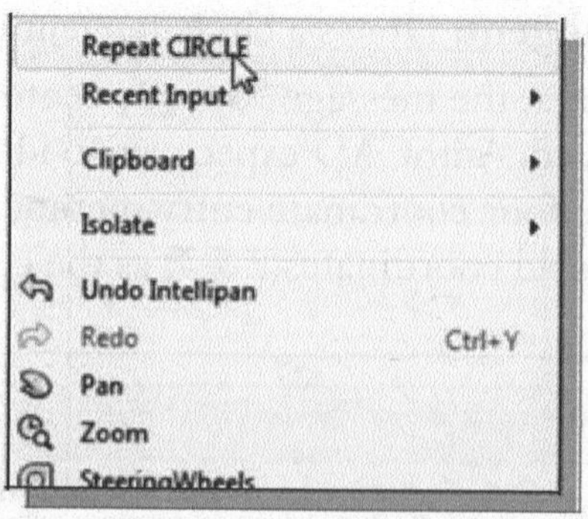

Fig.8.48: Repeat the Circle Command

12. In the command prompt area, the message "Specify Radius of circle: <2.50>" is displayed. The default option for the Circle command in AutoCAD is to specify the radius and the last radius used is also displayed in brackets.

13. Inside the graphics window, right-mouse-click to bring up the popup option menu and select Diameter as shown.
14. In the command prompt area, enter 1.5 as the diameter. Specify Diameter of circle<2.50>: 1.5[ENTER]

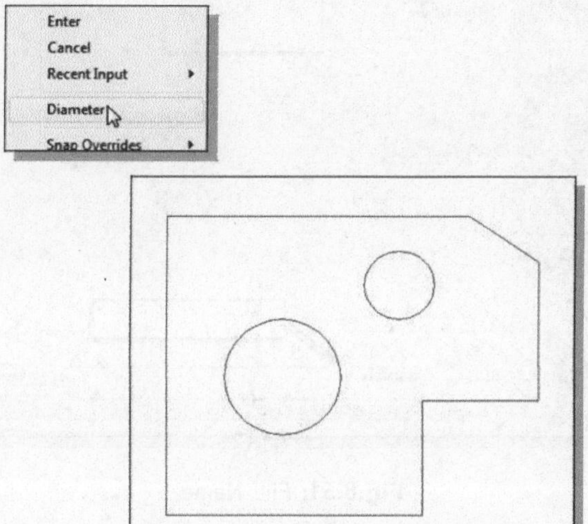

Fig.8.49: Command prompt area for specify diameter of Circle

Saving the CAD Design

1. In the Application Menu, select: [Application] □ [Save]
2. Note the command can also be activated with the quick-key combination of [Ctrl]+[S].

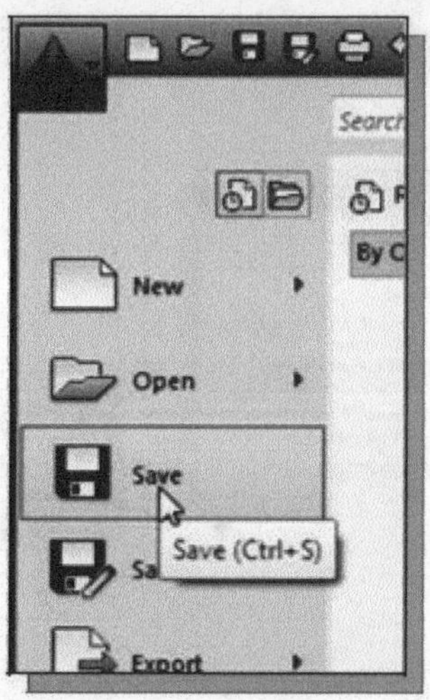

Fig.8.50: Save the CAD design

3. In the Save Drawing as dialog box, select the folder in which you want to store the CAD file and enter Guide Plate in the File name box.

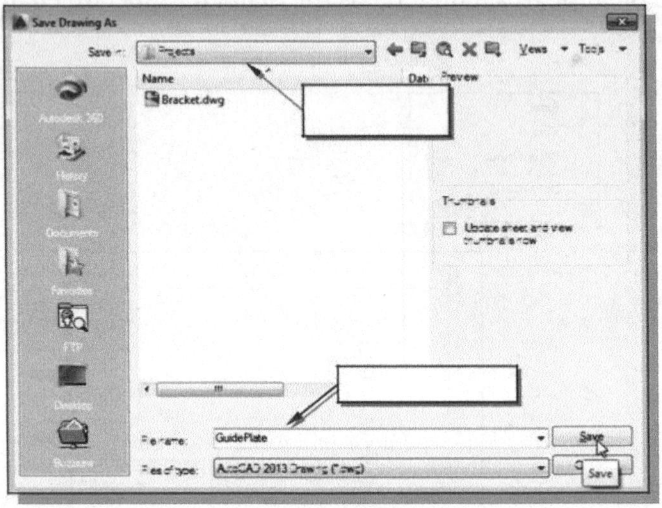

Fig.8.51: File Name

4. Click Save in the Save Drawing As dialog box to accept the selections and save the file. Note the default file type is DWG, which is the standard AutoCAD drawing format.

Close The Current Drawing

Several options are available to close the current drawing:

1. Select [Close]□[Current Drawing] in the Application Menu Bars Shown.
2. Enter Close at the command prompt.
3. The third option is to click on the [Close] icon located at the upper-right-hand corner of the drawing window.

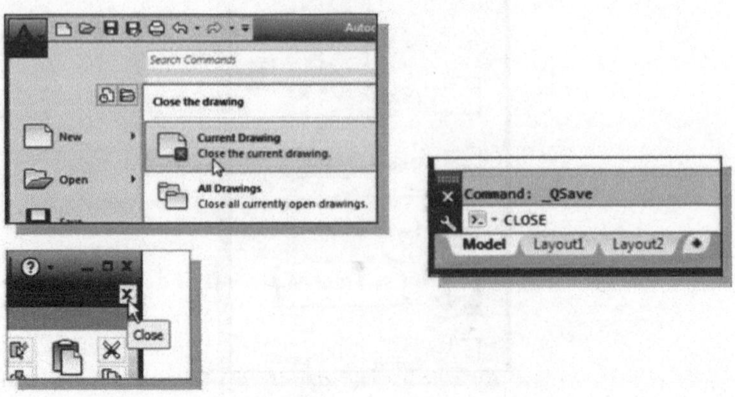

Fig.8.52: Close the current drawing

The Special Design

Example: To create the drawing shown in Fig.8.53 using more of AutoCAD's drawing tools.

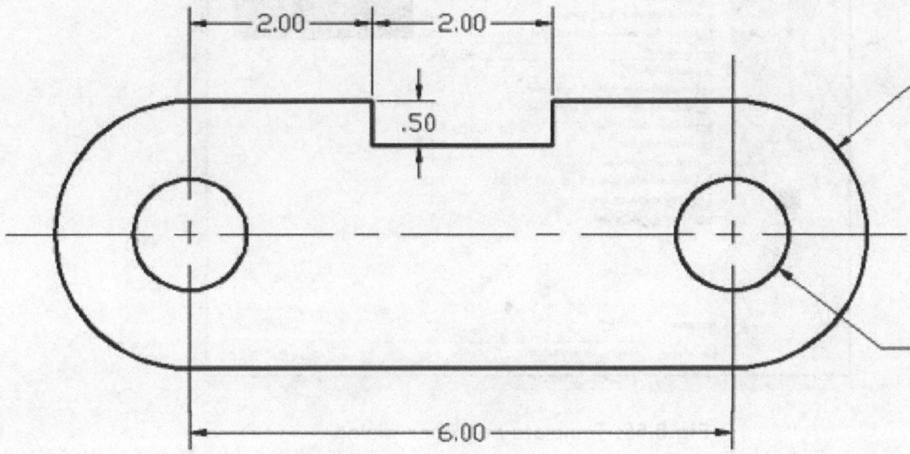

Fig.8.53: Drawing shows more command of AutoCAD's Tools

Start New Design

1. In the Application Menu, select [New] to start a new drawing.

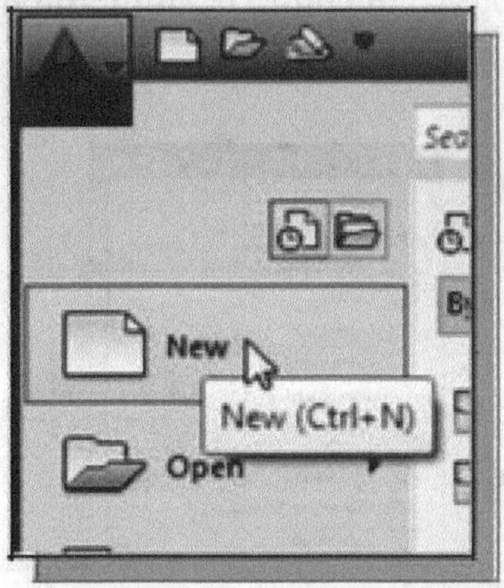

Fig.8.54: Selection of New Drawing

2. The Select Template dialog box appears on the screen. Click Open to accept the default acad.dwt as the template to open.

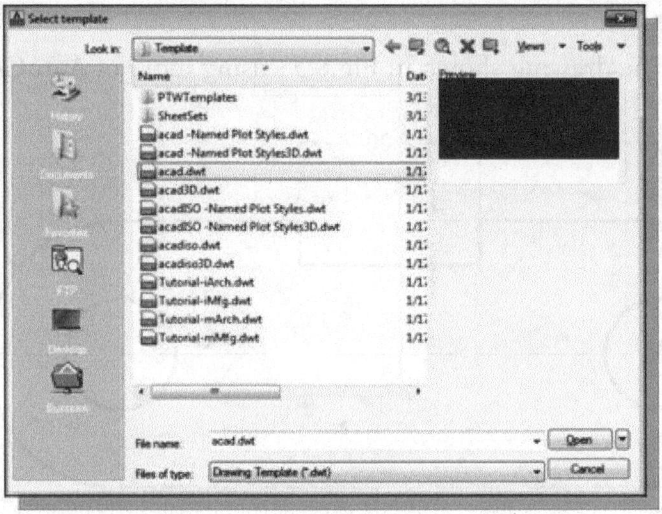

Fig.8.55: Template box open dialog

- The dwt file type is the AutoCAD template file format. An AutoCAD template file contains pre-defined settings to reduce the amount of tedious repetitions.

Drawing Units Setup

- Every object constructed in a CAD system is measured in units. Determine the system of units within the CAD system before creating the first geometric entities.

1. In the Menu Bar select: [Format] □ [Units]

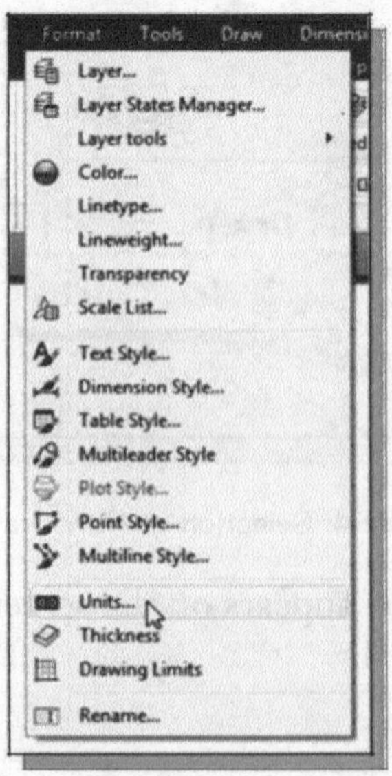

Fig.8.56: Selection of drawing units

- The AutoCAD Menu Bar contains multiple pull-down menus where all of the AutoCAD commands can be accessed.

2. Click on the Length Type option to display the different types of length units available. Confirm the Length Type is set to Decimal.

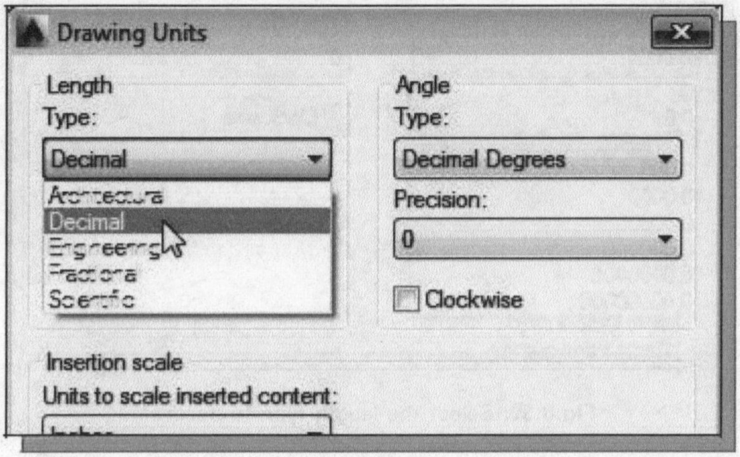

Fig.8.57: Different types of length units

3. Examine and check the other settings that are available in the pull down menu and tool box.

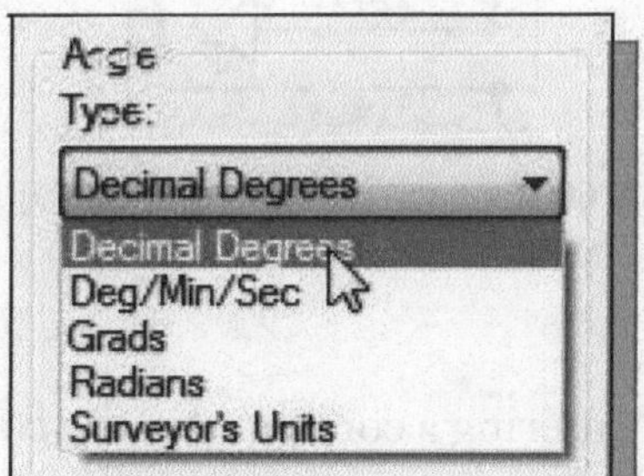

Fig.8.58: Setting of the tool box

4. In the Drawing Units dialog box, set the Length Type to Decimal. This will set the measurement to the default English units, inches.

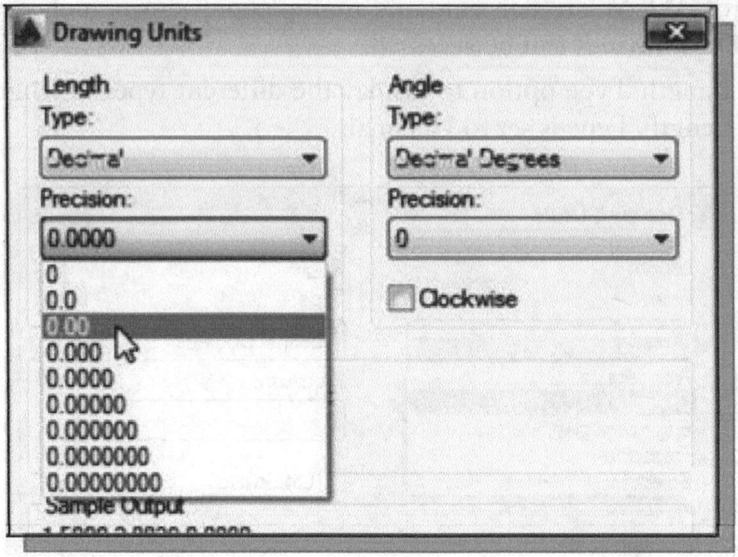

Fig.8.59: Select the length type to decimal

5. Set the Precision to two digits after the decimal point as shown in the above figure.
6. Click OK to exit the Drawing Units dialog box.

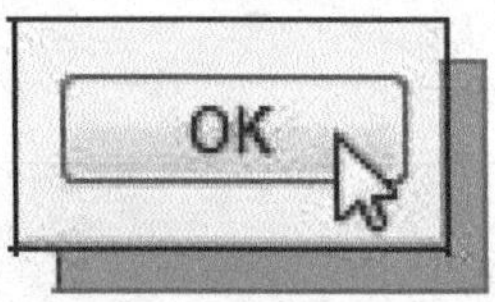

Fig.8.60: Exit the drawing unit dialog box

Drawing Area Setup

- The Drawing Limits by entering a command in the command prompt area. Setting the Drawing Limits controls the extents of the display of the grid. It also serves as a visual reference that marks the working area. It can also be used to prevent construction outside the grid limits and as a plot option that defines an area to be plotted/printed. Note that this setting does not limit the region for geometry construction.
- In the Menu Bar select: [Format] □ [Drawing Limits]

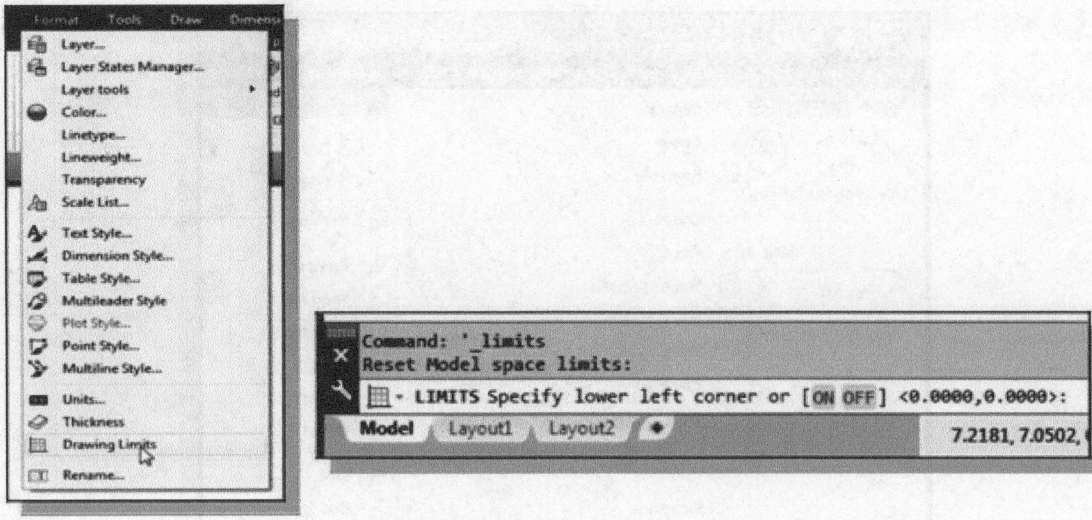

Fig.8.61: Selection of drawing limits

1. In the command prompt area, the message "Reset Model Space Limits: Specify lower left corner or [On/Off] <0.00,0.00>:" is displayed. Press the ENTER key once to accept the default coordinates <0.00,0.00>.
2. In the command prompt area, the message "Specify upper right corner<12.00,9.00>:" is displayed. Press the ENTER key again to accept the default coordinates <12.00,9.00>.

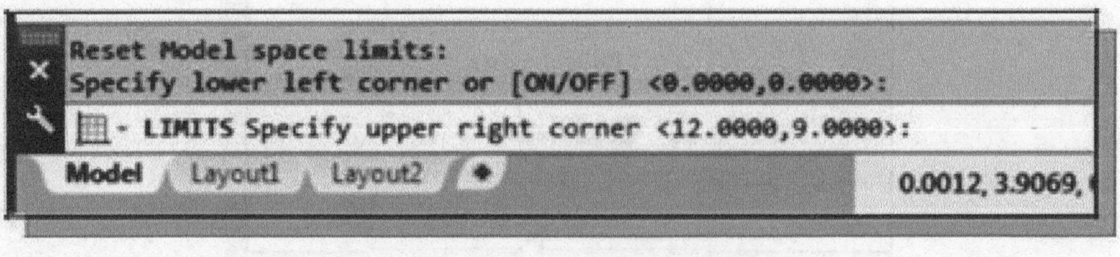

Fig.8.62: Reset model space limit

3. Now, move the graphics cursor near the upper-right corner inside the drawing area and note that the drawing area is unchanged. (The Drawing Limits command is used to set the drawing area, but the display will not be adjusted until a display command is used.)
4. Inside the Menu Bar area select:[View] □ [Zoom] □ [All]
   - The Zoom All command will adjust the display so that all objects in the drawing are displayed to be as large as possible. If no objects are constructed, the Drawing Limits are used to adjust the current viewport.
5. Move the graphics cursor near the upper-right corner inside the drawing area, and note that the display area is updated.

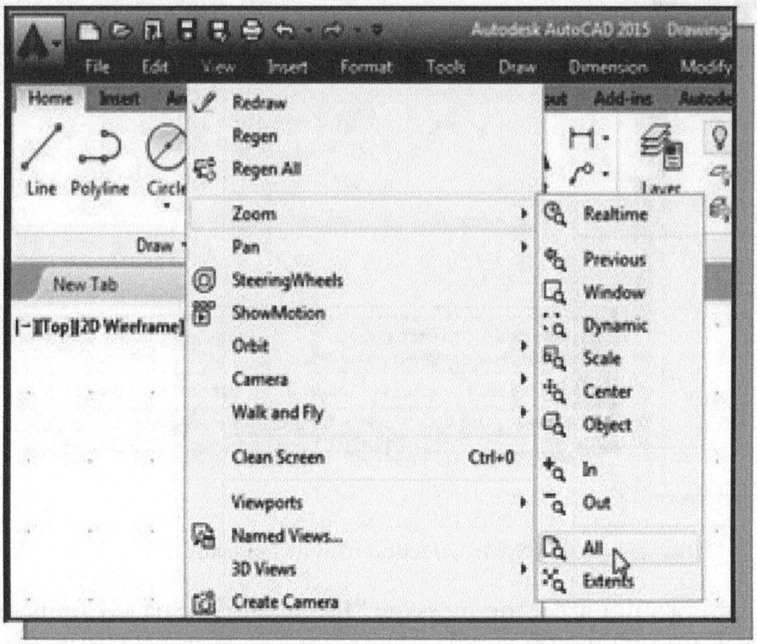

Fig.8.63: From menu bar view, zoom all

6. In the Status bar area, right-mouse-click on Snap Mode and choose[Snap Settings].

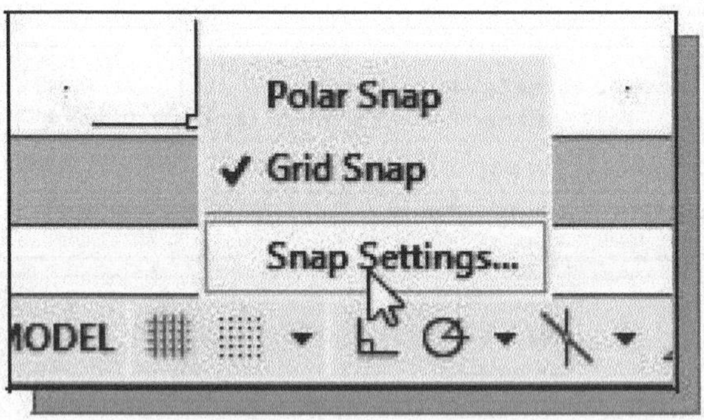

Fig.8.64: Snap Setting

7. In the Drafting Settings dialog box, switch on the Snap and Grid options.

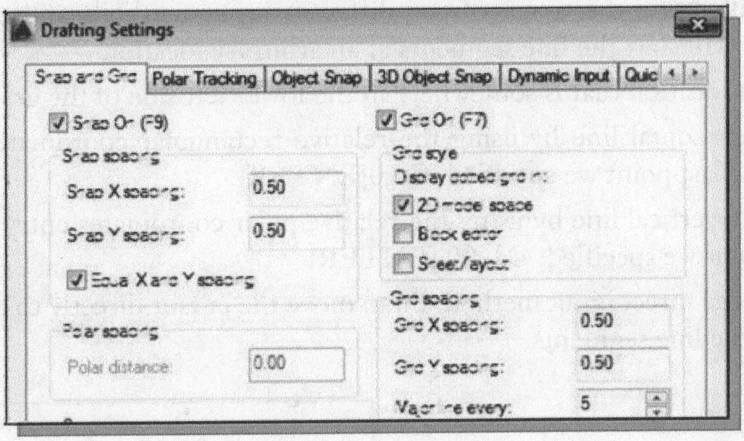

Fig.8.65: Drawing Setting

- EXIT the Drafting Settings dialog box and reset the status buttons so that only GRID DISPLAY and SNAP MODE are turned ON as shown.

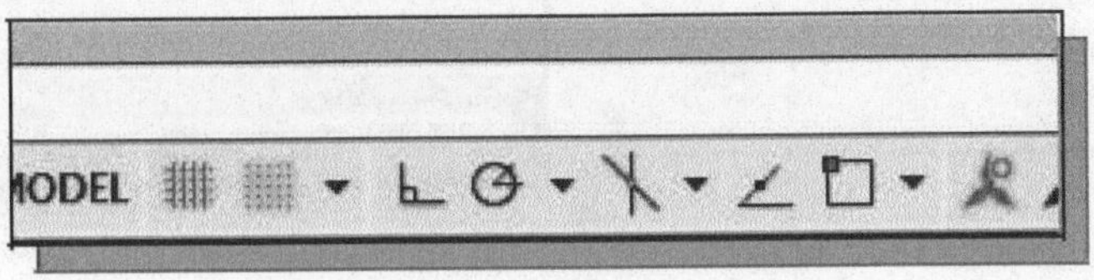

Fig.8.66: Exit the Drawing Setting

Using the Line Command

1. Select the Line command icon in the Draw toolbar. In the command prompt area, near the bottom of the AutoCAD graphics window, the message "_line Specify first point:" is displayed. AutoCAD from the user to identify the starting location of a straight line.

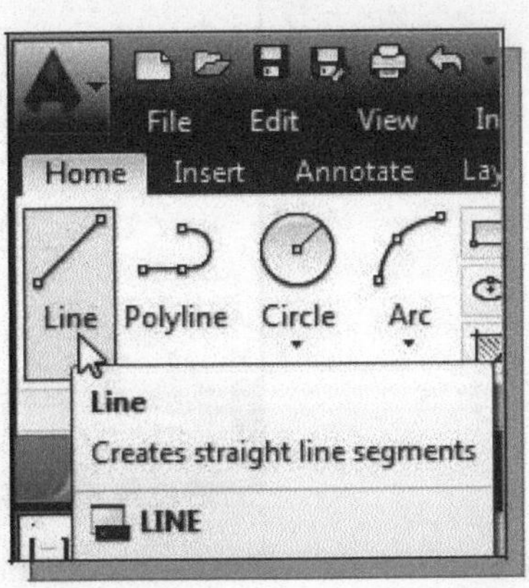

Fig.8.67: Selection of Line Command

2. To further illustrate the usage of the different input methods and tools available in AutoCAD, it will start the line segments at an arbitrary location.
   - Start at a location that is somewhere in the lower left side of the graphics window.
3. It create a horizontal line by using the relative rectangular coordinates entry method, relative to the last point we specified: @6,0[ENTER]
4. Next, create a vertical line by using the relative polar coordinates entry method, relative to the last point we specified: @3<90 [ENTER]
5. Next, it uses the direct input method. First, move the cursor directly to the left of the last endpoint of the line segments.

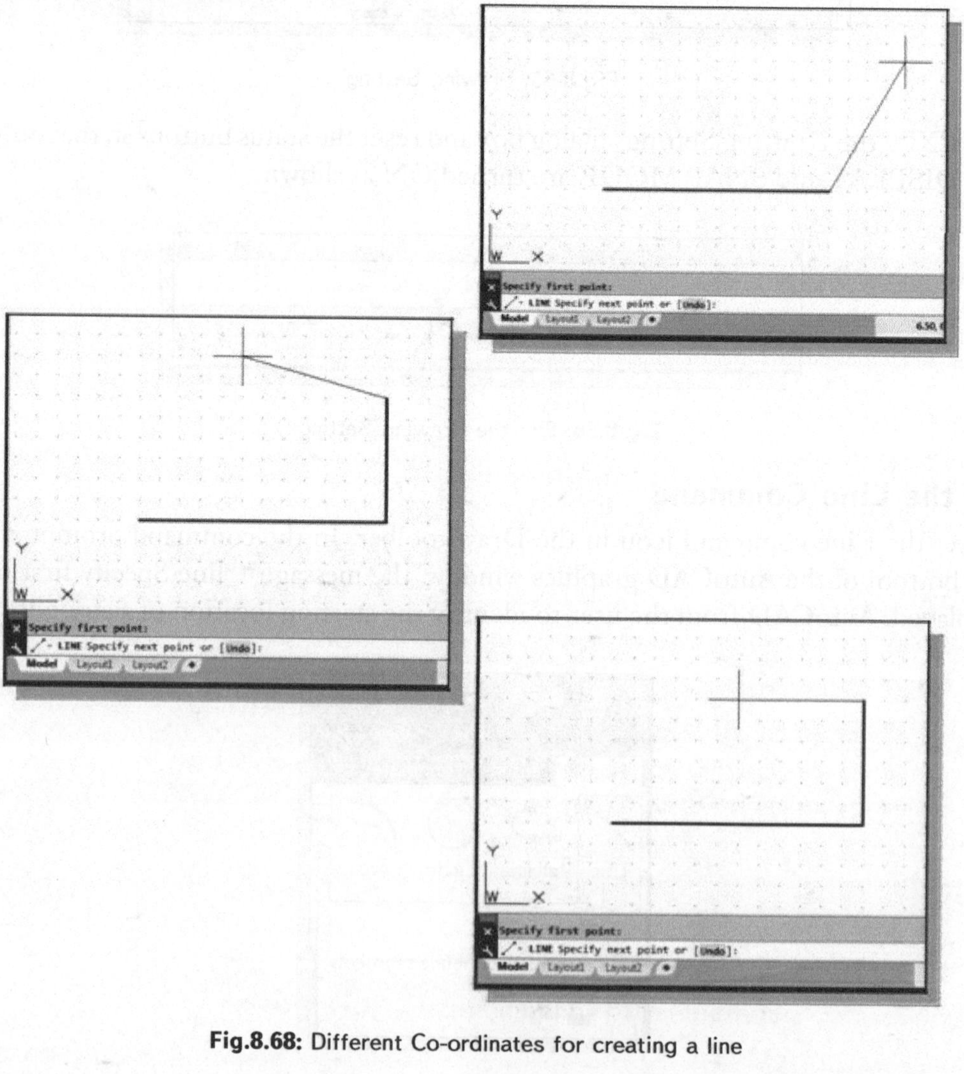

Fig.8.68: Different Co-ordinates for creating a line

6. Use the direct distance entry technique by entering2 [ENTER].

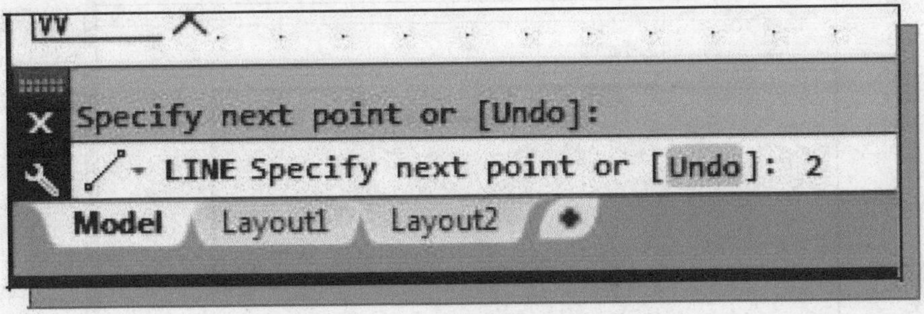

Fig.8.69: Specify next point for line

7. Repeat the above steps and create the four additional line segments, using the dimensions as shown.

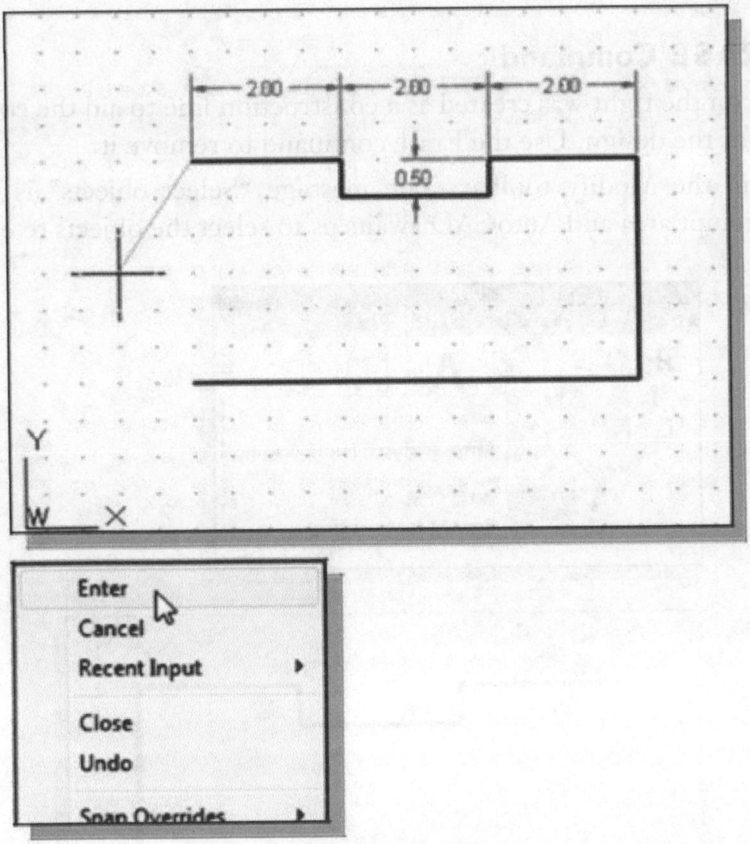

Fig.8.70: Repeat steps for line segments

8. To end the line command, either press the [Enter] key on the keyboard or use the Enter option, right-mouse-click and a popup menu appears on the screen.
9. Select Enter with the left-mouse-button to end the Line command.

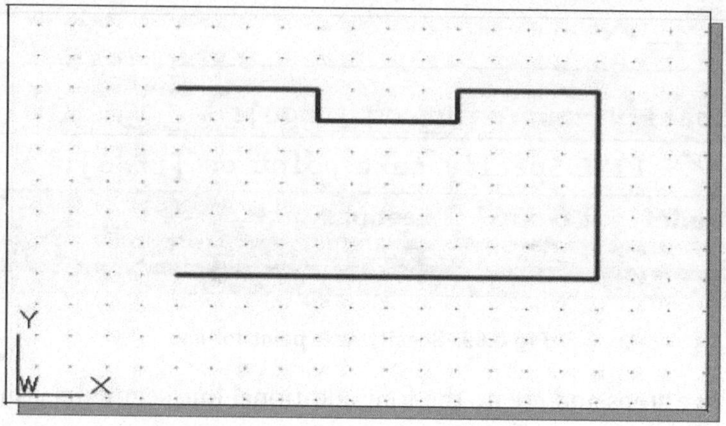

Fig.8.71: End of Line Command

Using the ERASE Command

The vertical line on the right was created as a construction line to aid the construction of the rest of the lines for the design. Use the Erase command to remove it.

1. Pick Erase in the Modify toolbar. The message "Select objects" is displayed in the command prompt area and AutoCAD awaits us to select the objects to erase.

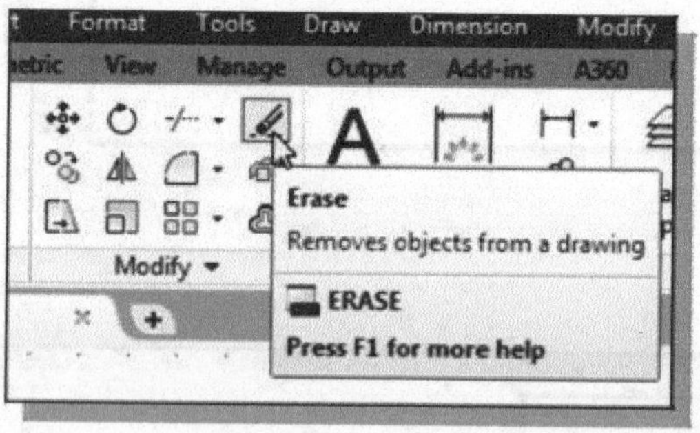

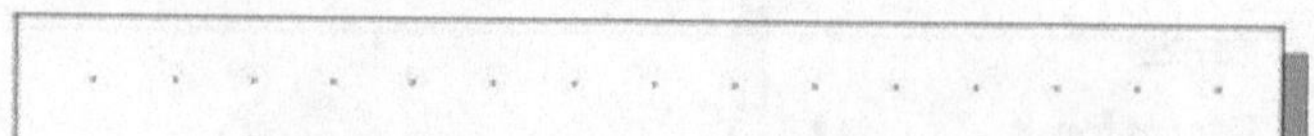

Fig.8.72: Selection of Erase Command

2. Select the vertical line as shown.
3. Click once with the right-mouse-button to accept the selection and delete the line.

Using the ARC Command

1. Click the down-arrow icon of the Arc command in the Draw toolbar to display the different Arc construction options.
   - AutoCAD provides eleven different ways to create arcs. Note that the different options are used based on the geometry conditions of the design. The more commonly used options are the 3-Points option and the Center-Start-End option.

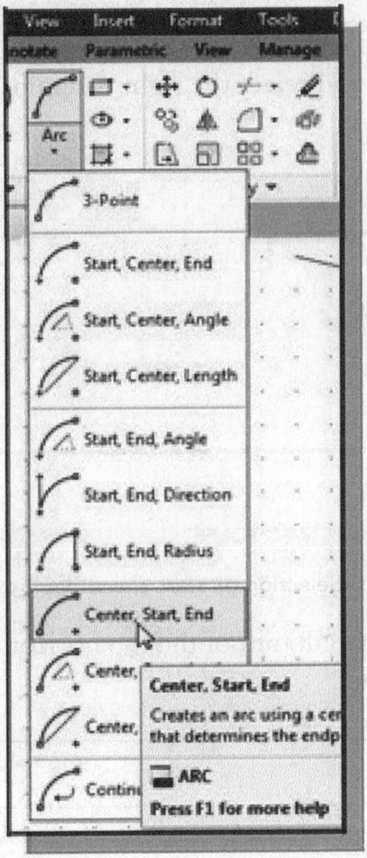

Fig.8.73: Selection of Arc Command

2. Select the Center-Start-End option. This option requires the selection of the center point, start point and end point location, in that order, of the arc.
3. Move the cursor to the middle of the two horizontal lines and align the cursor to the two endpoints as shown. Click once with the right-mouse-button to select the location as the center point of the new arc.

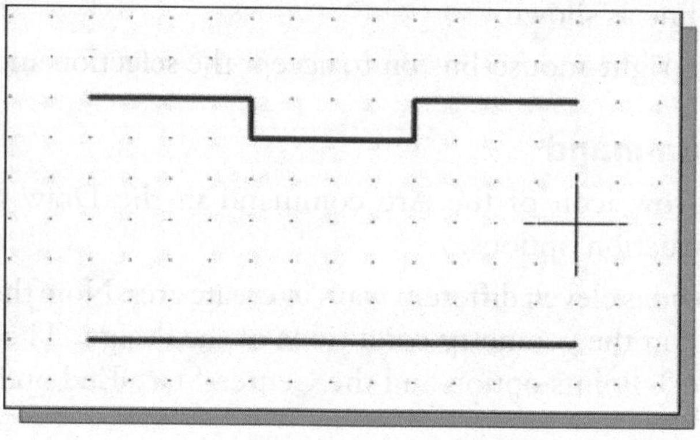

Fig.8.74: Select the location for the center point of New Arc

4. Move the cursor downward and select the right endpoint of the bottom horizontal line as the start point of the arc.

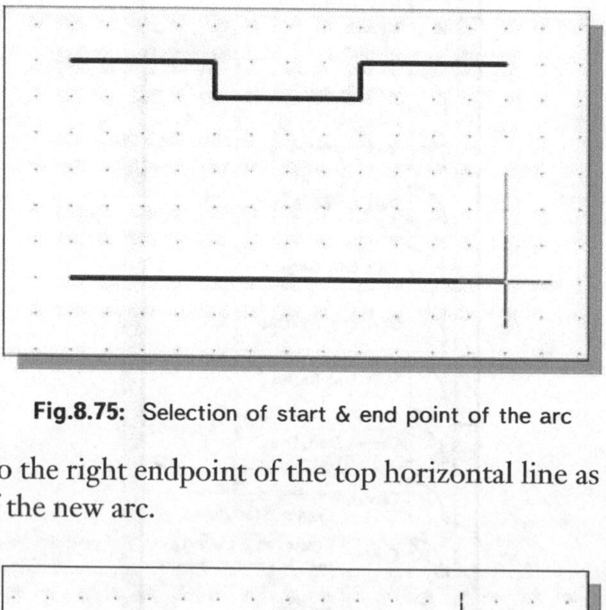

Fig.8.75: Selection of start & end point of the arc

5. Move the cursor to the right endpoint of the top horizontal line as shown. Pick this point as the endpoint of the new arc.

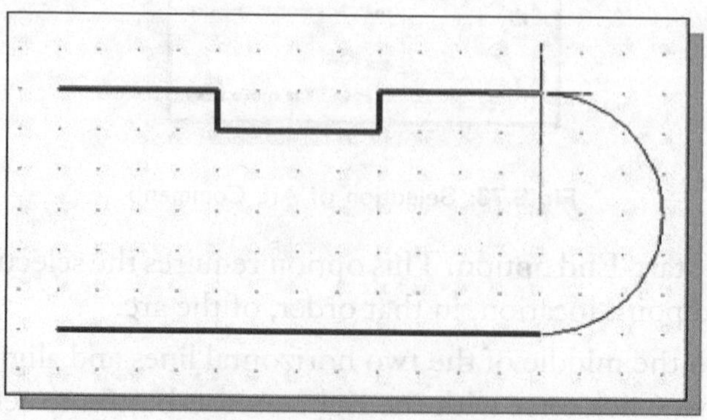

Fig.8.76: Arc is Constructed

6. Repeat the above steps and create the other arc. Note that in most CAD packages, positive angles are defined as going counterclockwise; therefore, the starting point of the second arc should be at the endpoint on top.

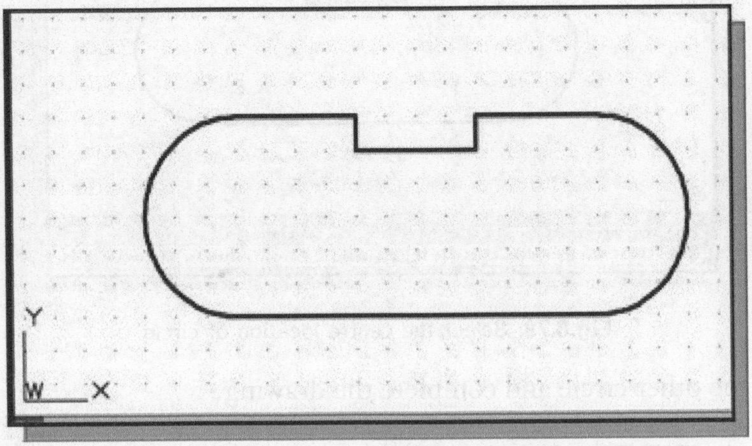

Fig.8.77: Repeat of Arc Command

Using the CIRCLE COMMAND

1. Select the [Circle]□[Center, Diameter] option.

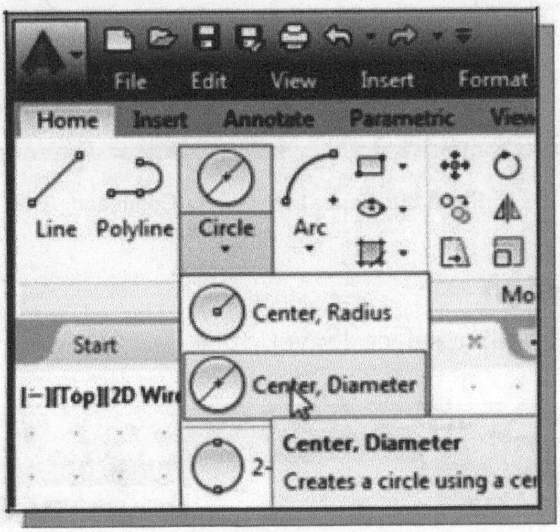

Fig.8.78: Selection of Circle Command

2. Select the same location for the arc center as the center point for the new circle.
3. In the command prompt area, the message "Specify diameter of circle:" is displayed. Specify diameter of circle: 1.25[ENTER]

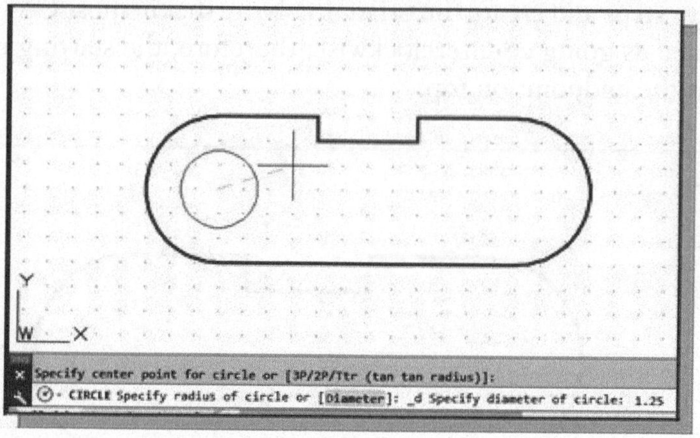

Fig.8.79: Select the centre location of circle

4. Now, create the other circle and complete the drawing.

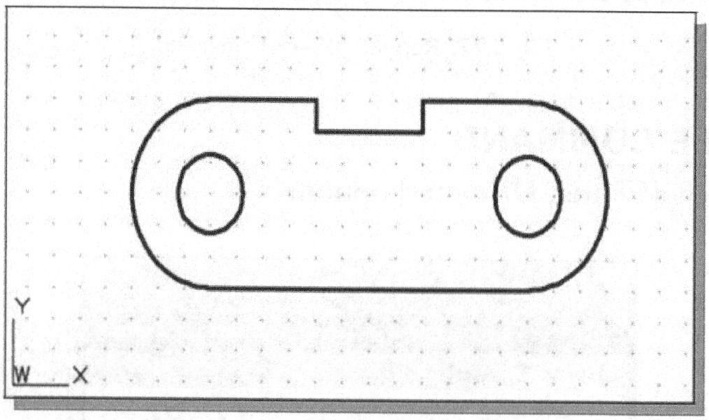

Fig.8.80: Repeat the Circle Command

Saving the CAD Design

1. In the Quick Access Toolbar, select: [Save]

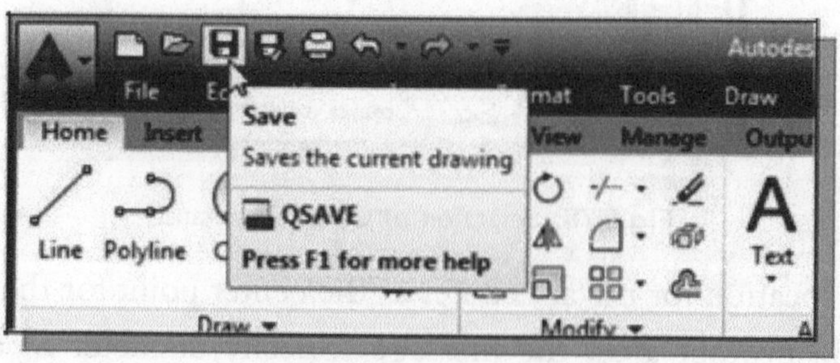

Fig.8.81: Save the drawing

2. Note the command can also be activated with the quick-key combination of [Ctrl]+[S].

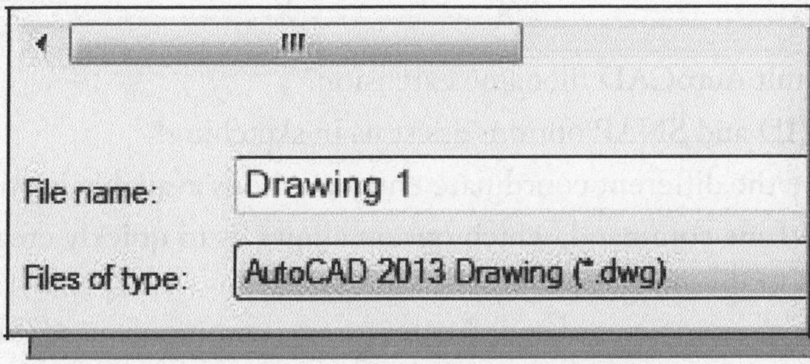

Fig.8.82: Quick Key Command for Saving

3. In the Save Drawing As dialog box, select the folder in which user want to store the CAD file and enter Drawing I (File name) in the File name box.
   - Click Save in the Save Drawing As dialog box to accept the selections and save the file. Note the default file type is DWG, which is the standard AutoCAD drawing format.

Exit Auto-CAD

- To exit AutoCAD, select Exit AutoCAD in the Menu Bar or type QUIT at the command prompt. Note the command can also be activated with the quick-key combination of [Ctrl]+[Q].

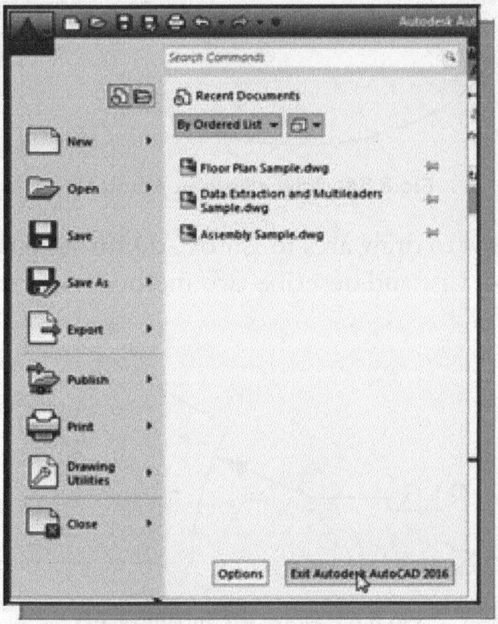

Fig.8.83: Exit Auto-CAD

General Questions

1. What are the advantages and disadvantages of using CAD systems to create engineering drawings?
2. What is the default AutoCAD filename extension?
3. How do the GRID and SNAP options assist us in sketching?
4. List and describe the different coordinate entry methods available in AutoCAD.
5. When using the Line command, which option allows us to quickly create a line-segment connecting back to the starting point?
6. List and describe the two types of coordinate systems commonly used for planar geometry.
7. Which key do you use to quickly cancel a command?
8. When you use the Pan command, do the coordinates of objects get changed?
9. Find information on how to draw ellipses in AutoCAD through the Autodesk Exchange, and create the following arc. If it is desired to position the center of the ellipse to a specific location, which ellipse command is more suitable?

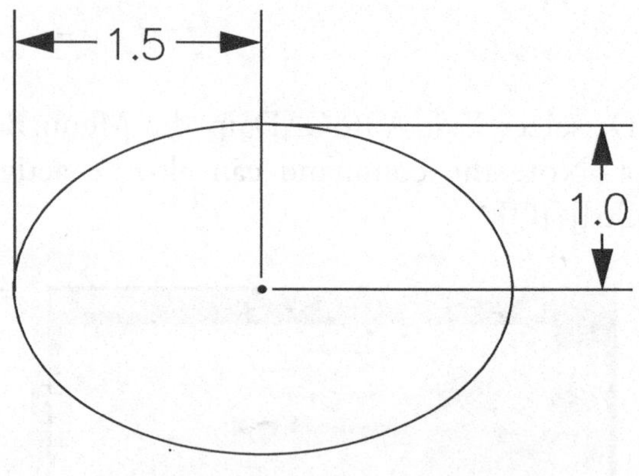

Fig.8.84: Draw ellipse in AutoCAD

10. Find information on how to draw arcs in AutoCAD through the Autodesk Exchange and create the following arc. List and describe two methods to create arcs in AutoCAD.

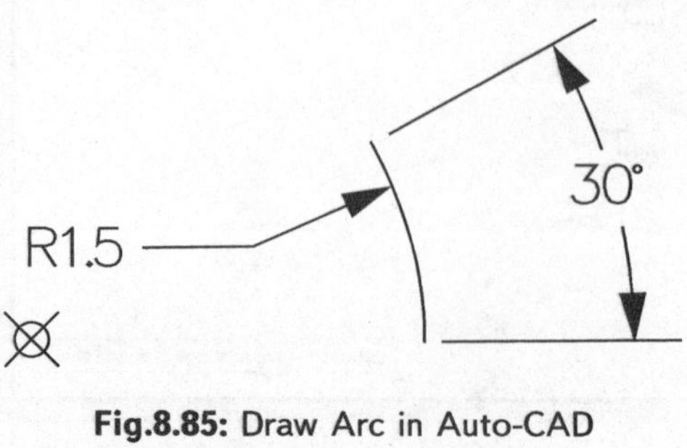

Fig.8.85: Draw Arc in Auto-CAD

Exercises: Make the drawings as mentioned blow in figures 8.86 to 8.89 using AUTOCAD SOFTWARE.

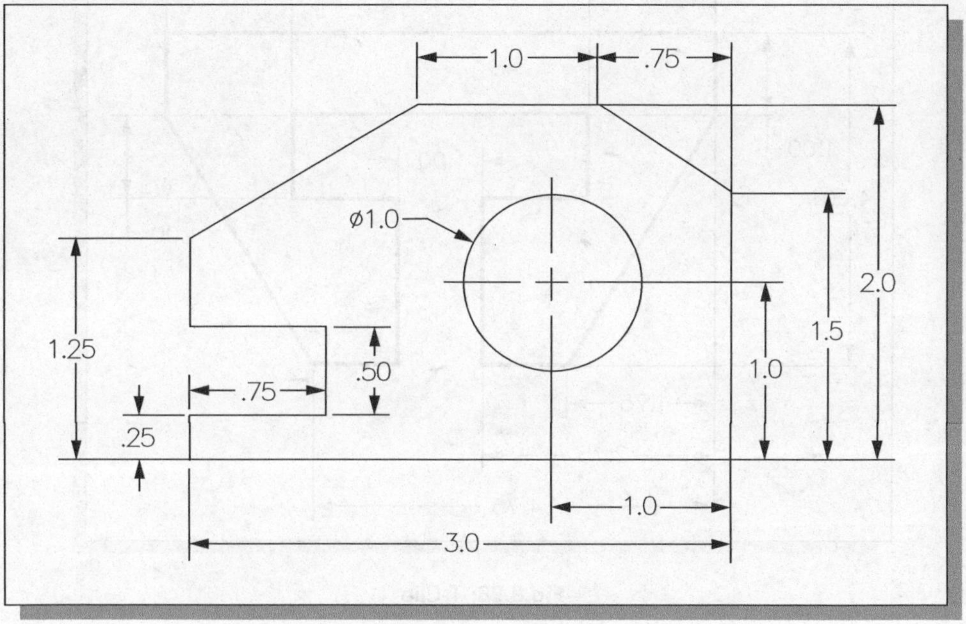

Fig.8.86: Angle Spacer

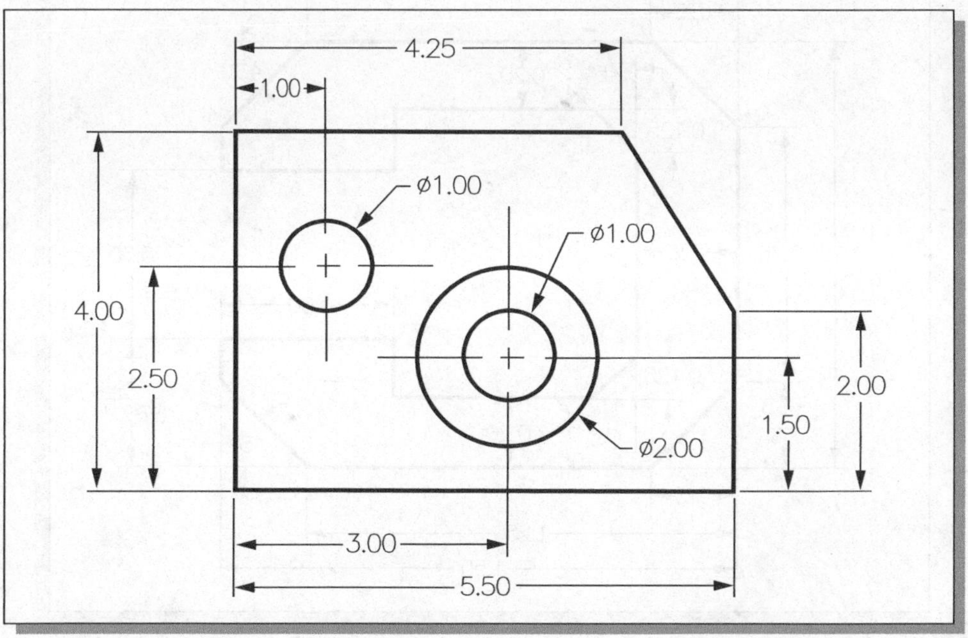

Fig.8.87: Base Plate

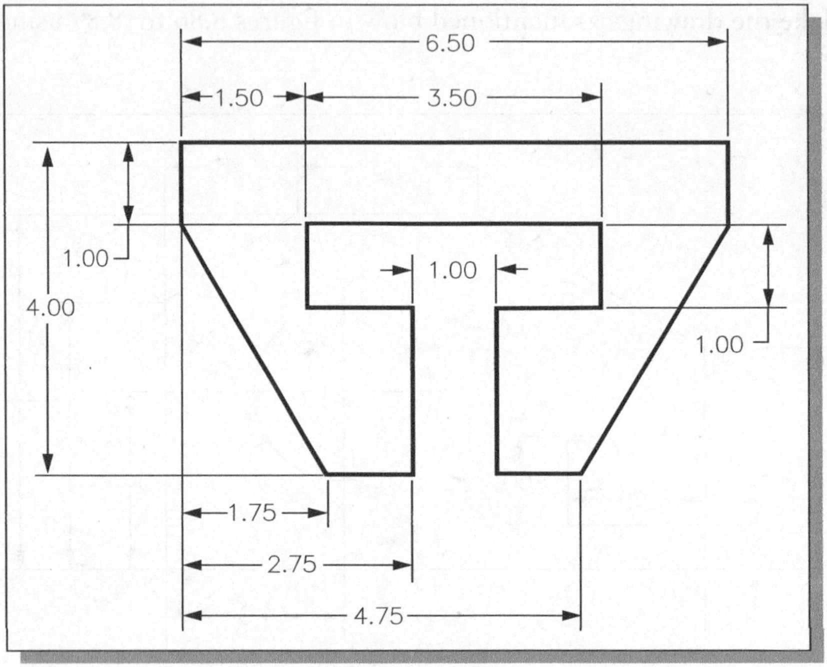

Fig.8.88: T-Clip

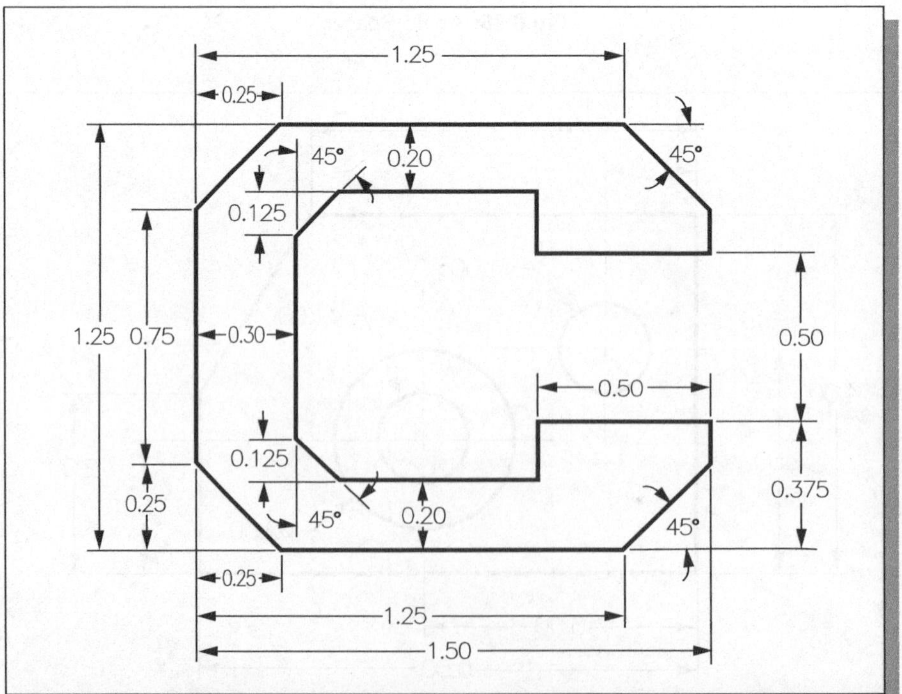

Fig.8.89: Channel Plate

8.2 SOLID WORK

SolidWorks is a solid modeling computer-aided design (CAD) and computer-aided engineering (CAE) computer program.

Scope

SolidWorks is a solid modeler, and utilizes a parametric feature-based approach to create models and assemblies. Parameters can be either numeric parameters, such as line lengths or circle diameters, or geometric parameters, such as tangent, parallel, concentric, horizontal or vertical, etc. Numeric parameters can be associated with each other through the use of relations, which allows them to capture design intent.

Design intent is how the creator of the part wants it to respond to changes and updates. For example, you would want the hole at the top of a beverage can to stay at the top surface, regardless of the height or size of the can. SolidWorks allows the user to specify that the hole is a feature on the top surface, and will then honor their design intent no matter what height distance later assign to the can.

Features refer to the building blocks of the part. They are the shapes and operations that construct the part. Shape-based features typically begin with a 2D or 3D sketch of shapes such as bosses, holes, slots, etc. This shape is then extruded or cut to add or remove material from the part. Operation-based features are not sketch-based, and include features such as fillets, chamfers, shells, applying draft to the faces of a part, etc.

In an assembly, the analog to sketch relations are mates. Just as sketch relations define conditions such as tangency, parallelism, and concentricity with respect to sketch geometry, *assembly mates* define equivalent relations with respect to the individual parts or components, allowing the easy construction of assemblies. SolidWorks also includes additional advanced mating features such as gear and cam follower mates, which allow modeled gear assemblies to accurately reproduce the rotational movement of an actual gear train. Finally, drawings can be created either from parts or assemblies. Views are automatically generated from the solid model, and notes, dimensions and tolerances can then be easily added to the drawing as needed. The drawing module includes most paper sizes and standards (ANSI, ISO, DIN, GOST, JIS, BSI and SAC).

8.3 CATIA

CATIA is a **computer aided three-dimensional interactive application** multi-platform software suite for Computer-Aided Design (CAD), Computer-Aided Manufacturing (CAM), Computer-Aided Engineering (CAE), Product Lifecyle Management (PLM) and 3D (3 Dimensional).

Scope of application

Commonly referred to as a 3D Product Lifecycle Management software suite, CATIA supports multiple stages of product development, including conceptualization, design (CAD), engineering (CAE) and manufacturing (CAM). CATIA facilitates collaborative engineering across disciplines around platform, including surfacing & shape design, electrical, fluid and electronic systems design, mechanical engineering and systems engineering.

Mechanical engineering

CATIA enables the creation of 3D parts, from 3D sketches, sheetmetal, composites, molded, forged or tooling parts up to the definition of mechanical assemblies. The software provides advanced technologies for mechanical surfacing & BIW. It provides tools to complete product definition, including functional tolerances as well as kinematics definition. CATIA provides a wide range of applications for tooling design, for both generic tooling and mold & die.

Design

CATIA offers a solution to shape design, styling, surfacing workflow and visualization to create, modify, and validate complex innovative shapes from industrial design to Class-A surfacing with the ICEM surfacing technologies. CATIA supports multiple stages of product design whether started from scratch or from 2D sketches.

Systems engineering

CATIA uses the open Modelica language in both CATIA Dynamic Behavior Modeling and Dymola, to quickly and easily model and simulate the behavior of complex systems that span multiple engineering disciplines.

Electrical systems

CATIA v5 offers a solution to facilitate the design and manufacturing of electrical systems spanning the complete process from conceptual design through to manufacturing. Capabilities include requirements capture, electrical schematic definition, interactive 3D routing of both wire harnesses and industrial cable solutions through to the production of detailed manufacturing documents including formboards.

Fluid systems

CATIA offers a solution to facilitate the design and manufacturing of routed systems including tubing, piping, Heating, Ventilating & Air Conditioning (HVAC). Capabilities include requirements capture, 2D diagrams for defining hydraulic, pneumatic and HVAC systems, as well as Piping and Instrumentation Diagram (P&ID). Powerful capabilities are provided that enables these 2D diagrams to be used to drive the interactive 3D routing and placing of system components, in the context of the digital mockup of the complete product or process plant, through to the delivery of manufacturing information including reports and piping isometric drawings.

Industries

CATIA can be applied to a wide variety of industries, from aerospace and defense, automotive, and industrial equipment, to high tech, shipbuilding, consumer goods, plant design, consumer packaged goods, life sciences, architecture and construction, process power and petroleum, and services.

8.4 PTC CREO OR PROE

PTC Creo, formerly known as **Pro/ENGINEER**, is a 3D CAD/CAM/CAE feature-based, associative solid modeling software. It is one of a suite of applications that provide solid modeling, assembly modelling, 2D orthographic views, finite element analysis, direct and parametric modelling, sub-divisional and NURBS surfacing, and NC and tooling functionality for mechanical designers.

Scope

Creo Elements/Pro PTC's parametric, integrated 3D CAD/CAM/CAE solution, is used by discrete manufacturers for mechanical engineering, design and manufacturing.

Creo Elements/Pro can be used to create a complete 3D digital model of manufactured goods. The models consist of 2D and 3D solid model data which can also be used downstream in finite element analysis, rapid prototyping, tooling design, and CNC manufacturing. All data are associative and interchangeable between the CAD, CAE *and CAM modules without* conversion. A product and its entire bill of materials (BOM) can be modeled accurately with fully associative engineering drawings, and revision control information. The associativity functionality in Creo Elements/Pro enables users to make changes in the design at any time during the product development process and automatically update downstream deliverables. This capability enables concurrent engineering – design, analysis and manufacturing engineers working in parallel – and streamlines product development processes.

Creo Elements/Pro is a parametric, feature-based modeling architecture incorporated into a single database philosophy with advanced rule-based design capabilities. It provides in-depth control of complex geometry, as exemplified by the trajpar parameter. The capabilities of the product can be split into the three main headings of Engineering Design, Analysis and Manufacturing.

Product Design

It offers a range of tools to enable the generation of a complete digital representation of the product being designed. In addition to the general geometry tools there is also the ability to generate geometry of other integrated design disciplines such as industrial and standard pipe work and complete wiring definitions. A number of concept design tools that provide up-front Industrial Design concepts can then be used in the downstream process of engineering the product. These range from conceptual Industrial design sketches, reverse engineering with point cloud data and comprehensive free-form surface.

Analysis

Creo Elements/Pro has numerous analysis tools available and covers thermal, static, dynamic and fatigue finite element analysis along with other tools all designed to help with the development of the product. These tools include human factors, manufacturing tolerance, mould flow and design optimization. The design optimization can be used at a geometry level to obtain the optimum design dimensions and in conjunction with the finite element analysis.

Surface Modeling

Creo has good surface modeling capabilities also. Using commands like Boundary blend and Sweep we can create surface models

Manufacturing

Creo is a family or suite of design software supporting product design for discrete manufacturers. The suite consists of apps, each delivering a distinct set of capabilities for a user role within product development.

8.5 NX CAD

NX for Design is an integrated solution that helps you develop innovative new products. With leading-edge design tools and technologies, NX streamlines and accelerates the product development process. Unlike CAD-only solutions and closed enterprise solutions, NX delivers the highest integration between development disciplines in an open, collaborative environment.

Design Advantages

Fast, Flexible, Efficient Product Design

NX design tools are superior in power, versatility and productivity. You can work faster and more efficiently in the full range of design tasks, from 2D layout through 3D modeling, assembly design, drafting and documentation.

Work Seamlessly with Data from Other CAD Systems

With synchronous technology, NX allows you to directly use models created with other CAD systems. You can import and modify CAD geometry from any source with speed, ease and efficiency. NX is the solution of choice for multi-CAD, collaborative design.

Power and Capacity for Complex Products

NX assembly design tools are ready for the most complex assemblies, even those with thousands of parts. You can create full multi-CAD digital mockups with NX to quickly identify issues and resolve problems.

Integrated Design Validation

To help you fulfill customer and engineering requirements, NX offers integrated, automated design validation capabilities. You can continuously monitor your designs for compliance with company and industry standards, and more easily produce designs that achieve your goals and customer requirements.

Visual Analytics Improve Decision-Making

With NX visual reporting and analytics, you can instantly gather product and process information and visualize its impact in the context of the 3D design. Visual synthesis of PLM data accelerates the design process and improves decision-making.

8.6 ANSYS

It is an American Computer-aided engineering software. Ansys publishes engineering analysis software across a range of disciplines including finite element analysis, structural analysis, computational fluid dynamics, explicit and implicit methods, and heat transfer.

8.6.1 ANSYS Workbench

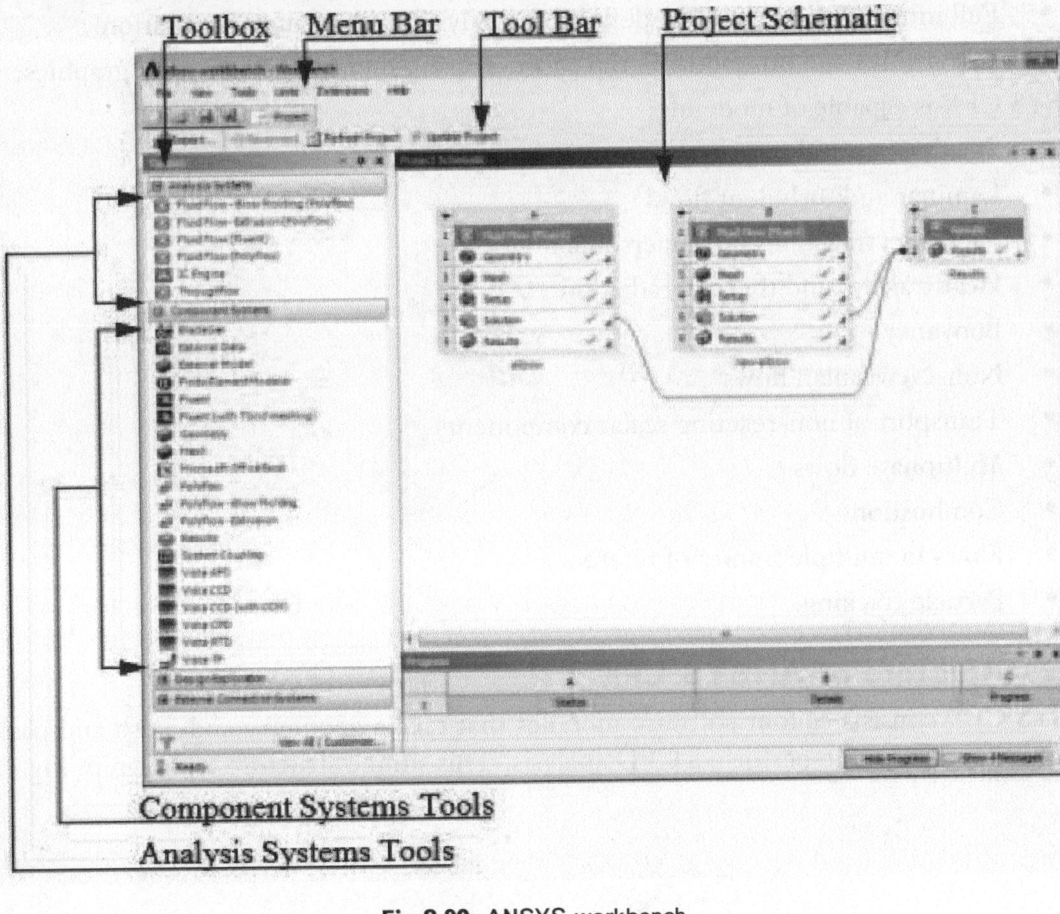

Fig.8.90: ANSYS workbench

8.6.2 Structural Analysis

ANSYS Mechanical is a finite element analysis tool for structural analysis, including linear, nonlinear and dynamic nature of studies. This simulation product provides finite elements to model behavior, and supports material models and equation solvers for a wide range of mechanical design problems. ANSYS Mechanical also includes capabilities for thermal analysis and coupled-physics capabilities involving acoustics, piezoelectric, thermal–structural and thermo-electric analysis.

8.7 FLUID DYNAMICS TOOLS

8.7.1 CFX

ANSYS CFX is a general purpose Computational Fluid Dynamics (CFD) software suite that combines an advanced solver with powerful pre- and post-processing capabilities.

It includes the following features:

- An advanced coupled solver that is both reliable and robust.
- Full integration of problem definition, analysis, and results presentation.
- An intuitive and interactive setup process, using menus and advanced graphics.

ANSYS CFX is capable of modeling:

- Steady-state and transient flows
- Laminar and turbulent flows
- Subsonic, transonic and supersonic flows
- Heat transfer and thermal radiation
- Buoyancy
- Non-Newtonian flows
- Transport of non-reacting scalar components
- Multiphase flows
- Combustion
- Flows in multiple frames of reference
- Particle tracking.

8.7.2 Structure of ANSYS CFX

ANSYS CFX consists of four software modules that take a geometry and mesh and pass the information required to perform a CFD analysis. This simple structure is shown in Fig.8.91.

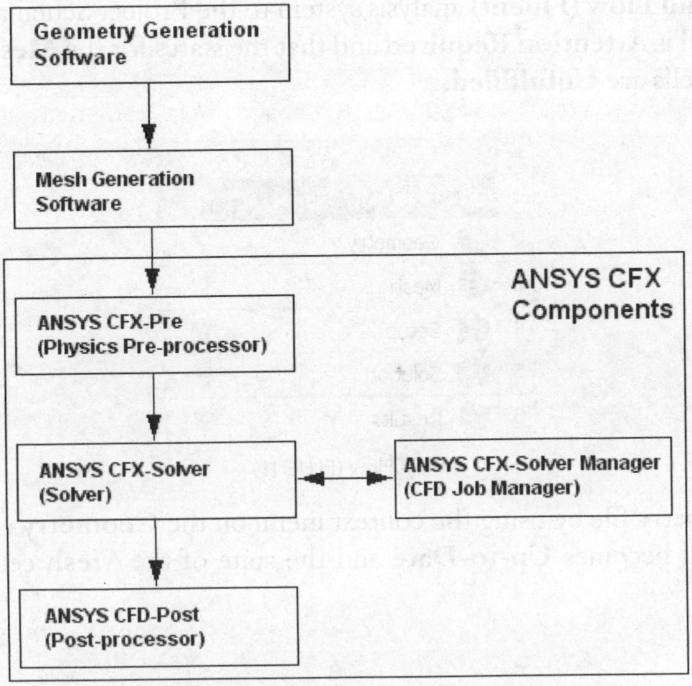

Fig.8.91: Structure of ANSYS CFX

8.7.3 Fluent

ANSYS Fluent is a state-of-the-art computer program for modeling fluid flow, heat transfer, and chemical reactions in complex geometries.

ANSYS Fluent is written in the C computer language and makes full use of the flexibility and power offered by the language. Consequently, true dynamic memory allocation, efficient data structures, and flexible solver control are all possible. In addition, ANSYS Fluent uses a client/server architecture, which enables it to run as separate simultaneous processes on client desktop workstations and powerful compute servers. This architecture allows for efficient execution, interactive control, and complete flexibility between different types of machines or operating systems.

ANSYS Fluent provides complete mesh flexibility, including the ability to solve your flow problems using unstructured meshes that can be generated about complex geometries with relative ease. Supported mesh types include 2D triangular/quadrilateral, 3D tetrahedral/hexahedral/pyramid/wedge/polyhedral, and mixed (hybrid) meshes. ANSYS Fluent also enables you to refine or coarsen your mesh based on the flow solution.

8.7.4 Fluent Analysis in Workbench

This example describes when the files that are generated and used by Fluent are written and how the cell states change as you work with a Fluent-based system in Workbench.

1. Add a new **Fluid Flow (Fluent)** analysis system to the Project Schematic. The state of the **Geometry** cell is **Attention Required** and that the states for the **Mesh, Setup, Solution,** and **Results** cells are **Unfulfilled.**

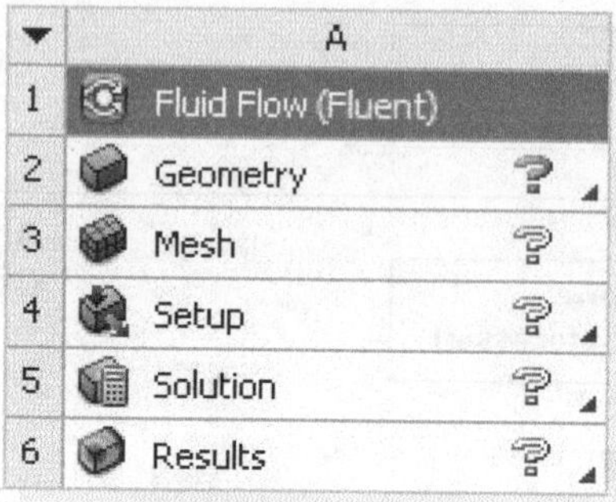

Fluid Flow (FLUENT)

2. Import a geometry file by using the context menu on the **Geometry** cell. The state of the **Geometry** cell becomes **Up-to-Date** and the state of the **Mesh** cell becomes **Refresh Required.**

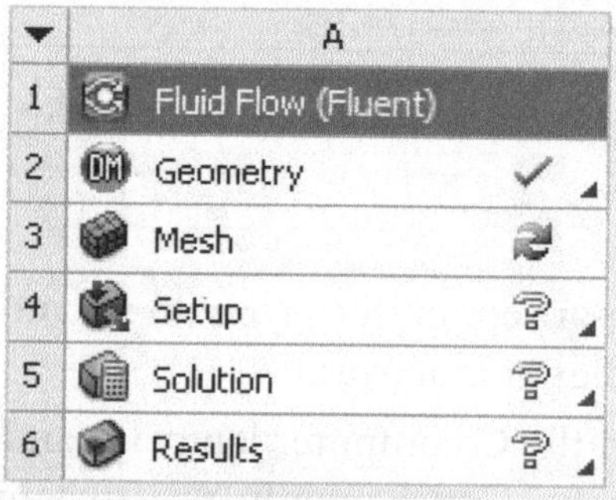

Fluid Flow (FLUENT)

3. Double-click the **Mesh** cell. The ANSYS Meshing application launches and loads the geometry file. The state of the **Mesh** cell becomes **Update Required.**

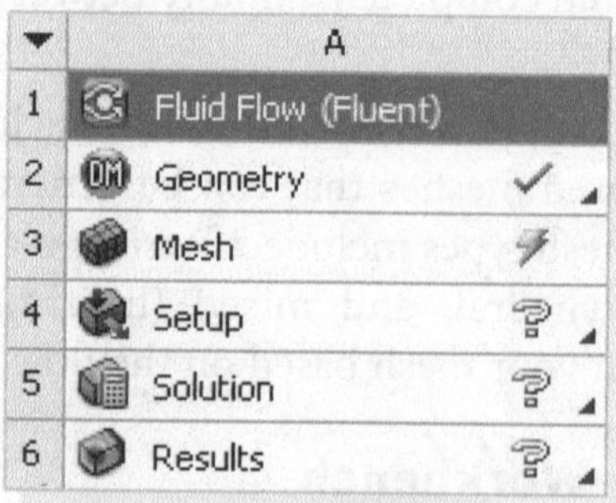

Fluid Flow (FLUENT)

4. In the ANSYS Meshing application, specify settings for the mesh, then select the **Update** command. The mesh is generated, the mesh (.msh) file is written, the state of the **Mesh** cell becomes **Up-to-Date**, and the state of the **Setup** cell becomes **Refresh Required**.

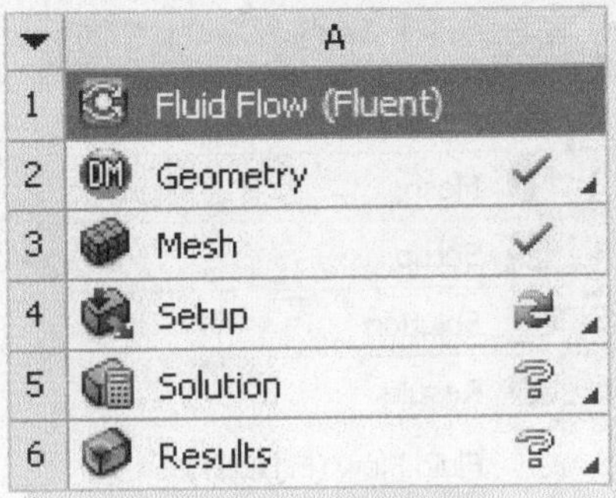

Fluid Flow (FLUENT)

5. Double-click the **Setup** cell. Fluent launches and loads the mesh file. The state of the **Setup** cell becomes **Attention Required**.

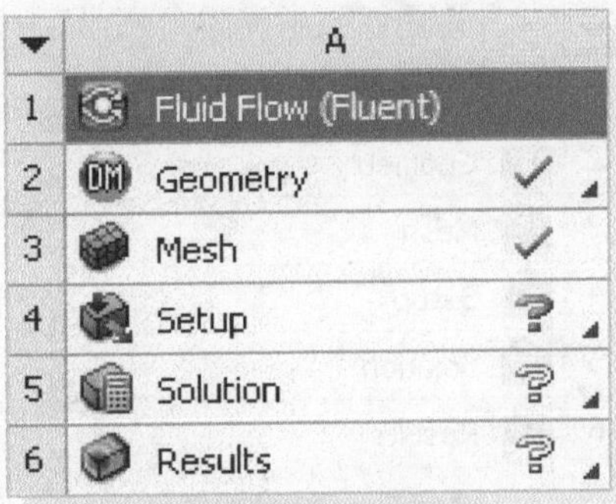

Fluid Flow (FLUENT)

6. In Fluent, specify boundary conditions, initialize the solution, and enter a non-zero number of iterations on the **Run Calculation** task page. The state of the **Setup** cell becomes **Up-to-Date**, and the state of the **Solution** cell becomes **Refresh Required**.

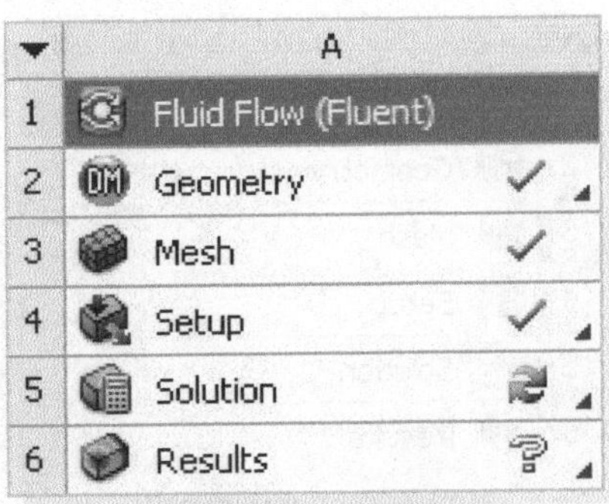

Fluid Flow (FLUENT)

7. In the Fluent application, select the **Calculate** button. The settings (.set) file is written and iterations begin. The state of the **Solution** cell becomes **Update Required**.

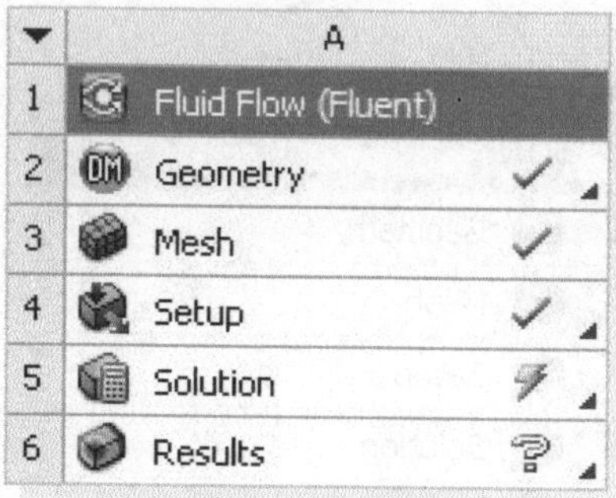

Fluid Flow (FLUENT)

Iterations are completed, or the solution meets the convergence criteria. The state of the **Solution** cell becomes **Up-to-Date** and the state of the **Results** cell becomes **Refresh Required**.

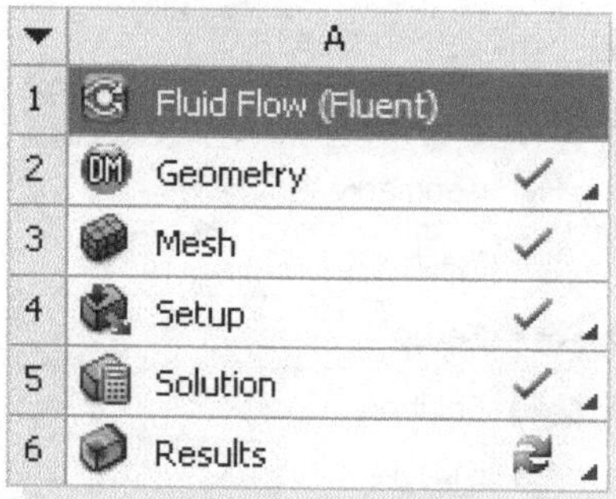

Fluid Flow (FLUENT)

8. Double-click the **Results** cell. CFD-Post launches.
   The case (.cas) and data (.dat) files are written, CFD-Post loads the case and data files, and the state of the **Results** cell becomes **Up-to-Date**.

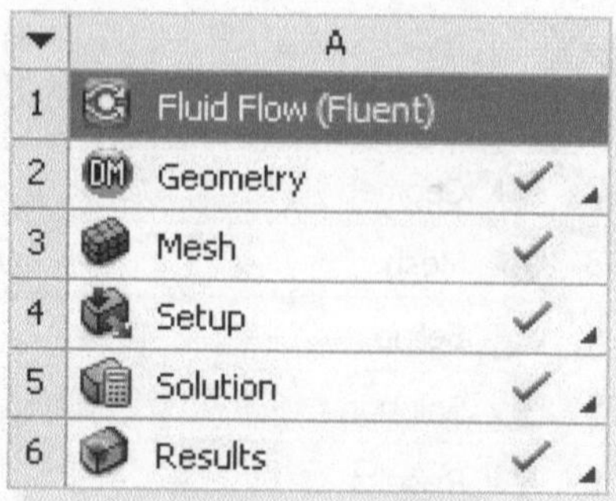

Fluid Flow (FLUENT)

8.7.5 ANSYS HFSS

ANSYS HFSS is a Finite Element Analysis tool for simulating full-wave electromagnetic fields. HFSS incorporates finite element, integral equation, and hybrid methods to solve a wide range of microwave, RF and high-speed digital applications.

Viva Voce Questions

1. What is CAD?
2. What is graphic's package?
3. How many computer aided graphics systems. What are they?
4. What is digitizer?
5. What are the applications of locators and selectors?
6. What do you understand by drawing limits and extents?
7. What is layering concept?
8. How do you begin a new drawing?
9. How do you select an existing drawing for editing?
10. How to exit from Auto-CAD?
11. List 5 important edit commands and mention their applications.
12. List the utility commands.
13. Differentiate between DIM and DIMI commands.
14. List the categories of dimensioning commands.
15. Distinguish between normal, outer-most and ignore styles of hatch command.
16. When do you use plot and prplot commands?
17. Explain how a line can be drawn by
    (i) Cartesian coordinate method.
    (ii) Incremental form and
    (iii) Polar coordinate form.
18. How to draw an ellipse? Explain.
19. Give the procedure for describing a polygon of 7 sides of side 30 mm.
20. What are the various modeling techniques on acad?
21. What do you understand by point command?
22. What is view ports?
23. What are the options available on viewports command?
24. What are the applications of ANSYS?
25. What is CFX, Fluent?

REFERENCES

1. *Dhawan R.K., A Text Book of Machine Drawing, S. Chand, Revised Edition, 2006.*
2. *Narayan K.L., Machine Drawing, New Age International Publishers, 2006 and 2009.*
3. *Lakshminarayanan & Mathur M.L., Machine Drawing, Jain Brothers, 14th Edition.*
4. *Bhatt N.D., Machine Drawing, Charotar Publishing House Pvt. Ltd., 49th Edition, 2013.*
5. *Gill P.S., A Text Book of Machine Drawing, S.K. Kataria & Sons, 2013.*
6. *Siddeshswar N., Kannaiah P., Shastry VVS, Machine Drawing, Tata McGraw Hill, 2017.*
7. *Ostrowsky O., Engineering Drawing with CAD Applications, ELBS, 1995.*
8. *Bhattacharya Basudeb, Machine Drawing, Oxford University Press, 2011.*
9. *Bhatt N.D., Engineering Drawing, Charotar Publishing House Pvt. Ltd., 53rd Edition, 2014.*
10. *http://knowledge.autodesk.com/autocad/learnexplore/caas/cloudhelp*
11. *https://ansys.com*
12. *https://mech.iitm.ac.in/Production%20Drawing.pdf*
13. *hhttps://www.slideshare.net/umeshchikhale/assembly-and-details-machine-drawing-pdf*
14. *Indian Standard IS:696-1972 to come up with IS:10714-1983. ISO and BIS Convention or Code. CHAPTER 2. https://www.ikbooks.com/home/samplechapter?filename=151 Sample-Chapter.pdf*
15. *https://www.scribd.com/presentation/268486404/Mini-Drafter-PPT*

MACHINE DRAWING

O.P. JAKHAR, AMIT MATHUR

FEEDBACK FORM

1. Which topics from your examination point of view are inadequately or not covered in this book?

____

____

2. Is there any misprints/ mistakes/ factual inaccuracy in this book? If so, please specify.

____

____

3. What is your assessment of this book as regards the presentation of the subject-matter, expression, precision and price in relation to the other recommended books available on this subject?

____

____

4. Which competing books you regard as better than this? Please mention their author and publishers.

____

____

5. Any further suggestions/comments you would like to make for the improvement of the book?

____

____

PS: *If needed, please attach a separate sheet.*

Name : ____________________

College : ____________________

Address : ____________________

Email : ____________________

Mobile : ____________________

Please mail the feedback form at:

KHANNA BOOK PUBLISHING CO. (P) LTD.

4C/4344, Ansari Road, Daryaganj, New Delhi-110002

You can also email this feedback form at contact@khannabooks.com or Whatsapp at +91 – 99109 09320

BEST FEEDBACK WILL BE REWARDED SUITABLY